THE STORY OF
BIG CREEK

REVISED EDITION

THE STORY OF
BIG CREEK

REVISED EDITION

By

David H. Redinger

with contributions from

Edith I. Redinger
and
William A. Myers

Printed in Hong Hong by Palace Press

10 9 8 7 6 5 4 3 2 1

Library of Congress Cataloging-in-Publication Data

Redinger, David H.
The Story of Big Creek / by David H. Redinger; with contributions
from Edith I. Redinger and William A. Myers. — Rev. ed.
            p.   cm.
Includes index.
ISBN 0-9628236-8-6 (hardcover)
1. Hydroelectric power plants—California—Big Creek Region—History.
2. Southern California Edison Company—History.
I. Redinger, Edith I. II. Myers, William A., 1947-   . III. Title.
TK1424.C2R44   1998
333.91'4'097949—dc21   98-42701
                                                                  CIP

Book production by   Color photography by Greg
Ironwood Press   O'Loughlin and Mitch Kaufman,
2968 West Ina Road #285   Southern California Edison Corporate
Tucson, Arizona   85741   Communications Department

Table of Contents

Foreword

E LECTRICITY IS VITAL TO OUR modern society, yet most consumers take its availability for granted. At the flick of a switch, light is provided or work performed, with little thought as to how the unseen force was created and put there. Few are aware of the tremendous system of power plant, transmission line and distribution wires that is needed to provide electric service, or of the human effort needed to build, maintain and operate that system.

For decades, one of the important sources of the electricity used in Southern and Central California by customers of the Southern California Edison Company has been the powerhouses of the Big Creek Hydroelectric Project. This book is the history of that project, one of our nation's great engineering achievements. It was written by David Hubbard Redinger, who spent virtually his entire professional life involved with the project. Since its first publication is 1949, The Story of Big Creek has come to be recognized as a classic story of enterprise and personal labor from the early years of America's electric utility development.

The Big Creek Project was begun back in 1910, at a time when the region's remote mountain canyons were virtually inaccessible. To move the thousands of men and tons of supplies to the isolated construction sites, a railroad and connecting network of roads first had to be built. The power plants that arose along the rushing mountain streams were marvels of technology and giants of their era.

The story of the Big Creek Project has come a long way in the half-century since Dave Redinger wrote of his experiences. New dams, lakes and powerhouses have been added and older facilities modernized to provide even more energy for an ever-growing Southern and Central California. One of the newer reservoirs even bears Redinger's name, in gratitude to his lifetime of labor at Big Creek.

David Redinger is legendary among employees of the Southern California Edison Company. He looms as the man who oversaw the construction of the Big Creek Project during its dynamic early years, when the

Previous pages: This dramatic eagle's-eye view of the Big Creek Project was drawn in the mid-1920s.
Artist unknown, from the Edison Collection

project earned the reputation as the largest hydroelectric development ever built entirely by private enterprise.

Dave Redinger arrived at Big Creek on August 13, 1912. As a young civil engineer just a year out of college, his experience was limited, but he enjoyed outdoor life and quickly fell in love with the area. When he got off the train at Cascada that early morning in August, Redinger had no thought that it would be any different for him, but he was wrong.

David Redinger retired from the Edison Company in 1949, having worked for the company and its predecessors for 37 years, all but a year or so of that time at Big Creek. He had progressed from rodman to surveyor to project engineer to superintendent of Northern Division Hydro Generation. Upon his retirement, he was asked by Harry Bauer, then Edison's Chairman and Chief Executive Officer, to write of his experiences of the Big Creek Project. The result was *The Story of Big Creek,* first published in 1949.

The book immediately became popular among all who knew and loved Californiaís Sierra Nevada Mountains. Its chatty narrative contains a wealth of fascinating information about early construction methods, the Edison Company, the Big Creek Project and the mountains. It is a valuable resource, providing an insight back to a time in America's history when private enterprise was the primary force for public good.

The Big Creek Project that Dave Redinger reluctantly left behind at his retirement has grown in the ensuing years to accommodate a tremendous increase in the demand for electricity in Southern and Central California's burgeoning communities.

Altogether, there have been four distinct periods of construction in the history of the Big Creek Project. The early work, called "The Initial Development," was begun by Henry Huntington's Pacific Light & Power Corporation in 1910. In this phase, three dams were built to form Huntington Lake reservoir, and Powerhouses No. 1 and No. 2 were placed into operation.

The second period of construction began in 1917, when the Southern California Edison Company absorbed Pacific Light & Power. This phase began with the raising of the dams impounding Huntington Lake, and continued with the construction of Powerhouses No. 8, No. 3 and No. 2A.

Dave Redinger participated in, and wrote about, the first two phases of the Big Creek Project. When he retired, Big Creek's powerhouses provided some 300,000 kilowatts of generating capacity to the Edison system. The project's capacity was more than doubled by the third phase of construction that was just beginning at his retirement. With the fourth phase additions completed, Big Creek's plants aggregate over 1,288,000 kilowatts of capacity. Dave Redinger would still recognize "his" project, but he would be impressed by that which has been accomplished by modern engineering techniques.

Along with the completion of Balsam Meadows in 1987, the Big Creek Automation Project was also nearing completion. The scope of this job was to consolidate the operation of the eight powerhouses on the Big Creek system to one central location at Big Creek No. 3.

Automation was no stranger to the Big Creek Project. Portal Powerhouse and Mammoth Pool Powerhouse were built to be automated plants in the late 1950s, and Big Creek No. 4 and Big Creek No. 2/2A were converted to "supervisory" control from remote locations in the 1970s.

The task of the Automation Project was to install "local controllers" in each of the plants and tie them to a "master controller" at Big Creek No. 3. This was a difficult task as many of the plants were designed to have an operator on site and did not lend themselves to automation. Eventually, these obstacles were overcome and the plant operators went to dayshifts only.

The Automation Project was completed in late 1988 and has been used to control the Big Creek Project ever since. However, computer technology is ever-changing. The original equipment is now aged and replacement parts have become hard to get. Enter the "New Automation Project," which includes replacement of all of the "local" controllers in the plants and the "master" controller at Big Creek No. 3. At the John S. Eastwood Powerstation, the pump portion of the project was commissioned in 1991. This required extensive installation, calibration and testing of equipment.

This single-circuit transmission tower stands on a hillside overlooking Dam No. 7 and Redinger Lake in the background. Towers of this design were pioneered in 1913 for the original Big Creek development. Today, 220,000-volt transmission lines on several different rights-of-way feed Big Creek power into the Edison system.
Joseph O. Fadler Photo, from the Edison Collection

One of the most apparent of which is the 13,000 horsepower pony motor that is mounted on top of the motor/generator and used turn the 450-on pump/generator rotor in the pump direction to 400 rpms. where the unit is then synchronized to the system. When the unit is on line in the pump mode, it uses 170 megawatts (MW) of power to pump 1,400 cubic feet of water per second uphill to the forebay. This is done in the off-peak hours when power is inexpensive. Then during peak hours this water is used in conjunction with additional water from Huntington Lake to run the unit in the generate mode, producing as much as 207 MW of power to meet peak demand.

This installation completed the Balsam Meadows Project and brought with it a flexibility in how the Big Creek Project is used to make the "Hardest Working Water in the World" work that much harder.

In 1996 Hydro embarked on a project called the Maintenance Planning and Scheduling Process, which would identify, plan, schedule and document maintenance activities in all of Hydro.

There have been many, many years of expertise on the maintenance of the equipment in Hydro most of it residing in the heads of the people involved. This process will get that information into a system where it can be readily accessed and utilized for future planning.

In early January, 1997 a severe rain storm hit the Big Creek area, causing damage throughout the region. The most significant was extensive impairment to the intake structure for Big Creek No. 3 at Dam 6.

In order to optimize the outage required to repair the damage, which virtually shuts down the project, with the exception of Eastwood, a plan was devised to complete the annual maintenance outages on all the units in a three-week time frame. This plan required additional manning supplied by the Steam Division.

The down time was kept to a minimum. An added bonus was that this was a great partnership between divisions that has created relationships that continue today.

It is interesting to note that January 1997 was the wettest month on record at Big Creek and that February through September of 1997 was the driest.

In April, 1998, Southern California Edison, along with the rest of the California electric utility industry, embarked on the new market whereby Big Creek power generation was bid into the California Power Exchange. This was the start of a new era where power is a commodity and subject to the forces in the marketplace. Hydro is a strong player in the market largely due to its flexibility and availability.

As you can see, a lot has changed at Big Creek since Dave Redinger first published his memoirs of the project. To keep this book current, new chapters have been added that were penned by his wife, Edith Redinger, and also by William A. Myers. We have also included beautiful color pictures from the talented staff photographers at Southern California Edison.

Opposite page: This 1986 view looks down the penstocks toward Big Creek Powerhouse No. 3 below. The banded pipes at left and center are from the original installation of the 1920s; the newer pipes at right are from the 1948 and 1981 additions. *Photographer unknown, from the Edison Collection*

I
Introduction

MANY OF MY FRIENDS have suggested that I put on paper the story of Big Creek, and my association of thirty years with the project bearing its name. Although I had been considering such a task for some time, I did not make a final decision to write the story until impetus was given me by Harry J. Bauer, Chairman of the Board of Directors of the Southern California Edison Company.

The name "Big Creek" includes not only the small settlement where our field headquarters have always been located, but the entire project, covering hundreds of square miles.

A résumé of my own background may afford an explanation as to how I became associated with the project.

A few days before graduating from the University of Kansas with a degree in civil engineering in 1911, I received a temporary appointment on a United States Government investigation in Alaska, involving the Bering River Coal Fields. This area, along with Controller Bay, formed the basis of much controversy in Washington at that time. The appointment came by telegram from the Commissioner of the United States General Land Office, Washington, D.C., and I must say it gave me one of the greatest thrills of a lifetime. I still have the original message. Since the appointment came shortly before commencement, a special examination had to be arranged and given quickly to allow me to meet the June 1 sailing from Seattle. I have always been grateful to Dean F. O. Marvin for the consideration he extended in making it possible for me to take advantage of a most unusual opportunity, particularly for a new college graduate.

My qualifications for work with coal arose out of my experience in the five-year period between my high school and college courses, which I spent in and around the mines and coal fields of Colorado. A large portion of this time was spent with an uncle, H. C. Nicholls, who operated several mines in the southern part of that state. Through this association I came in contact with his mining engineer, M. S. Hibbard, retained for the engineering necessary for the proper functioning of such underground work. I was assigned to assist him on each of his monthly trips to the mines. Eventually, I was

Dave Redinger, not long after his arrival at the Big Creek Project in 1912.
Redinger family album, from the Edison Collection

14

Dave Redinger's first job after graduation was on a survey trip to Alaska, mapping locations for coal fields and other large mineral deposits. The location of this camp is not known, but it illustrates the primitive conditions endured on this job.
Dave Redinger Photo, from the Edison Collection

spending all of my time in this manner, and accompanied Mr. Hibbard on trips to many of the large mines in other parts of the state. One day I made the decision to return to my native state and enter college. Mr. Hibbard maintained contact with me during the four years I was in college, and made possible my appointment on the Alaskan work, when he was given full responsibility for that project.

Upon completing the field work in Alaska, the crew engaged there, with the exception of one man, returned to Seattle, where final details were completed in the office. George Parks, a member of the party, remained in Alaska, and in due time was appointed Governor by President Coolidge.

On my return to Seattle, like many others from the North, I made my headquarters at the Frey Hotel, which had just been completed. This hostelry seemed to be a favorite rendezvous for many of the Alaska "sourdoughs." At the hotel I made the acquaintance of H. P. Banks, a chemical engineer who had also just returned from Alaska, and this chance acquaintance developed into a warm friendship which has continued to the present. It was he who was responsible for my coming to Big Creek.

In the course of several weeks, Mr. Banks mentioned that a large hydroelectric development was being started in the High Sierra of California, and that a college mate of his was connected with its construction. Mr. Banks contemplated going to the job himself, and wondered if I would be interested. Not having been to California, and knowing nothing whatever about hydroelectric development, I was eager for such a chance, particularly since my government assignment was drawing to a close. Midsummer of 1912 found both Mr. Banks and me at Big Creek—he as a chemist in charge of the cement-testing laboratory, and I as a transit man. On my way down from Seattle I had thought I would look over the Big Creek job, and after a few months probably go on to other "pastures." Little did I realize that the year 1947 would find me still keenly interested in and enjoying my connection with the project. My good friend Mr. Banks spent several years in the Edison Right-of-Way Department in Los Angeles and then returned to Seattle,

where he played a major role in a successful manufacturing concern.

After having spent a large part of my life in close association with the development of such a large project in all its phases, and having seen it grow from nothing to what it became, is it any wonder I have formed more than just a "bread and butter" attachment for these things built by man—to say nothing of the natural grandeur of the scenery which is so much a part of them?

D. H. REDINGER

Big Creek, California

1949

Dave entitled this picture "The Last Day in Camp at Dick Creek, Alaska." These engineers seem ready to return to the delights of "civilized" Seattle! One member of this group, George Parks, became a Territorial Governor of Alaska.
Dave Redinger Photo, from the Edison Collection

II

John S. Eastwood

A NATURAL QUESTION one might raise concerns the identity of the man who first recognized the power possibilities in this region and, therefore, is responsible for the birth of the Big Creek-San Joaquin Hydroelectric Project. Surely credit for this should go to John S. Eastwood, engineer, who made numerous trips into the Big Creek country—his first, according to Mrs. Eastwood, in 1886. Mr. Eastwood was born in Scott County, Minnesota. On August 13, 1924, at the age of sixty-seven years, he was drowned or died of a heart attack while swimming in Kings River. At the time of his death he was investigating the Pine Flat Project below Trimmer, California. In one of his notes, written to General W. H. Hart in July 1902, he described himself as a "railway engineer of quite wide experience." In 1884 he had made a reconnaissance for a railway from Fresno to Pine Ridge, which is about ten miles below Shaver Lake, and was running lines for power development during 1900 and 1901. Besides being an engineer, Mrs. Eastwood has informed us, her husband loved the mountains and was a keen student of forestry—so much so that by placing his hand on a tree in the dark he could name its kind. She has written that during the latter part of 1886 and for a year or more following, Mr. Eastwood was a timber expert for a large lumber company, for which he also located and built tramways for sawmills.

He had become much interested in electric power transmission, and saw the possibility of developing power for Fresno. In 1894 he made the first examinations of the ground of the North Fork of the San Joaquin, and during the spring of 1895 the San Joaquin Electric Company was organized, with him as vice president, chief engineer, and superintendent. The capital stock was $800,000, all of which was subscribed by seven directors—six of them subscribing $500 each, and Mr. Eastwood $797,000. The plant was finished April 14, 1896. Mrs. Eastwood writes that she had the honor of touching the button that put the great dynamos and machinery in motion in the substation at Fresno, while Mr. Eastwood was listening in over the telephone at North Fork, thirty-seven miles away. At that time this was the longest transmission line in the world. This must have been the original Crane Valley

The large volume of water carried by this rushing Sierra torrent even in the late summer months persuaded John Eastwood to name it "Big Creek."
C. C. "Pop" Laval Photo, from the Edison Collection

18

Several of John Eastwood's original drawings for his proposed Big Creek plants still survive in Edison Company files. This drawing was prepared to show the relative strengths of, and quantities of materials required for, traditional gravity arch and rock-filled dams, as compared with Eastwood's own innovative multiple-arch dam design. Eastwood strongly believed that because the gravity-arch (called the "Croton Profile") and the rock-filled designs used vastly greater quantities of material than his "buttressed concrete," or multiple-arch design, they were poorly suited to remote construction projects such as Big Creek.
Edison Collection

Plant, alongside of which now stands the A. G. Wishon Powerhouse of the Pacific Gas & Electric Company, on the shore of Kerckhoff Lake. In a grassy plot in front of the old building, for all to see, stands one of the first generators, with a copper plaque indicating it as such. The plant was in operation June 1896 to 1910, making it the forerunner of the present large system.

In 1914 Mr. Eastwood was requested to write the early history of the San Joaquin Electric Company. It contains, among many others, this interesting paragraph:

> Shortly after the completion of the plant, a longer distance of transmission was made in Utah, which was again exceeded by us building to Hanford, a distance of seventy-nine miles. In this connection, it is a pleasure to state that I did all of the preliminary work in what is now the largest plant on the Pacific Coast, the longest transmission in the world, and the highest head in the world, that which is used for the large plant, the Big Creek development of the Pacific Light & Power Corporation. (The predecessor of the Southern California Edison Company.)

With respect to the Big Creek Project, Mrs. Eastwood has written that she cannot give the exact date when her husband made the surveys, but she is definite on this—that he had studied and investigated the water power possibilities of the Big Creek country before the San Joaquin Light & Power Company went into the hands of a receiver in the fall of 1899. He had kept the knowledge of his investigation to himself, as he wanted to be sure of his water findings. When the San Joaquin Light & Power Company failed, he remarked to Mrs. Eastwood, who says that she shared in his secret, "I could

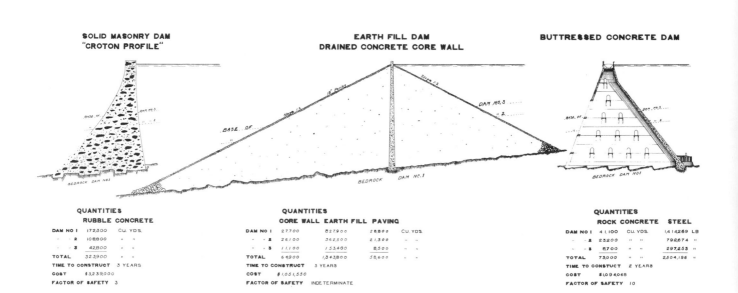

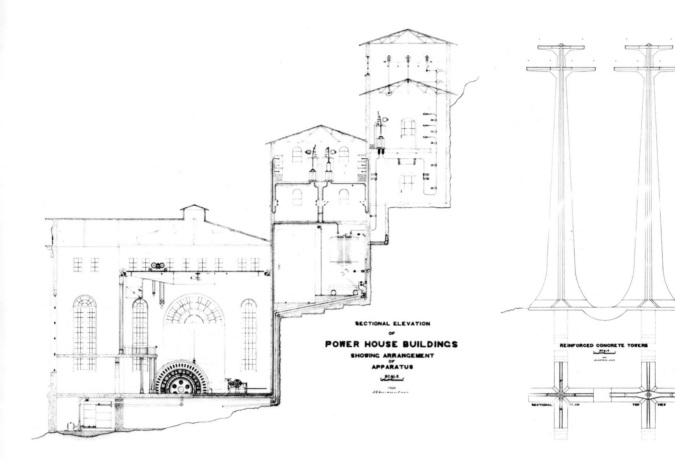

SECTIONAL ELEVATION
OF
POWER HOUSE BUILDINGS
SHOWING ARRANGEMENT
OF
APPARATUS

REINFORCED CONCRETE TOWERS

organize a new company, and could have a much greater power project than the San Joaquin Light & Power Company, but I don't think it would be right." So he offered the results of his investigations to the succeeding company—the Pacific Light and Power Corporation—and merged all his interests in the Big Creek Project, going out of the San Joaquin Company without one cent. He was in the mountains in 1900, five weeks at one time, making surveys, looking into the possibilities of a greater power project in the Big Creek country. In the *Fresno Bee* of May 8, 1941, "Fresno's Yesterdays Forty Years Ago," there appeared this item:

> John S. Eastwood, Civil Engineer of the Mammoth Power Company of San Jose, had a large crew of men in the mountains east of Fresno, where they were making a survey for a tunnel and flume.

In September, 1902, he organized a survey party, and from his files I quote from a letter written to W. G. Kerckhoff about one month after he had the party in the field:

> Big Creek, October 7, 1902. It gives me great pleasure to inform you that I have completed the surveys for a tunnel line to the junction of Pitman and Big Creeks, and I can place before you the most remarkable power project yet presented.

Two more of Eastwood's early drawings reveal his proposals for Big Creek. A multi-leveled powerhouse was to be located at the junction of Pitman Creek and Big Creek, the site where Powerhouse No. 1 was later in fact built, although to a different architectural style. The other drawing reveals another flash of Eastwood's genius, a design for prestressed concrete transmission towers, rather than the traditional wooden or steel poles. Such concrete towers were not used at Big Creek, but later were experimented with elsewhere.
Edison Collection

19

John Samuel Eastwood (1857-1924) was involved in civil engineering projects in the San Joaquin Valley and the High Sierras for almost all of his career. Although his development of the thin-shell multiple-arch dam was controversial during his lifetime, it made a major contribution to civil engineering. In addition to the Big Creek Project, the invention of the multiple-arch concrete dam is John Eastwood's most enduring legacy.
Courtesy Mrs. Jean Browning

Albert G. Wishon, one of the pioneer electric power entrepreneurs in the San Joaquin Valley, is seen in a photo taken in his later years, when he was President of the San Joaquin Light and Power Corporation.
Hartsook Photo, Courtesy Pacific Gas & Electric Company

Powerhouse No. 1, of the Southern California Edison Company, now stands at the junction of the two creeks which Mr. Eastwood mentions in the preceding letter.

In the party of September 1902 was A. Emery Wishon, who, until his death in 1948, was executive vice-president of the Pacific Gas & Electric Company. In one of his letters to me, with reference to this particular crew, Mr. Wishon states there were two such parties, one being headed by Mr. Eastwood, the other by Louie Manuel. The surveys were described as starting at Shaver Lake, and continuing to what is now Huntington Lake, where lines and levels were run to determine quickly the available storage capacity of the reservoir, and where cross-sections were taken of the proposed Dams 1 and 2. The surveys also included the running of a line over Raiser Pass to determine the length of tunnel necessary to bring in the South Fork of the San Joaquin River. This idea was carried out in later years when the Florence Lake Tunnel, later named Ward Tunnel, was driven, connecting Florence and Huntington Lakes.

Mr. Wishon also stated that he walked with Mr. Eastwood to the top of Raiser Mountain at a point overlooking the Big Creek country, the South Fork of the San Joaquin, and Jose Basin. Mr. Eastwood spent several hours describing to Mr. Wishon, then just a youngster, the full project he had in mind—and, as far as our present Powerhouse No. 2 is concerned there have been few changes from Mr. Eastwood's original ideas—but from there down the canyon, the project has been developed differently than was contemplated by him.

It is interesting to learn that one of Mr. Eastwood's plans, as related by Mr. Wishon, involved driving a shaft through the solid granite of Kerckhoff Dome, to be lined with light steel filled in behind with concrete. It was his thought at the time that such a shaft, to serve as a penstock, would be a great saving, and something entirely original.

One day during the same period, Mr. Wishon brought into camp a piece of marble he had found in the Big Creek Canyon, and showed it to Mr. Eastwood. The latter became very enthusiastic over it, and spent several days and evenings sketching a power house which he planned to build with the local product. This sample was taken from the site known today as the Wishon Marble Quarry, located about midway between our Big Creek No. 1 and No. 2 Plants. For many years, the Wishons faithfully made the necessary annual assessment work on this claim.

A. G. Wishon, at the time he was president of the San Joaquin Light and Power Corporation, in a letter dated January 3, 1929, stated that Mr. Eastwood was never on the payroll of his company but on that of the Pacific Light & Power Corporation instead. According to Mrs. Eastwood, he received only a small salary—just sufficient for living expenses— during the several years he was engaged on the preliminary work of the Big Creek Project, because the future seemed bright. At last he lost everything.

During the summer of 1923 I had the pleasure of taking Mr. Eastwood over a large part of the Big Creek work completed at that time. He was a quiet, unassuming man, keenly interested in everything he saw on this, his first trip since the construction was started. The place where he wanted to make his longest stop was at Stevenson Creek, on our Lower Road. He stood

The prominent granite dome that towers over the site of Big Creek Powerhouse No. 1 was named by John Eastwood for William G. Kerckhoff, an early investor in Eastwood's power projects. Kerckhoff became the President of the San Joaquin Light & Power Company, which grew out of Eastwood's original San Joaquin Electric Company.
C. C. "Pop " Laval Photo, from the Edison Collection

Fast-flowing streams falling down steep mountainsides first attracted John Eastwood to the hydroelectric potential of the High Sierras. Years before anyone else, Eastwood worked to develop this energy source for the benefit of California communities.
C. C. "Pop" Laval Photo, from the Edison Collection

speechless for a while, looking up at the 1,600-foot cliff above us, and then commented that he was just thinking how easily he had just reached this point, as compared to a trip many years before on which he had such difficulty getting in and out.

Mr. Eastwood became interested in dam construction, and is credited with having developed the theory of the multiple-arch type, like that at Florence Lake.

The naming of Kerckhoff Dome, in honor of W. G. Kerckhoff, is credited to Mr. Eastwood. It is most unfortunate that nothing in this whole area has ever been named for the man who had the courage, vision and ability to recognize the power possibilities in this part of the Sierra. His brother made a similar comment to me when I called on him in Fresno a few years ago.

III

San Joaquin &
Eastern Railroad

WITH THE ARRIVAL of the years 1910 and 1911, the Pacific Light & Power Corporation was faced with serving a rapidly increasing population, and something had to be done to take care of the load which was likewise increasing throughout Southern California. Some idea of this growth and development may be had when it is recalled that the population of the city of Los Angeles was 105,000 in 1905, 500,000 in 1914, and 1,810,000 in 1944.

The company realized that additional generating capacity for electricity must be provided to meet the demands of the electric railways and commercial needs, since its plants were already operating at practically full output. Seventy-five percent of their capacity was steam-generated, and it was desirable to replace it with hydroelectric power, which could be supplied then at less cost. In any large power system good operating practice requires a fairly even division between steam and hydro plants to ensure dependable service. When the hydro plant gets into trouble—and this does happen—the steam plant must be called upon to make up the difference. The advantage was apparent, too, of the less variable cost for water power generation, as compared to the more viable and increasing cost of steam power produced with fuel oil. Today the cost per barrel of fuel oil has risen to a price more than double that prevailing in 1911 and 1912.

In 1911 the operating capacity of the Pacific Light & Power system was about 75,000 horsepower, distributed among ten plants, including Redondo Steam Station. Compare that with today's capacity of the Southern California Edison System, which is approximately 2,000,000 horsepower from a total of twenty-four hydro plants, four steam plants, and one diesel plant. To provide additional power, negotiations were entered into with the San Joaquin Light and Power Corporation, whereby the Pacific Light and Power Corporation acquired the rights, filings, etc., necessary to proceed with the development of the Big Creek Project. Practically all the capital stock of the latter corporation was owned by Henry E. Huntington, who also owned the entire capital stock of the Los Angeles Railway Corporation.

White railbus No. 501 was used by the San Joaquin and Eastern Railroad to carry small groups of passengers. Dave Redinger states that it was known as the "White Elephant," and was unpopular with riders and the railroad's operating staff. This 1920 picture shows the railbus just beginning its downhill trip to El Prado. Big Creek Powerhouse No. 1 is in the background.
G. Haven Bishop Photo, from the Edison Collection

One of the first problems encountered involved transportation, as the site of the proposed development was in the Sierra Nevada mountains fifty miles from the nearest railroad. Hauling by twelve or fourteen mule teams was impractical for several reasons—the early completion desired, distances involved, and steep grades to be encountered in the handling of enormous tonnage.

The decision was made by the Pacific Light & Power Corporation to build a railroad, and the San Joaquin & Eastern Railroad Company was organized as a subsidiary. A contract was made with the Stone & Webster Construction Company of Boston, and authority was given to proceed with construction on January 26, 1912. Prior to this date, though, about December 1, 1911, a reconnaissance party was in the vicinity of Friant, seeking the best route through the foothills to reach Auberry. At that time Friant was, and it still is, the terminus of a branch of the Southern Pacific, and became the site of the huge Friant Dam, constructed by the United States Bureau of Reclamation. The location selected for the junction with the Southern Pacific was named "El Prado," and was six miles south of Friant and eighteen miles from Fresno.

Ground was broken on February 5, 1912, and the last spike was driven on July 10, completing the fifty-six miles to Big Creek. Building this much standard-gauge railroad in 157 days constituted a record for such work. The survey crews had to hustle to keep ahead of construction, as time was of the essence after the job was once started.

There was nothing available for such construction in the way of the modern equipment we have today—such as tractor-type shovels, bulldozers, motor-operated graders and scrapers, dump trucks, carryalls, etc.; consequently, all work had to be done by team and scraper, wheelbarrows, and hand drilling. There was not even one of the old railroad-type steam shovels used, except for a few dipperfuls on the Big Creek end by one being moved through to "The Basin" (Huntington Lake). All drilling for blasting, instead of being done with the present-day type of hammer drills, was done by hand, with the well-known single- and double-jack methods. The former is done by one man holding his own drill with one hand and wielding the sledge with the other. The latter method involves two men, one holding the drill with one or both hands while the sledgehammer is slung by the other man. Woe be unto the hammer wielder, too, if he missed the drill. A real old-time double-jacker never missed, but until he had proved his skill to the satisfaction of his helper, the latter might use a handle to hold the drill, for his own safety, although such practice was considered to be only for amateurs.

Old records reveal some other interesting things. The work was carried on seven days per week, and at least ten hours per day. The maximum number of men on the payroll at one time was 1,270 in March of 1912. The average from January through May was about 800 men. The average wage paid was between twenty-seven and twenty-eight cents per hour. The turnover was large, because men did not have to look far for work. It was unusual for a man to have more than 100 hours' time in a month, and timekeepers did not have to worry much about classifications, which consisted almost entirely of laborers, teamsters and drillers.

There were 1,100 curves in the railroad, the maximum curvature being sixty degrees. The sharpness of these curves limited both passenger and freight cars to thirty-six feet in length. There was always a notation on requisitions for material and supplies that shipments must be made in cars not exceeding that length. Occasionally, there would be an error and some shipper would get his order into a longer car, thereby requiring the cargo to be reloaded at Fresno or El Prado.

The need for such respect for the sharp curves was impressed upon me while on my first trip to Big Creek. It was said to be about the first regular run, and we left El Prado in the forenoon of August 12, 1912, arriving at Big Creek at 3:00 a.m. the following day. The train literally felt its way above Auberry, but in spite of the care taken, several car steps were either damaged or torn off by overhanging rocks on curves.

Standard rod engines were used between the valley and Auberry, the division point. But because of steep grades above, which reached a maximum of 5.6 percent, geared locomotives such as Shays and Climaxes were used between Auberry and Big Creek. These geared engines, pulling their respective trains on the climb up the mountain, would make a terrible fuss, the noise being comparable to the New York Central's Century roaring through the Mohawk Valley.But where the Century would be making eighty to one hundred miles per hour, the Shay or Climax might be going five or six mph.

For some years, until 1926, railroad tickets read "to Cascada," but mail

The first few miles of the SJ&E were easy to construct, but as the Sierra foothills were reached, heavy cutting and filling became necessary. This crew stopped long enough to have their picture taken at "the front," somewhere near Dry Creek, early in 1912.
Stone and Webster Photo, from the Edison Collection

El Prado (Spanish for "the meadow") aptly described the starting point of the San Joaquin and Eastern Railroad. In this early 1912 view, the Southern Pacific's Friant Branch runs to the left in the foreground, and the SJ&E main line curves away in the center. Notice the carpenters building a water tank in the center of the picture, a sure sign that the railroad was still under construction.
Stone and Webster Photo, from the Edison Collection

would be addressed "Big Creek," although they were the same place. John B. Miller, then Chairman of the Board of the Southern California Edison Company, was responsible for dropping the name Cascada. He preferred "Big Creek," which to him was more typical of the country's ruggedness and the big outdoors. There was some confusion, also, in the local mail service, since there was a post office, "Cascada," in California.

The railroad was the principal means of transportation for many years for the employees and their families, and the general public was also served through a total of twenty-two stations. Business was so brisk for a long time that the Big Creek depot was open day and night—a distinction usually enjoyed only by large city stations.

The main highway to the San Joaquin Valley was not oiled in those days,

This rare photo shows a construction train on the SJ&E in the spring of 1912. By this time, the railroad had been built far into the rugged fastness of the High Sierra, and was nearing the future site of the town of Cascada (Big Creek). The exact location of the "head of steel" is uncertain.
Collection of William A. Myers

and was usually closed by winter conditions from November to March or April, depending upon severity of the winter and earliness of the following spring. Due to heavy snow in January 1913, there was a period of nineteen days when there was no train in or out of Big Creek. Several miles of track had to be cleared of three to five feet of snow to release a locomotive snowbound below Big Creek. One hundred fifty men did the job by hand. Some used wooden shovels, hurriedly improvised. One man broke his shovel, and, there being no replacement at hand, the foreman sent him on ahead to another group as "straw boss." Such quick promotion was the cue for the "accidental" breaking of other shovels to such an extent that methods had to be changed forthwith. Local telephone communications with the train dispatcher at Auberry were disrupted, and Roy Walker, station agent at Big Creek throughout the life of the railroad except for a few months, walked five miles to West Portal to make contact. He took two train orders before failure of the telephone line between him and the dispatcher, and remained at his post for five days until an engine came from Auberry, there being no communication in the meantime. During his sojourn he was furnished meals by a construction family living in a tent nearby, and to his utter amazement, his meals were served on Haviland china.

Often referred to as "slow, jerky and expensive," the San Joaquin & Eastern occupied a place unique in the annals of railroads. A trip over it was long to be remembered, especially if one were at all subject to *mal de mer* (motion sickness). There were other things more pleasant. One could board the train at the Southern Pacific Depot in Fresno early in the morning, and for those desiring something special, a parlor car was available in later years. If it was crowded at the start—and it frequently was—the passengers would thin out rapidly and move to another car when the conductor called for the extra fare. In summer, we enjoyed open cars with canopy tops, called "Bleachers."

Fair speed could be attained between El Prado and Auberry, where the geared locomotives would replace the rod type for the 3,000-foot climb to Big Creek. Shortly after leaving El Prado the conductor would ascertain the number of box lunches required, and these would be put aboard at Stevenson Creek. It was interesting to see how quickly the dogs along the way learned the daily schedule, and were on hand for tidbits thrown out by passengers.

As the train struggled up the grades, one could look several thousand feet below and see the San Joaquin River winding like a shiny ribbon through the canyon. When one grew tired of this, there were lofty peaks to admire, snow-capped in winter, which would begin to peek out in the distance, and near the journey's end there were the lovely waterfalls at the base of Kerckhoff Dome. Such a delight it was, when sufficient altitude had been made, to be among the grand old pines, to enjoy the mild aroma—such as can come only from them—wafting through the open car windows. Now and then there would be a smell resembling witch hazel, from bear clover—so called, it is said, because it is not clover and the bears do not like it. It belongs to the rose family. What a relief too, after having left the hot valley—air conditioning, of course, had not arrived—to feel and breathe the pure, cool air that only mountains can supply.

A favorite stunt of each conductor, and one which afforded amusement for the passengers, was to leave the train at the beginning of a long, sharp curve near Webstone, walk across the neck, and get aboard on the far side.

The supervisory personnel, headed by W. H. Dresser and H. L. Wheeler, would scoot over the rails in special equipment, of which there were several pieces, each consisting of a touring-car body fitted with flanged steel wheels. A roller coaster could offer no more thrills for the uninitiated than the first trip on one of these contraptions. There was much uncertainty of the thing's making the sharp curves, as reflected by the foot pressure on the front floor boards. One's fears would be relieved but little, if on some of the curves he happened to relax enough to even glance down into a deep and precipitous canyon.

In the early summer, passengers interested in wildflowers would have a treat through the foothills when "baby blue eyes," gold poppies, "snow in the mountains," Mariposa lilies, and blue lupine were at their best. Further along there would be the Judas tree, or "red bud," and near Hairpin they could see a few bushes of the lovely Carpinteria California. A ranger of the local Forest Service, reputed to speak authoritatively on wildflowers of the area, says this location, including Tollhouse Grade, is the only place in the world where this rare flower grows. Besides its fame for rarity, it has the further distinction of small seeds—15,600,000 to the pound. Late in the fall, Indians could be seen harvesting acorns and storing them in grass-covered containers high on stilts for safety against birds and animals.

Although probably not recorded in the archives, it should be mentioned that the stork paid a visit on one trip. Conductor Tucker and one of his brakemen shared honors in "entertaining" the bird. Despite the improvised facilities, the principals could not have fared better in the maternity ward of a hospital.

Hundreds of thousands of tons of material and supplies, and many thou-

The so-called "speeder," an automobile body on railroad wheels, was a popular means of transport on the San Joaquin & Eastern Railroad. Here, a group of Pacific Light & Power officials visits Indian Mission Siding, a short distance above Auberry, on April 11, 1914.

Pacific Light & Power Photo, from the Edison Collection

sands of men, were transported during the busy life of the railroad. One year the freight receipts amounted to over $1,000,000. The usual freight train would consist of four cars for one engine, and seven with a double-header.

With completion of the major construction in 1929, there was not much to foresee in the way of freight, express or passenger traffic, all of which had been dwindling for some time. Automobiles had been coming into more general use, and were supplemented by a bus line operated between the Big Creek area and Fresno by W. R. Miles. Even the mail contract had forsaken the railroad for the faster bus service. Eventually—March 6, 1930—the bus line was taken over and operated by the railroad, until October 16, 1934, when it was sold to Fortier's of Fresno, which has continued operation to the present. Rail service reached a stage where trains were being run only as often as was required under the franchise. I recall being picked up one day in the vicinity of West Portal. The crew was most accommodating, even between stations, in view of such light traffic. The train consisted of an engine and caboose, and there was only one passenger when I got aboard. I was twitting the conductor, Walter Low, about his light payload, and he pointed to a carton containing half a dozen two-inch pipe valves which was the only freight item.

The inevitable arrived, and the railroad was abandoned in 1933. On August 15 the last train, consisting of an engine and caboose, made its last run in and out of Big Creek, with Ernest Root at the throttle. It can really be said that Spike Meehan, who took the first locomotive into Big Creek, then known as "Cascada," on July 13, 1912, also handled the throttle on the last run, since it was he who, as hostler at Auberry, had prepared the engine for the final trip. There was nothing unusual the day the last run was made to herald the passing of this railroad, unique in many ways, which had played a major role in the development of one of the world's largest power projects.

It required some time for the Big Creek residents to become accustomed to the quietness of the canyon, no longer echoing with the train's whistle, so welcome for many years, or with the grinding of wheels on the distant curves. The reaction of some was in direct contrast to the thrill and excitement manifested on the day—twenty-one years before—when the first locomotive had noisily labored its way alongside the little station, which at that time consisted of one tent.

All rolling stock, rail and ties were removed and sold, and subsequently the right-of-way reverted to the landowners, the largest being the United States Government. The greater portion became a public road, particularly between Hairpin and Indian Mission. Between Indian Mission and Shaver Crossing, where it joins the state highway, the upper portion is impassable in winter. To the passerby nothing remains but an occasional station sign or water tank as a reminder of what was once a unique railroad.

IV

Initial Development

I N THE EARLY 1890s, and long before the San Joaquin & Eastern Railroad was thought of, the Fresno Flume & Irrigation Company, for its own operations at Shaver, extended the county road north about two miles to what was known as Griffin's Shake Camp. Following the surveys made in 1902 by Mr. Eastwood, the San Joaquin Light & Power Company, under the direction of A. G. Wishon, continued the road and completed it into Big Creek in 1909, preparatory to starting development of the Big Creek Project. The same year the J. G. White Company constructed for Wishon's company the present Pitman Creek weir, also one across Big Creek. The latter had to be destroyed in 1912 when Dam 4 was built. These weirs, like all such structures, were for the purpose of securing data on stream flow, since such information is of primary importance in connection with water power development.

So far, the plans of Wishon's company did not include a road to The Basin (later named Huntington Lake), as it was contemplated that freight and passengers would be transported by an incline cableway. The ground clearing for this had already been done. Mr. Wishon told me he made a special trip to Los Angeles to promote the construction of a road about which there was disagreement among the directors. His sales talk, apparently, had some effect, and the present road was built in 1910, with an outfit consisting of ten men, one team, a plow and a scraper. H. B. Howard and Charlie Miller, with hand level and tape, were the engineers. Maximum grade of 12 percent was intended, but due to the lack of full cooperation on the part of the directorate for a road of any kind, there resulted one much steeper stretch just above the "saddle" which remains a bugaboo to many motorists, and which can easily be identified on almost any hot day by cars stalled due to overheating.

Negotiations had been completed for the Pacific Light & Power Corporation to take over, and contracts for designing and constructing what is known as "the initial development" were executed early in 1912 with the Stone and Webster Engineering Corporation, which was then building the railroad to Big Creek. Headquarters which had been established in Old

These rock drillers are clearing a path for the high-pressure penstock pipeline to Powerhouse No. 1. The tripods that hold the compressed air drills were nicknamed "spiders," and were developed specifically to deal with the steep terrain encountered on the Big Creek Project.
Stone and Webster Photo, from the Edison Collection

32

This view of Camp No. 2, later the town of Cascada (now Big Creek), was taken from the south side of Big Creek Canyon on February 16, 1913. The absence of snow is unusual for the time of year, but it did enable the work to go faster. The penstock for Powerhouse No. 1 is in the early stages of construction, at upper right.
Stone and Webster Photo, from the Edison Collection

Town, on the south bank of Pitman Creek, were moved to the present location, then called Camp No. 2, late in 1911. Bunkhouses were being built, and the mess hall had been opened early in December.

The first automobile to reach Big Creek from Auberry, via Indian Mission, Stevenson Creek and Dawn, arrived on December 11, 1911, the occupants being S. L. Shuffleton, F. M. Thebo, Arthur F. Blight, A. C. Criddle, and Bill Wright. As far as Dawn, which became a station, the route traveled by this party was almost identical to that over which the railroad was built shortly thereafter. From Dawn the car came via Camp 6 over a newly constructed road which joined the present state highway at the foot of the Shaver grade. This junction is the beginning of what we now call our Lower Road.

The area that Big Creek occupies is said to have been used by Potter and Freeman as a sheep range in 1870-71, and was known as Big Creek Flats. In 1902 when John Eastwood made his principal surveys, and up to the development of the project, the area was called Manzanita Park.

Some enlargement of headquarters was still under way when I arrived by train at three o'clock in the morning of August 13, 1912. In those days men carried their own bedrolls, or "bindles," and were known as "construction

stiffs." Another favorite term for one's bedroll in construction parlance was "crumb pile"—from "crumb," which the soldiers of the First World War called "cootie." "Crumb boss" was the name for a caretaker around bunkhouses, since he had to "ride herd" over the occupants, many of whom in those days were quite apt to be pediculous (louse-infested). "Bull cook" later became the more common name.

Because of the early hour of my arrival—dawn was breaking in the east–I crawled into a huge pile of shavings in the unfinished office building until six o'clock, when the mess hall triangle sounded "all out." After breakfast the "crumb boss" suggested I provide myself with a mattress, and directed me to the nearest barn, one-half mile distant, where I obtained a large armful of straw. He then assigned me to a bunk, of which there were three tiers around the inside of the bunkhouse. It is strange how quickly straw can harden in a bed where the only springs are boards. Being a greenhorn, I was happy to have one of the bottom bunks. After the first night I learned why the uppers were so much more desirable. In a lower bunk, one got chaff and dirt in his face every time the fellow above moved or turned over. The old and reliable Sibley stove in the center of the room not only furnished too much or too little heat, depending upon the location of the bunk, but served as a drier for all the damp or wet clothing hanging around. Outside plumbing thrived in all its glory, and no one can fully appreciate how cold water can be until he tries to wash in an outside trough at six a.m., with the thermometer hovering between "zero" and "freezing," making no particular effort to go higher. At such times it wasn't much of a disappointment to find the water line frozen.

After having contacted W. D. Shannon and Arthur Blight, construction and division engineer, respectively, I was assigned temporarily to the party headed by Harry Banks for work on Tunnel No. 2, which eventually would carry the water from Powerhouse No. 1 to No. 2. Austin B. Mason was in

The builders of Big Creek worked hard and ate hard. This view of the dining hall at Camp No. 1 gives an intriguing glimpse into the harshness of their environment, in which a hearty meal was one of their few pleasures.
Stone and Webster Photo, from the Edison Collection

34

The engineers, surveyors and rodmen from Camps 1, 2 and 7 got together one Sunday in August 1913 to have their picture taken. Dave Redinger, who had been working at Big Creek for a year, is kneeling in the front row, fifth from left.
Stone and Webster Photo, from the Edison Collection

direct charge as tunnel engineer, Harry Banks handled the transit, and H. B. Howard and I managed the tape, level rod and paint bucket.

Our job was to keep the tunnel crews driving in the proper direction and at the correct elevation. Nine adits, each providing two headings, or faces, were employed to expedite driving. An adit, the opposite of an exit, may be thought of as a side entrance to a tunnel anywhere between two portals. An adit may be on the same grade as a tunnel, or at a steep angle. If vertical, or nearly so, it would be called a shaft. Since there were so many headings, and because the work was on a twenty-four-hour basis, our party at times would be "run ragged" because blasting would occur at any hour. It was our job to go in after each round was fired, to give direction and grade, or elevation, for drilling the next. Like a train crew, we were on a call basis.

Along the tunnel "battlefront" the thunderous report from each dynamite blast was terrific, and the echoes would reverberate through the Big Creek Canyon, up and down, across and back, as though infuriated by the interference of the canyon walls. Zeus himself could not have done a better job.

The pistol drill was used (the much-improved hammer-type drill would come later). A blacksmith shop stood at the mouth of each adit for the sharpening of the drill steel, which was done by hand. Today, most sharpening is done with a mechanical sharpener operated with compressed air. Instead of storage battery or trolley locomotives for hauling out blasted rock or muck, we used mules. It was amazing to observe the intelligence of these animals. They would function almost automatically—practically the only need for a driver was to see that they did not head for the stable during a trip outside, instead of returning for another load. The cars were loaded by hand, as the mechanical loaders had not yet been developed.

By keeping progress charts, it was easy to forecast the date when any two headings should break through. To be on hand for the final check in line and grade just after a breakthrough was an event in which our party was always keenly interested, since it would be the final test of the accuracy of our work. The closures were good, both in alignment and grade or elevation. When the checks were made, especially of alignment, it was always a favorite stunt of the fellow who had gone beyond the breakthrough to hold his pencil or plumb bob at least one foot off line. This gave the instrument man a shock, since he would not know whether or not his helper was holding the pencil on the proper point, and fearfully would signal him in the direction that coincided with the line carried forward. What a sigh of relief the instrument man would produce when he learned that both lines came together on the lead pencil.

On one of my travels through Fresno, en route to Big Creek, I remained overnight at the Grand Central Hotel. It was extremely hot, and with many others I spent most of the night, until chased out by the "cops," in the Court House Park trying to keep cool. In checking out of the hotel the following morning, I arranged to have one large suitcase kept in storage for about thirty days, leaving it on the floor in the lobby. Imagine my amazement when I returned one month later, after my first payday, to be greeted by the suitcase sitting in exactly the same spot where I had left it, intact in all respects, and well blanketed with dust.

During my first travels over the job, I kept running across a most likable and busy little chap with rosy cheeks, who had a smile for everyone, and whom I took to be one of the "common herd" along with the rest of us. One day he asked if I were the fellow who had recently come down from Seattle, how I liked my job and if I were being treated all right. Finally, I asked him what he was doing, and it was then I learned he was Rex C. Starr, the ubiquitous assistant to the superintendent, Mr. Thebo. He appeared quite young to be holding such a responsible position, but I learned later that even though he had not been long away from his alma mater, he had been through a previous power development in the Pacific Northwest.

Mr. Thebo and Mr. Starr were the kind of men the employees liked to see around, not the kind they would try to dodge—unless Starr was biting his fingernails. Then, look out!

Automobiles and trucks had not yet come into extensive use. Instead of these, there were many horses, mules and wagons—enough to have served adequately any of the large circuses.

There was only one automobile—a touring car—in the entire area. It was for the use of Mr. Thebo, and whenever a trip was contemplated to Huntington Lake, he would summon several men to accompany him to help push the car up the steep grades. Men soon learned to be unusually busy or hard to find whenever the car appeared in front of the superintendent's office.

One day I was asked to proceed to The Basin and check the alignment in Tunnel No. 1, about which there was some question. My party happened to be at Big Creek No. 2. At about two o'clock in the afternoon we picked up our paraphernalia and started to hike up the trail to West Portal, 2,000 feet in elevation and about two miles distant. Transportation was limited in those days to "shanks' mare." I carried the heavy Berger transit, hoping we might be lucky enough to catch a ride from West Portal to Big Creek on "the peddler," the name applied to the engine serving the tunnel camps. No such luck—so we walked the five miles following railroad track, and after a short rest started the six-mile hike from Big Creek around the road to The Basin and Dam No. 1. There was nothing in sight in the way of a team and wagon, even at Big Creek. We made Camp 1A just in time for supper, somewhat the worse for wear after the thirteen-mile hike and the 4,000-foot climb. However, we felt better after our meal, and proceeded to check the underground tunnel line, finishing the job in time for breakfast. The underground alignment was found to be considerably in error. (Today no one even thinks of going anywhere without using a car.)

Another job was to locate the set stakes for four cottages, which were the first permanent structures built. Although first occupied by Thebo, Starr, Shannon, and Roberts of the Stone and Webster staff, they eventually became the homes of operating employees. Little did I realize on that August day in 1912 that I would be concerned with these same houses in 1947.

The Basin, 2,000 feet higher and directly above Big Creek, was the origin of a local witticism with respect to the Big Dipper as seen from Big Creek. One night an alert observer, recognizing the relation, wisecracked, "I see the Dipper is up in the Basin tonight." The "Basin" was renamed as Huntington Lake shortly after construction began, in honor of Henry E.

Tunnel No. 1 was dug to carry water from Huntington Lake to the top end of the pipeline going to Powerhouse No. 1. This view of a working face in that tunnel was taken in March of 1913. Notice the complete absence of hard hats!
Stone and Webster Photo, from the Edison Collection

Huntington—but it didn't really "take" until about 1914. When people become accustomed to a name, it is about as difficult to change it as changing a horse to a new stall.

A large construction job, especially one having prospects of continuing for some time, is always a good lure for the sprouting of various enterprises—some of them worthy—in the area. The names Pressley, Alviso, Imhoff and Aggergaard became familiar to all old-time Big Creekers as the forerunners of the few businesses remaining. Big Creek's first store was built by Frank Alviso early in 1912, across the road from the present U.S. Forest Service garage. He sold out four years later to Imhoff and Aggergaard, the latter becoming sole owner in 1921. Aggergaard put up a new and larger store that year where Rasmussen's now stands. The former was destroyed by fire in the summer of 1930. Some competition appeared in 1916 when Pressley, an ex-conductor on the Southern Pacific, built a small store nearby, specializing in tobacco, punch boards and slot machines—also, in cashing checks. Big Creek stores, apparently, appealed to railroad conductors, as E. H. Barnett, formerly of the San Joaquin & Eastern, bought out Pressley and operated the place along with a string of pack stock. William Solomon came along, bought out Barnett, dismantled the building and built a new one, including a garage.

Mr. Thebo was anxious to have something better than bunkhouse quarters for guests. He encouraged A. O. Smith, of Clovis, to put up a hotel in 1913, adjacent to and just west of the present U.S. Forest Service garage. Later, several floored tents, or "rag houses," were erected opposite to handle the overflow. The hotel business was brisk enough by 1914 to encourage William Thrower, an ex-forest ranger, to build his Big Creek Hotel near the present site occupied by the Forest Service gasoline pumps. Naturally, in those days such a building was on the rustic order, lacking many present-day features—one being insulation against cold and noise. This was especially noticeable in the bathroom, which was separated from the main rooms by a thin, rough panel, affording one most extensive publicity; attending its use was a fearful sound that resembled that of the ice on the Yukon River breaking up in the spring. Thrower sold his hotel in 1920 to Ludwig Schurich, the owner of the present Big Creek Hotel. The former hotel was destroyed by fire in 1929.

Early in January 1913, trouble developed in Camp No. 3, one of the tunnel camps and my headquarters. Men were complaining about the food. The climax was reached one night after supper when a group arrived at the mess hall with "blood in their eyes,"carrying rope, allegedly to hang the cook! Word had gone ahead that such a move was under way, and as the advance guard went in the front door, the chef went out the back and disappeared. He never did return to that area. Coincident with the total tie-up set off by this outbreak, a heavy storm set in. The snow, four and five feet deep, would have made it impossible to continue effectively with the work for at least two weeks. The San Joaquin Light & Power Corporation was furnishing power for the job, and the storm caused the failure of a half-mile span of the transmission line just outside headquarters camp, leaving the entire job without light and power. Even Dick Stout, chief electrician, was unable to restore service for two weeks. It was fortunate that the commissary and warehouse had a large supply of candles on hand.

When Austin Mason left in February 1913, the assignment of tunnel engineer was given to me. I had been transit man and assistant engineer for some time. Banks had returned to the field laboratory to devote all his time to making and testing samples of cement and concrete, along with any other construction materials which might come his way. The greater part of the work went ahead on a seven-day-per-week basis—some of it twenty-four hours a day.

Tunnel Superintendent Criddle's transportation consisted of a horse and cart; Arthur Blight and I each had one of those rail-borne, three-wheeled contraptions called "speeders." They were quite nice to use on the down-grade, but not so pleasant to pump on the uphill return. Some thrill for us, too, when we met the "peddler" on a sharp curve and had to yank the speeder off the track in a hurry—much to the amusement of the engine crew.

During that summer the job was again closed down for about a month, to recuperate from financial difficulties. Mr. Huntington came to the rescue, putting up his own collateral to ensure completion of the work that was then under way.

There was not much in the way of special amusement in those days, and on Sundays those lucky enough to be off would head down the trail for Carlson's Hotel, now the location of Camp Sierra, for one of the chicken dinners made famous by Mrs. Carlson and her daughter, Pauline. The chicken would be piled so high in front of us we had to "eat our way out," not difficult to do even though it was flanked on all sides by Pauline's hot biscuits. Boy, how we did enjoy the change to a woman's cooking, with "frills" not put out by the camp mess halls! Such "eases," including wonderful dinners from the hands of Mr. and Mrs. Banks, along with the most gracious hospitality, will never be forgotten.

As a result of the work my party had been doing—checking overhead and underground lines—it acquired the name "prezacts," a combination of "precision" and "exact." Such work required the use of spring balances on the steel tape lines to ensure equal tension in measuring distances. Corrections in steel tape measurements were made for temperatures either above or below the standard of 62F. In later years accuracy was facilitated by the use of a steel tape calibrated in Washington, D.C., by the Bureau of Standards, and which was carefully guarded and used only when necessary for checking the tapes in daily use.

Provision for storage of water was necessary, and The Basin, at an elevation of 7,000 feet, filled this requirement. To make it into a reservoir, however, three large concrete dams had to be built. In addition to the three darns, the initial development included Powerhouses 1 and 2, two tunnels (one four miles in length, the other three-quarters of a mile), one 84-inch flow line that was 6,600 feet long, four high-pressure pipelines, or penstocks, each about one mile in length, and a double transmission line 248 miles long to operate at the highest voltage—150,000 volts—ever used commercially. An early start on such construction was vital because the schedule called for the first powerhouse and one transmission line to Los Angeles to go into service July 1, 1913, followed by the second plant and line by October 1. With such objectives it was necessary that the reservoir be ready to impound water

Camp No. 2, located at the end of the railroad from the San Joaquin Valley, was the principal supply point for outlying camps. Here, two butchers cut some of the hundreds of tons of meat consumed monthly by the construction workers at Big Creek.
Stone and Webster Photo, from the Edison Collection

Even in deepest winter, with the fleshpots of Fresno seemingly a world away, payday was an important event in the lives of Big Creek's construction workers. These men are lined up in wet January snow at Camp No. 2 to pick up their gold coins from the paymaster.
Stone and Webster Photo, from the Edison Collection

GOING AFTER U.S. MAIL
JAN. 15/13 Nº 151

Although construction work continued through the depths of the winter of 1912-13, the Big Creek Project seemed very isolated from the outside world. Getting the U.S. Mail from the railhead at Camp No. 2 to the most distant camps was a necessary, if difficult, task.
Stone and Webster Photo, from the Edison Collection

from the 1913 spring runoff; otherwise, there would be one year's loss of water and, naturally, the same delay in time. In all such mountain power systems, the water is gone until the following year if it is not retained as the snow melts in the spring.

Camps, of course, had to be established for all such operations, and Camp 2, the headquarters, was already flourishing. The plans provided that the camps serving the two areas accommodate a total of 2,000 men. Camp 1, in the bottom of the reservoir area about three-quarters of a mile northeast of Dam No. 1, was the location from which all gravel was obtained for the concrete going into the dams and pertinent structures. The alphabet was used extensively to identify other camps in the area. Camp 1A served principally during the construction of Dam No. 1. Camp 1B took care of Tunnel No. 1. Camp 1C, located where Huntington Lodge now stands, cared for those working on Dam No. 2. Camp 1D, somewhat down the canyon, was the base for the installation of the 84-inch flow line, and the men engaged in building Dam No. 3 lived in Camp 1E. So many camps, instead of one central location, were justified because a camp near the job had advantages over dis-

Camp 1E was located at the site of Dam No. 1, one of the three dams built to impound Huntington Lake. Despite the 36-inch snowfall recorded in this January 1913 picture, construction work went on.
Stone and Webster Photo, from the Edison Collection

The permanent housing built at the town of Big Creek seemed luxurious compared to the tents and bunk houses provided for the construction forces. This village was the nerve center of Edison operations in the Big Creek region.
Stone and Webster Photo, from the Edison Collection

tant quarters. The area involved was so large that, to serve the various sites, thirteen miles of standard-gauge construction railroad had to be built, and nine locomotives, together with over a hundred standard railroad freight cars, were provided. The greater portion of such equipment was used in the Huntington Lake area, all of it being moved up the incline cableway. A second incline was constructed from West Portal on the San Joaquin & Eastern Railroad to Powerhouse No. 2. Both inclines were a little over a mile long, rising about 2,000 feet, with the maximum grade about eight percent—a rise of eighty feet vertically in one hundred feet horizontally. The incline cars were standard railroad flats with a "strong back" on the lower end to prevent loads from sliding, and were kept in service permanently. Thousands of tons of material, equipment and supplies were handled without serious mishap.

Clearing and excavation at the sites of the three dams started during the summer of 1912, as did the driving of Tunnel No. 1.

Compared to present-day equipment, the guy derricks and skips used in excavation for the dams were slow but sure. The pouring of concrete for Dams No. 1 and No. 2 continued through the winter, even though low temperatures prevailed. Steam pipes under canvas were the protective measures used to prevent freezing. Dams No. 1 and No .2 were completed shortly after the first of the year 1913, leaving Dam No. 3, the smallest one, trailing behind because trouble was experienced in excavation. Bedrock was deep, and much more difficult to reach than the foundation for either of the other two dams. The three sluice gates in the bottom of Dam No. 1 were closed for the first time on April 8, 1913, causing Big Creek to halt abruptly, accustomed as it had been to cascading down the canyon since time immemorial. Such was the beginning of the reservoir to be known later as Huntington Lake.

The reservoir area was, quite naturally, largely covered with trees many of which were cut from a boat as the water rose at the time of the first filling. Such a method explains why stumps stand as much as twenty feet high when water is at low stage. There was no time to dispose of the trees after they were cut, and they remained where they fell. This was a serious mistake, as we found in later years. Today government regulations demand a good cleanup of such areas, and any power company would not want it otherwise—not only from the standpoint of good housekeeping but also because of relief from subsequent trouble caused by floating debris. In later years, large expenditures have been made to remove many of these "sinkers," which usually float large end up and became a general nuisance, to say nothing of being unsightly.

The forests were literally full of engineers, or "S.I.'s" as they are called in construction vernacular—from the first letters of the legendary backwoods spelling "Sivil Injuneer."

The engineers' quarters at The Basin were located on the spot later occupied by Huntington Lodge. Several of the men made pets of chipmunks, numerous in these parts. A large enclosure was made with suitable wire netting, adjacent to the building, and boxes were arranged with material for nests. The little fellows were easy to tame, and afforded no end of amusement during the long winter evenings with their antics. Small holes were cut in the partition between the pen and the main room of the building. It was amusing to watch them enter through these holes, scamper around the room, and end up in various pockets looking for peanuts, of which they were very fond, and of which they usually found plenty. Let a stranger enter, and they would scatter in all directions, resulting in a traffic jam at each exit. Soon a head would reappear at each hole, and before long all would venture in again. If the stranger sized up to their satisfaction, all well and good, but if he made any suspicious moves or gestures, the mad scamper would be on again. Once a workman who was going home for a few days to Los Angeles took a dozen

At the top of Incline No. 1, an extensive system of standard-gauge trackage, nicknamed the "Basin Railroad," served gravel quarries, construction camps, a sawmill and all three dam sites. Here, construction engine No. 7, with a flatcar purchased from the Tonopah and Goldfield Railway, stands at the top of the incline, about to take several well-dressed ladies on a Sunday tour of The Basin. Judging from the expressions of the men at left, such visits were rare.
Pacific Light & Power Photo, from the Edison Collection

chipmunks to his children—or at least started out with that number. He made the trip by train. The little pets-to-be were carried in a suitable ventilated box; everything was lovely. The workman stopped at one of the large stores in downtown Los Angeles to make some purchases for the family. Somehow the cage was accidentally knocked off the counter. The lid came off, releasing the occupants, and they scattered throughout the place. With much effort on the part of many employees, a few of the chipmunks were found that day—one being discovered in the pocket of a new overcoat. The manager, naturally, was deeply concerned over possible damage to goods and assigned special help to round up the little fellows. It was several days, even with the help of some of the members of the fire department, before a full accounting could be made—allowing everybody to rest more easily.

The concrete foundation for Big Creek Powerhouse No. 1 was poured during March 1913, followed in April by the one for Big Creek No. 2. The work on both plants was progressing satisfactorily, and No. 1 was complet-

This February 1913 photo shows workmen preparing the bedrock for the foundations of the west end of Dam No. 3, the largest of the three that were to impound Huntington Lake.
Stone and Webster Photo, from the Edison Collection

ed, when No. 2 met with disaster. Just as the roof was finished, and before the concrete had a chance to set, fire broke out in the adjacent carpenter shop and spread to the concrete forms, enveloping the entire structure. Consequently, the huge roof fell upon the upper floors, causing major damage. The extensive repairs delayed the plant's going into service until December 18, 1913. Although Plant No. 1 did not go into regular service until November 10, when the transmission line was completed, it had been delivering power to local circuits since October 14.

The initial development utilized the water from Huntington Lake through a total fall of nearly 4,000 feet. Subsequent development increased the fall to upward of 6,000 feet. It may be of interest to see how the water performs. Let us follow its course from the reservoir through screens, or rack bars, into the large intake tower, thence through the twelve-foot tunnel, three-quarters of a mile long. The screens, which are necessary and common for all such structures, prevent the passage of moving debris. Connecting with the tunnel today are two pipes of 84-inch and 60-inch diameter, called flow lines, which are each a little over one mile in length. The high-pressure pipelines, or penstocks, are connected to the lower end of the flow lines, and extend down the steep mountain side to Powerhouse No. 1. They terminate at the powerhouse in eight nozzles, each six inches in diameter, one for each water wheel, and two water wheels for each unit, from which the water discharges at a velocity of about 350 feet per second. These jets, almost like bars of steel, discharge across an open space of a few inches to strike the buckets of the water wheels. A tremendous impact might be expected, but the shock is relieved

Stone and Webster No. 11, which began life in 1866 as Central Pacific No. 24 "Montana," is hard at work in the gravel pit in The Basin in February of 1913. Trainloads of gravel were carried several miles to a crushing and mixing plant, where the rock was made into concrete for the three dams then under construction on the perimeter of The Basin.
Stone and Webster Photo, from the Edison Collection

46

This picture of Dam No. 1, taken in February 1913, shows the foundation being prepared for the first pour of concrete. The elaborate wooden trestlework was needed to hoist the mixed concrete and chute it down onto the work face.
Stone and Webster Photo, from the Edison Collection

since the part of the bucket, when first touched, is nearly parallel to the jet. The water's course over the surface of the buckets is momentary, and without much pressure and velocity it falls into the tailrace. For the drop of 2,100 feet, the pressure at the water wheels is between 900 and 1,000 pounds per square inch. The control of pressure and the economical use of water at varying loads is provided for, each wheel having a governor, so that maximum efficiency can be obtained from a unit by using one or both wheels according to load demand. The size of the jet, or the amount of water being discharged, is regulated by a needle valve controlled by the governor, and excessive changes in pipeline pressures are relieved by bypass openings back of the nozzles, also controlled by the governor. After reaching the tail-

By May of 1913, each of the three dams at The Basin was virtually complete. Here, work crews are pouring an eastern "wing wall" extension to Dam No. 1. By this time, with much of the original "Basin Railroad" flooded by the rising waters of the reservoir, a two-foot narrow-gauge tramway was being used to deliver mixed concrete to each work face.
Stone and Webster Photo, from the Edison Collection

A boatload of officials tours the growing reservoir that will soon be named Huntington Lake. Due to the need to capture the spring runoff in 1913, the reservoir began to be filled before the ground could be entirely cleared of trees. For some time after, floating debris had to be regularly removed from the surface of the lake.
Stone and Webster Photo, from the Edison Collection

Big Creek Powerhouse No. 1 arose at the junction of Pitman Creek and Big Creek, on exactly the site proposed by John Eastwood a decade earlier. By April 1913 work was well under way. This view looks west down Big Creek Canyon, with the town of Cascada (Big Creek) just out of the picture at the right.
Stone and Webster Photo, from the Edison Collection

The most difficult engineering problem encountered during the initial development of Big Creek was the design and manufacture of steel pipe having sufficient strength to withstand the tremendous pressures generated by the water during its final precipitous fall into the powerhouses. This "penstock pipe" was built in Germany by the famed Krupp Works, using metallurgy similar to that needed for cannon barrels. This dramatic view shows the penstock being laid up the 80 percent grade above Powerhouse No. 1 during August of 1913.
Stone and Webster Photo, from the Edison Collection

race, the water, instead of continuing unchecked down the natural canyon, must repeat its first performance because its job is only half done—and is again impounded, this time by Dam No. 4 across Big Creek just below Powerhouse No. 1. The water passes through a four-mile tunnel and into the high-pressure lines, through which it is carried to the wheels in Powerhouse No. 2.

The high-pressure pipe for the four units installed during the initial development—two in each of the two plants—was made in Germany. When it was laid, the work was started at the powerhouse and the sections placed uphill, the lines being kept full of water as they grew in length. The water allowed a lower and more even temperature to be maintained, and in warm weather would hold the pipe movement in the trench to a minimum. It is amazing how pipelines will react to temperature changes—crawling around like snakes if care is not taken. The practice of providing expansion joints was adopted in later years, but since there are none in these older lines they were backfilled—that is, covered with earth. The lap-welding process for making the longitudinal seams had been developed and used extensively in Germany in the manufacture of pipe for such purposes. Two Germans were sent to Big Creek by the factory, to remain during the installation of its product, to represent the manufacturer and to be of possible assistance in laying the pipe. Those of us on the job did not realize there was any great difference in rank between the two until our attention was directed to the situation quite forcibly. Some reference was made to Katagan about his partner, Kawalski, whereupon Katagan retorted indignantly, "He iss not my partner—he iss my man."

Mr. Shuffleton, western manager for Stone and Webster, was in general charge of the initial development. Although he did not spend much time

P.H"² FROM ROAD CROSSING.
J.O.1142—Nº 664. 10.15.13.

here, he made frequent visits to keep in close touch with the progress. A self-made man, he was second to none when it came to handling difficult construction, no matter how large or complicated. If there were a pumping problem—and most construction jobs have many—one was sure to find him there. He had a way with pumps, particularly secondhand ones, and after getting them on the job he certainly could make the "darn" things perform wonders. It mattered not how wet, muddy, or otherwise disagreeable a location for a pump might be, he would be found there, covered with mud and grease from his black derby to his feet. He never bothered about coveralls, staying with it until the pump was working to his satisfaction. Scornful of slide rules, he had his own methods, and quite frequently would quickly correct, through his mental processes, a fellow using a "guessing stick."

He was disdainful of carrying luggage, and took long trips without so much as a hand bag. The only time I ever saw him with any kind of a bag was once in Fresno. He apologized for the luggage, explaining that Mrs. Shuffleton was along.

The gradient of the penstock pipe down to Powerhouse No. 2 was not quite as steep as that to Powerhouse No. 1, but the same extra-strong Krupp-built pipe was used. This October 1913 view looks down the pipeline toward a still incomplete powerhouse.
Stone and Webster Photo, from the Edison Collection

This view of Unit No. 1 in Powerhouse No. 1 shows how each generator was flanked by two "Pelton" water wheels. This was done to equalize the tremendous forces placed on the common shaft joining the water wheels to the generator. At this time, Big Creek's two powerhouses employed the largest Pelton-style water wheels ever built.
Stone and Webster Photo, from the Edison Collection

Visitors to this project have been legion, and I can truthfully say that of them all, Mr. Shuffleton was outstanding. During a visit here several years ago, he was, as usual, most entertaining in every way and keenly interested in everything, no matter what nor how small. During this trip he remarked to Mrs. Redinger that he had been too busy for many years to bother with vacations, whereupon she inquired how he managed to get married. He explained that it occurred when there was a lull in construction and he was not very busy for a few days. Unfortunately, I never had the chance to hear Mrs. Shuffleton's version.

Late in November 1913, while I was temporarily stationed in a camp at Indian Mission checking over a trunk telephone line, I received a message from Big Creek headquarters that, along with hundreds of other men, I was being laid off, the initial development by Stone and Webster having reached completion except for final cleanup.

At 1:15 a.m., December 1, 1913, the first penstock failure occurred when a flanged joint pulled apart in the right-hand leg of Line No. 2, Big Creek No. 1, just above the public highway. The weather was cold and the heavy spray, spreading completely over the nearby steel transmission tower, froze, causing it to collapse. The powerhouse was flooded, not only with water but

also sand and mud—and, of course, was put out of commission. Steam pumps were rushed into service to help clear the basement. The San Joaquin Light & Power Corporation came to the rescue with power for light circuits and crane operation during the emergency .

At completion of the initial development, this plant had the highest head in this country. The word "head" is used in hydraulics to designate the vertical distance between reservoir level and the water wheels. The water wheels and the generators were the largest of their type built at that time.

Some idea may be had of the growing demand for power in the territory served then, by the fact that when construction began it was planned to provide 40,000 kilowatts of capacity. The plan had to be revised and the plants built to deliver 60,000 kilowatts from the substation, with liberal provisions throughout for increases in capacity. To provide for future demands, the transmission lines were built for three times the capacity first contemplated. About this same time a large proportion, 78 percent, of the company's power sold, was used by electric railways, the Los Angeles Railway operating 355 miles, and the Pacific Electric, 868 miles of interurban lines in Southern California.

In the extent and value of its properties in 1914, together with its volume of sales, the Pacific Light & Power Corporation ranked as one of the largest and most successful public utilities on the Pacific Coast.

At the bottom end of the pipelines from the reservoir high above lies this complex casting, the "needle-valve housing." Inside this pipe, a long, slender "needle valve" travels back and forth to regulate the flow of water onto the water wheel, thus regulating the electrical output of the generators. This photo of one of the four needle valve housings in Powerhouse No. 1 gives an idea of the small hole through which the water must flow.
Stone and Webster Photo, from the Edison Collection

On October 13, 1913, the first unit at Big Creek Powerhouse No. 1 began generating power for the local area. Although it would be another month before electricity would be delivered to Los Angeles, and several months' work remained before the "Initial Development" would be completed, John Eastwood's original dream, backed by Henry Huntington's financial strength, was at last fulfilled.
Stone and Webster Photo, from the Edison Collection

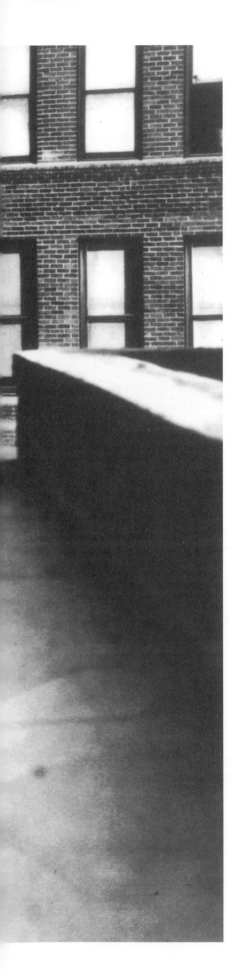

V
Intermission–World War I

As SOON AS THE first development was completed, the Stone and Webster forces moved out. In one respect, any construction job is like a large circus--even including the clowns. As soon as the "show" is over, the outfit moves elsewhere. Rex Starr became affiliated with the Pacific Light & Power Corporation as hydraulic engineer, with Arthur Blight as assistant. Hundreds of others scattered to the four winds. After the exodus there was a lull in the area with respect to major construction, but not with the two large powerhouses just completed. They settled down to grinding out kilowatts for rapidly growing Southern California, the job for which they were built.

On the door of one of the many offices in the newly built Marsh-Strong Building in Los Angeles, later renamed Rives-Strong, appeared the sign, "Banks & Redinger"—who were to take on various and sundry jobs of an engineering nature. We realized we had to seek new affiliations, and were of the opinion that while doing so, it would be desirable to have some spot to which we could return to "rest our legs." If, in the meantime, the sign should attract something, all well and good. Apparently we did not use the right kind of "fly paper," because nothing of consequence came our way, although we did have a few nibbles and much fun out of the venture for a while. Then the situation took on a different color, since office rent was not being donated and we had to live.

Banks and I were resting our "dogs" in the office one day, planning some more moves, when our phone (yes, we had one) rang. Both jumped as if it were a fire alarm. Starr was calling for Redinger, and wanted to know if he would be interested in a job. We had to present a good front, of course-or at least we thought we did—and indicated that we had several very good prospects at the moment, but that we would be glad to listen to any proposition, while at the same time being careful not to be "dropped off the hook." He was given time, with some difficulty, to hang up his receiver before I rushed into his office. The firm of Banks & Redinger dissolved shortly, both individuals going to work for the Pacific Light &

The principal steam power plant for Henry Huntington's Pacific Light & Power system was at Redondo Beach. The original units, installed in 1907, were giant reciprocating engines, but when additional units were needed in 1910, steam turbines were installed. Fuel oil for this plant was brought in via the Pacific Electric Railway. This March 1914 view of the Redondo Steam Plant shows how the plant appeared at about the time Dave Redinger briefly worked there.
Pacific Light & Power Photo from the Edison Collection

Power Corporation—and what a sigh of relief we gave. Starr sent me to the Redondo Steam Plant to do what was necessary to reinforce the pier supporting the large pipelines which carried the condensing water from the ocean to the boilers, as an unusually heavy sea was threatening serious danger. This assignment was cut short when a United States marshal suddenly appeared with a subpoena requiring my appearance in Seattle immediately, in connection with the Alaska coal land investigation on which I had been engaged before coming to Big Creek.

Upon my return to Los Angeles several weeks later, Starr took me to the Azusa powerhouse, now owned by Pasadena, to make some tunnel repairs. A bad cave-in had occurred between the intake and the powerhouse, causing a complete shutdown. After finishing this, I returned to Big Creek, located the intake portal of the tunnel to be driven between Powerhouses No. 2 and No 3 (the latter not yet built); also the outlet portal of the tunnel headed for Mammoth Pool on the San Joaquin River. Although both tunnels were started shortly thereafter—it was now June 1914—a slow schedule was adopted and followed until there was a change in plans at the time of an urgent need for additional power, resulting in the birth of Powerhouse No. 8.

Having located these portals, along with the first tangent of both tunnels, my party was preparing to move to headquarters when we heard about the forthcoming arrival in Big Creek of a large group of girls from the Fresno State Normal School. One can hardly imagine the excitement which resulted among the few engineers left at that time. It certainly put us on the *qui vive.* Fifty young women arrived on July 3, having enrolled in what was to

Pacific Light & Power's Azusa Hydro Plant was the oldest on its system, having originally been placed into service in 1898. Its unusual two-phase generators were a rarity. Dave Redinger also briefly worked here before returning to Big Creek in June of 1914.
Pacific Light & Power Photo, from the Edison Collection

become one of the major enterprises in this area, the summer school of the Fresno institution. The Fresno State Normal School had been established in 1911 and was renamed Fresno Teachers College in 1921. By an act of the State Legislature the present name, Fresno State College,was adopted in 1935.

The quarters occupied at Big Creek for that first summer session consisted of several of the rough buildings such as bunkhouses and mess hall remaining from the 1912-1913 construction. Such primitive accommodations did not encourage continuation of the project, but because of the Pan-Pacific International Exposition in San Francisco in 1915 there were no classes that year. By 1916 a site had been selected at Huntington Lake near the Huntington Lake Lodge, which had been built in the meantime, where the school flourished each summer until 1926, when it moved to a permanent base—a forty-acre tract adjacent to Lakeshore on the north side of the lake. At that location the school continued each season with an enrollment of 250 to 350, until war conditions prevented its operation in 1943, 1944 and 194~5. The sessions have always been very popular in such an environment, since the students could enjoy unusual recreation while making professional progress. The Black-Fore Military School of Los Angeles occupied for several years the site relinquished by the summer school near Huntington Lake Lodge.

It was amazing how much work we suddenly found close to headquarters after arrival of the summer school group, but our plans were quickly frustrated when we learned we were to leave Huntington Lake early on July 5 for reconnaissance along the upper South Fork of the San Joaquin River, twenty-five to forty miles distant by trail. This sudden change in plans did not interfere with our attending the dance at Big Creek the evening before— even though we knew we would have to hike to Huntington Lake afterwards in the wee small hours of the morning. We reached the engineers' quarters at

Pages 52-53: Los Angeles' streets were still dominated by the trolley car when Dave Redinger opened a private engineering practice early in 1914. This view of rush hour shows Los Angeles Railway trolley cars lined up on East Seventh Street, waiting their turn to cross the equally busy Main Street. All of these trolleys, and much of downtown Los Angeles, were receiving electricity from the new Big Creek power plants.
Charles Lawrence Photo, Courtesy Huntington Library and Art Gallery

Huntington Lake about four o'clock— allowing us about an hour before we would have to get breakfast and have our bedrolls ready to turn over to the packers by six o'clock. We did not think it worthwhile undressing, let alone opening our bedrolls, and scattered throughout the large room upstairs looking for a place to "flop." Suddenly it occurred to me that I might sneak into the only room in one corner of the spacious upstairs and "sleep soft." The room had been made, furnished and set aside for the use of the "brass hats," and usually the door was kept locked when unoccupied. I thought perhaps someone might have failed to lock it, and no one else in our group would think of making any investigation. There had been no "brass hats" around during the day, so to the room I went, feeling my way and being careful not to fall over anyone stretched out on the floor. The door was unlocked, and "what luck!"—so I thought. I opened it carefully, stepped inside, and closed it so quietly a mouse would not have been disturbed. I sat down on the bed, removed my shoes and started to undress, when there was a woman's voice. "What's going on here?" I didn't know one of the engineers had brought his wife along. Out the door I went, without my shoes, and as for sleep the next hour, I had none. It was not altogether the shock, but the only suitable spot I could find to lie down on quickly was on some cold folded canvas, part of our camp equipment going out with us that day.

There were two parties—one headed by H. L. Wheeler, the other by me—all men hiking except the packers. Saddle horses for such a group were not provided in those days, and if they had been offered we would have been very much surprised, if not offended.

The trip to Blaney Meadows, via Red Mountain and Hot Springs Pass, was broken by camping overnight on the way. Wheeler started his work on the right-hand side of the South Fork of the San Joaquin River, heading upstream, and I began on the other. A line of levels was carried all the way from Huntington Lake to Piute and Evolution Creeks. This was to determine the elevation above sea level of all important points of our work. We were investigating the feasibility of carrying water from the higher elevations across Hot Springs Pass and into the Huntington Lake watershed. We thought nothing of climbing as much as 2,000 feet each morning to our work, and over terrain as rough as one could find. I recall one experience while we were running our line around and far up on the side of the Pavilion Dome, a steep cliff. Handholds and toeholds along the sheer face were scarce, but we had become adept in the use of "skyhooks" under such conditions. I got into a spot from which I could not extricate myself without leaving my six-foot steel rod, which a chief of party carries when he goes ahead to assist in running a survey line. The rod, no doubt, is still there, as no one but an experienced alpine climber would ever attempt to scale such a cliff just for fun.

Blaine Riley, transit man, had a narrow escape when he slipped, but fortunately he was able to catch a handhold by letting loose of the Berger transit. A sheer drop of at least a thousand feet was below him.

A good idea of the terrain may be had by my saying that one day's run covered a total distance of only 100 yards. Our line was carried along on contour, and it was not unusual to look down on our camp, one to two thousand feet below. The camp was moved frequently enough to make our trips

as short as possible horizontally, but nothing much could be done about the vertical distances.

We were surprised and annoyed one morning upon arriving at the place on line where we had left our transit, tapes, axes, etc., the evening before, to find that during the night the string from our plumb bobs and the buttons from our coats and jackets had been eaten off and carried away. The transit could not be accurately set, of course, without a plumb bob, but we made do through that day, since a round trip to camp for anyone would have taken several hours. We profited from this lesson about the hazards of chipmunks.

For pastime on Sunday, if we did not work, we would usually take a "postman's holiday"—go on a hike and climb some mountain peak, the highest in the vicinity. Being so near, we couldn't pass up a visit to Evolution Lake, and several were unable to resist the temptation to climb Mt. Darwin, in spite of its elevation—almost 14,000 feet. The naming of the lake and mountain is credited to Theodore S. Solomons in 1895. It is only natural for one to call to mind the Darwinian theory when confronted with the names of the above lake and mountain, and those on government maps—Wallace, Spencer, Fiske and Haeckel—all close High Sierra neighbors and often referred to as "The Evolution Group of Philosophers."

The names or initials, with dates, carved on quaking aspens along the trails, attest to the fact our party went that way, but we were by no means the first, as we saw date scars from the 1870s.

At the outbreak of World War I our camp was located far up on Evolution Creek. "Sippi" Johnson, from headquarters, rode through the night and into the day, bringing instructions to "button up" the job and return to Big Creek.

The survey crews who laid out the initial development at Big Creek had to endure the most primitive living conditions. An unidentified crew of surveyor, rodman and axeman poses for a Sunday portrait near Halleck Creek, below Powerhouse No. 2. Dave Redinger lived in camps like this during the summer of 1914.
Collection of William A. Myers

The next morning, August 20, we were up before daylight, and believe me, that was early. Our bedrolls were quickly made ready for the packers, and after a hasty breakfast we headed for Big Creek on foot, some thirty five or forty trail miles via Blaney Meadows and Hot Springs Pass—all of us acting like a bunch of pack mules and saddle horses making for the corral after having been turned loose. Being in perfect trim for such a hike, we did not stop long enough for our light lunch, preferring to eat it on the fly, and literally slid down Pitman Creek into Big Creek. Our arrival was marred only by our method of entering camp. It was twilight, and to minimize embarrassment in case we should meet any women, we entered headquarters by a circuitous route. Even with such precautions we walked circumspectly at times, as the seats of our pants had been completely worn away by sliding over rocks.

On the trail we wondered whether any of the summer school girls might have remained at Big Creek, but concluded such a prospect was hopeless,

The most challenging surveying assignments at Big Creek was running levels and alignments for tunnels across the rugged back country terrain. Here, T. R. Bond and his party pose at an unidentified location, about 1912. Dave Redinger's survey trip to Blaney Meadows in the summer of 1914 took him to country like this.
Collection of William A. Myers

The most difficult job on a survey crew was that of "axeman." These men cleared away underbrush to provide the surveyors with a clear line of sight. This picture shows a survey party engaged in clearing a line for the construction of the San Joaquin & Eastern Railroad early in 1912. This was considered an "entry-level job" in the civil engineering profession, and Dave Redinger put in his share of time at this type of work.
Collection of William A. Myers

since we knew the summer session was scheduled to end August 15. We were delighted to find a few of those we had met on July 3 remaining over for a period of rest and relaxation, which was cut short by our arrival. The girls seemed not to object, and proceeded to entertain us royally with wonderful breakfasts and dinners, prepared and served in one of the old bunkhouses.

It should not be difficult for anyone to understand how ten days of such treatment affected us, after having had no meals prepared by such lovely hands for nearly two months. It was the forerunner of "disastrous" results for one member of the Fresno State College group who was the head of the Home Economics Department—because about three years later, and after much persuasion, she became Mrs. Redinger.

As a result of World War I, the company stopped all field work such as that which we had been doing, and again, along with the other members of both survey parties, I found myself laid off as of September 1, 1914.

For many years, a large part of Big Creek's electrical output powered the trolley cars of both the Pacific Electric and Los Angeles Railway companies. Each railway converted alternating current purchased from Edison into direct current. Valley Junction Substation was the largest on the Pacific Electric system. Built in 1911 to replace a smaller facility, it was rated at 3,500 kilowatts of capacity, and fed direct-current electricity to P. E.'s Pasadena Short Line, Covina-San Bernardino Line, and Pasadena via Garvanza Line. The latticed steel "pole" behind the substation is an Edison 66,000-volt transmission line feeding power into the Pacific Electric's 16,000-volt transmission system from a nearby Edison substation. This photo of Valley Substation and busy Valley Junction was taken in 1946.
Official Pacific Electric Photo, from the Collection of William A. Myers

This view of Phoenix looks west on Washington Street from its intersection at Central, about 1914.
Elizabeth Ullman Parsons Collection from the Arizona Historical Society

VI
We Winter in Arizona

THOSE OF US WHO had been turned loose were again in the market for a job. We wondered where we would find one, in view of our type of work being curtailed wherever possible on account of the European situation. We scattered in all directions. I found myself in San Francisco, where, coincidentally, I had been called by the United States Land Office to appear at another hearing in connection with the Alaska coal lands case. It was not long before several of the Big Creekers, including "Hank" Wheeler, the late O. J. Schieber, and me, thanks to "Ollie," were enjoying the "nosebags" of the U. S. Reclamation Service on the Salt River Valley Project at Phoenix, Arizona.

Naturally, the work involved irrigation problems, and for some time my party was located at Mesa, where we occupied a tent without a floor, in the U. S. Reclamation Service's mule corral—no foolin'—but the mules were nice and as gentle as mules know how to be. Two of them pulled us around in a regulation line wagon, and naturally we became quite well acquainted— so much so that they thought they should sleep with us in our crowded tent.

Walter Jessup (later the western representative of the American Society of Civil Engineers) had a deluxe tent, floored and screened, with even a kerosene heater, in a somewhat more secluded section of the corral than ours. Frequently, when it was unoccupied, we would take advantage, slip in and spend an enjoyable night amid such luxuries.

Some of the area we covered is today occupied either by a dude ranch or a swank hotel, such as the Arizona Biltmore and Camel Back Inn.

How well I recall being one of the thousands on hand to greet Barney Oldfield, that day in 1915, as he finished the historic nonstop run from Los Angeles to Phoenix. He was easy to recognize because of the ever-present cigar, and I can still see him and his mechanic as they roared through the outskirts of Phoenix while the tumultuous roadside throngs waved frantically and got spattered with mud, much of which the car threw at least fifty feet in the air. Besides affording the populace immense thrills, such endurance runs had much to do with the development of the automobile.

The rapid growth of Phoenix, clearly evidenced by this photo, was in part due to the extensive irrigation system developed by the Salt River Valley Project. In 1914 and 1915, Dave Redinger worked as a surveyor for the project, based in Phoenix and Mesa, Arizona.
Courtesy Arizona Historical Society

One Sunday morning in Phoenix, while walking to breakfast, I observed a heavy pall of black smoke. My favorite eating place, Gass Brothers Cafe, was engulfed in flames, and along with it was my weekly meal ticket purchased the night before. As was customary, I had left it with the cashier. As I did not have any change it was necessary to rouse some friends out of bed and "interview" them before I could eat.

Not long after this incident, I was on my way to the bank where I had recently deposited my limited funds. It was not smoke this time, but a large crowd in the street. There was a sign on the door—yes, you guessed it—announcing that the bank had failed. Again friends had to come to my rescue. Like the meal ticket, this loss was never recovered.

It afforded me pleasure, while in Arizona, to make preliminary arrangements for the monument which now stands near the El Tovar Hotel at the Grand Canyon, in honor of Major Powell, reported to be the first white man to make the hazardous trip down the Colorado River.

Phoenix, no doubt, will long remember New Year's Eve, 1915, when prohibition went into effect. All wet goods not consumed before midnight were carried away by the bottle, case, armful—any method available. I saw one man pushing a wheelbarrow down the street—full to the brim, like himself. Fixtures were yanked from their moorings, hauled, and even manhandled, through the streets—the all-night spirit being that of one huge carnival instead of a "swan song."

I have always been thankful for the Arizona experience because I learned not only to like the desert, the giant Saguaro cactus, the horned toads, but

The El Tovar, or Grand Canyon Lodge, at the South Rim of the Grand Canyon, was already an important tourist destination in 1915, when Dave Redinger surveyed the location for a monument dedicated to Major John Wesley Powell.
Courtesy Arizona Historical Society

also to appreciate fully the meaning of "the desert in bloom."

The Arizona assignment, coupled with three months in the employ of the California Highway Commission at San Luis Obispo and Bradley, constituted a period long enough to cause a break in continuity of service with the Pacific Light & Power Corporation, and the loss of three and one-half preceding years.

365

VII
Huntington Lake Lodge

A S THERE WAS NO HOTEL above Big Creek, the officials of the Pacific Light & Power Corporation became deeply interested in such a venture. After due consideration they reached a decision to build one at Huntington Lake. Such an undertaking appeared to have promise—especially in a mountain setting at an elevation of 7,000 feet, and with the railroad to serve the hotel. The Huntington Lake Hotel Company was formed as a subsidiary of the Pacific Light & Power Corporation, and the site selected was one beneath the pines on the south shore near the west end of the lake, readily accessible by road.

Huntington Lake Lodge was completed early enough in 1915 to allow it to be opened on July 4. H. M. Nickerson, who was associated with the Huntington Hotel in Pasadena, was engaged to supervise construction and to manage the hotel after it was opened. He returned for the 1916 season but had to relinquish management early because of illness. Mr. Huntington arranged for the services of Howard B. Brown, who headed the staff of the Alpine Tavern, the famous hotel at Mount Lowe, and he completed the season. Carl A. Babb, who had operated the Shasta Springs Hotel, became manager beginning with the 1917 season, and served through 1925. He was followed by Fred Williams, formerly of the Hughes Hotel in Fresno, who carried on from 1926 to 1931.

Considerable enthusiasm was shown for snow sports during the first winter after the lodge was opened. The Commercial Club of Fresno—sixty-five members strong—constituted the party making up the first "Ice and Snow Carnival," as it was called. The success of that outing is nicely described by George Wharton James of Pasadena, in his booklet, *Winter Sports at Huntington Lake Lodge,* dated Cascada, February 22, 1916. To my knowledge, that was the only such outing ever held in winter during the life of the lodge. The principal barrier to winter sports in the area, as far as the lodge was concerned, was the problem of keeping open the road between Big Creek and Huntington Lake under winter conditions. Justification for such heavy expense, along with that for operating the lodge, would have required

Famed Fresno photographer C. C. "Pop" Laval took a series of promotional photographs of the Huntington Lake Lodge about 1916. These pictures reveal the simplicity and innocence of an era that was soon to disintegrate under the stresses of World War I. Here, an unidentified family group sits in front of a rustic log structure known for many years as "Uncle Tom's Cabin." The main building of the lodge lies in the background.
C. C. "Pop" Laval Photo, from the Edison Collection

66

A clay court version of lawn croquet was another attraction of the Huntington Lake Lodge in its earliest years.
C. C. "Pop" Laval Photo, from the Edison Collection

This 1919 picture of the main room of the Huntington Lake Lodge clearly illustrates the rustic atmosphere that was its main attraction. Snowshoes, skis and a toboggan hint at the area's winter snowfall, while the bearskin on the wall reminds visitors of their remoteness from "civilization."
G. Haven Bishop Photo, from the Edison Collection

patronage larger than could have been expected in those days. For about the first ten years of operation, most of the guests came by train to Big Creek, where they were met and driven by bus up the 2,000-foot climb.

Naturally, the seasons were short, and although the hotel would open about June 1, guests would be few until the middle of that month unless the weather were unusually good. By the middle of September the lodge would close. It became a natural center for activities at the lake, continuing as such through the early 1920s.

The road around the north shore to the upper end of the lake was constructed in 1920 by the United States Bureau of Public Roads, the Isabella Construction Company being the contractor. The completion of this road really marked the beginning of what has become a large and popular summer resort, to the extent of about 400 individually owned cottages, several stores, hotel accommodations, Forest Service campgrounds, various schools and three post offices. On the south shore, but not accessible by road, Boy Scout camps have been established, and one large deluxe camp for boys. Prior to the construction of the road along the north shore, a few cabins were built, the material being ferried across the lake in rowboats. The first one built was intended for Henry E. Huntington, but he never saw it. Later the grounds were used by the lodge for entertaining its guests with barbecues and wiener roasts. The trips made across the lake to the camps on moonlit nights were picturesque and delightful. To add to the enjoyment, the boat usually towed a barge large enough to permit dancing. Long to be remembered is the full moon rising, especially on the nights, usually in August, when it appears to be pushing itself out of the very top of distant Red Mountain. This is a magnificent sight when seen from anywhere, and especially so if viewed from the northwesterly shores of the lake. The moon moves to the north each night, of course, and when it comes over the mountain on the south shore of the lake, the pine trees at the top are so clearly silhouetted that one can almost see the chipmunks running along the

68

Boating was not encouraged on Huntington Lake in earlier years, but the lodge used this launch to transport visitors to points around the lakeshore. This is the same boat that can be seen in the photo on page 47.
C. C. "Pop" Laval Photo, from the Edison Collection

limbs—except that they know better than to be out at that time of night.

Guests were always cautioned, when they went hiking or horseback riding, to stay on the well-blazed trails so as to take no chance of getting lost. If they insisted on going, and were not sure of themselves, they would be offered a guide to accompany them. On one occasion a woman guest was anxious to take a ride over some of the trails but did not want to be bothered with anyone accompanying her, insisting that she knew how to handle herself adequately in the mountains. Off she went—on the back of one of the best mountain horses the lodge owned. She became confused in the vicinity of Black Point. After losing the trail, and instead of allowing the horse free rein—he would have brought her back—she tied him to a tree, saddled and bridled, and started hiking. She was out overnight and said she had spent it sitting in a tree, since she was afraid of wild animals. Later in the day she appeared at one of our lower powerhouses, several mountain miles below, much bedraggled and exhausted. No one knew until then what direction to start on a search for the horse. He was found on the third day—the poor fellow still tied to the tree and ready for water and barley.

The lodge was the scene of many capacity gatherings, some sponsored by the Edison Company, and others, particularly conventions, on their own. It seemed to be a favorite spot for newspapermen to hold forth. Registered were many interesting guests, both local and from various parts of our own as well as foreign countries. One meeting I remember quite distinctly. The day after a convention of Pacific Coast lumbermen, I was having dinner in the lodge dining room, when Manager Babb told me a gentleman was waiting in the lobby and was quite anxious to see me. He gave his name as MacGregor, representing himself as being on the staff of the *Edinburgh Scotsman.* He wanted to learn all he could about the "wonderful power development then in progress in these parts," as he wished to give the story to his paper for the information of its readers throughout England and Scotland. He reported loss of his wallet on the train from Fresno that afternoon. Besides losing all the cash he had, he appeared to be more worried about the loss of his passport. I would have been apprehensive had it not been for presentation of a card bearing the name of a highly respected gentleman who had been in attendance at the lumbermen's convention the day before. The editor of *The Timberman* (Portland) had written a friendly introduction to me on his card, so all was taken to be in order. In those days, many men were being transported by train daily to the job, and steps were taken immediately to post notices in all camps, offering a reward for the return of the passport. No information was forthcoming. In the meantime, Manager Babb was asked to take care of MacGregor as a company guest.

Several days later, MacGregor was invited to my office, where he met George C. Ward, then vice-president in charge of all construction. MacGregor made an appointment with him that evening, and I was present. Mr. Ward took the time to give MacGregor quite a comprehensive story in considerable detail—in fact, enough to fill two stenographer's notebooks. Whether any of the notes he was making could be deciphered afterwards became questionable shortly to both of us. The morning after the interview, MacGregor came back to my office. More than a week had now elapsed, and not having heard anything about his allegedly lost wallet, he indicated his anxiety to reach the British Consul in San Francisco, pointing out that he could not accomplish much about a passport by wire. In Mr. Ward's presence, I asked MacGregor how much money he felt he would need to get to San Francisco and see him through until he could get his affairs in shape. The sum of $125 appeared to him to be sufficient. With Mr. Ward's approval (he had indicated on the side that he thought we should help the fellow) that amount was given him from our local funds. He departed to contact the British Consul and make necessary arrangements by cable to replace his passport and to secure additional funds.

Not having heard from MacGregor after two weeks, we sent a letter of inquiry to the editor of *The Timberman* in Portland, since his card had been used as MacGregor's introduction. The reply stated he had met MacGregor in Fresno upon the former's return from the convention at the lodge. After being told by MacGregor that he was on the staff of a paper, and was also a fellow countryman, the editor suggested he go to Big Creek and write up the project for the *Scotsman*. Feeling his responsibility for MacGregor's Big Creek trip, the editor cabled the *Edinburgh Scotsman*. No such person was known by any member of its staff. To add insult to injury, MacGregor, upon reaching Fresno the evening of the day on which he left Big Creek, met by chance a very good friend of mine in the Hotel Fresno. He convinced my friend that he, MacGregor, was also a very close friend of mine. As the result of his super-salesmanship, he obtained the loan of my friend's overcoat for use in San Francisco until he could buy one. Needless to say, the Edison Company remains $125 in the red, plus expenses at the lodge, and my Fresno friend was the one who had to buy the new overcoat.

After sixteen years of operation, the lodge closed at the end of the 1931 season, since which time it has served for three short periods to house construction crews, as well as the State Guard, on duty in this area during World War II.

VIII
We Rebuild a Large Flume

ON MARCH 11, 1916, I returned to the Pacific Light & Power Corporation as engineer for the summer, on the reconstruction of the Borel Flume where it crosses Kern River at Isabella. The conduit of which this flume is a part carries water to the Borel Power House from the Kern River, the intake being at Kernville. Six months were required for building the high concrete piers in the riverbed and for replacing the timber sub-structure of the large flume to be supported by these piers. The field work was done under the supervision of Bill Whitmire. The heavy bridge timbers and the cement were freighted by wagon from Caliente, the nearest railroad station, forty miles distant, over the old Walker Basin Road via Havilah. The present river road was not built until later years.

Common to almost all construction jobs are the words, "time is of the essence," and the one at Isabella was no exception. In order to have some relaxation and fun, we worked longer than our regular ten-hour shifts, there-by gaining enough time to allow us to take every other Sunday for a fishing trip. Several of the men had their families at Isabella for the summer. On the evening before the Sunday off, the wives would have prepared such items of food as are usually taken on a camping trip, but in quantity sufficient, one thought, to last for a week instead of over one night. Occasionally, there was a huge washtub filled with fried chicken. The large lumber wagon, piled high with bedding, eats and men, would leave ahead of Whitmire, who brought up the rear in his Model "T," loaded inside and out with women and children. Even the husky mules appeared to be just as anxious to get to Erskine Creek or Bull Run, where fishing was really good in those days. There must be something wrong with a man who does not enjoy some good companions, a campfire, the food cooked over it--especially coffee made in a gallon tomato can--and the prospects of snagging some wary trout on the morrow.

On one of our outings we came up rather shy on fried chicken. "Sippi" Johnson and I were delegated to go through the country and find the fryers (he always called them "gumps"). As we were returning to camp, from a

This early view of the interior of the Borel Hydroelectric Plant shows the five original generators installed when the plant was built. Subsequently modernized, the Borel Plant remains in operation today. *Pacific Light & Power Photo, from the Edison Collection*

ranch near Weldon, the jolting wagon shook the crate open. The chickens scattered in all directions but only one of us could enter in the chase because the other had to stay with the mules, there being no place to tie them. I could not run fast enough, and we returned to camp after dark with only a half dozen.

One day we received a report about a failure of the 84-inch steel flow line at Huntington Lake. Shortly after midnight on the morning of May 14, a circumferential joint pulled apart, the rivets having sheared because of the enormous side pressure of a slide from above. The entire hillside, saturated from the melting snow, had decided to move, and would not be thwarted by a mere man-made pipeline, even though it was large. It is strange how many major failures of various kinds occur at the most inconvenient hours. The damaged line was the only one at that time carrying water from Huntington Lake to the penstocks feeding Powerhouse No.1. Consequently, that plant was out of service until May 17 while repairs were being made. Steps had to be taken for harnessing the hillside permanently in case it should continue to be temperamental, because enforced outages of the plants below are serious. The present huge concrete structure, deeply and securely anchored, enclosing the large pipeline through the dangerous area, was built that summer. The design allows a slide to slip over the roof and down the canyon without disturbing the pipe in case the hillside should take another notion to "go places."

As the summer progressed, we learned of the proposed work for increasing the height of the Huntington Lake Dams. It appeared probable that we would move to that location with the completion of the flume repairs in September.

Previous pages: Pacific Light & Power's Borel Hydroelectric Plant in Kern Canyon is supplied by a long canal whose intake originally lay near Kernville. This massive wooden flume carried the canal waters over the Kern River at Isabella. Dave Redinger worked its reconstruction in the spring and summer of 1916.
Pacific Light & Power Photo, from the Edison Collection

Opposite page: The Borel Hydroelectric Plant was built by a subsidiary of the Pacific Light & Power Company. Named for Antoine Borel, an early business associate of Henry Huntington, the plant provided electricity to Huntington's growing trolley and utilities business in Southern California from 1904. The canal carrying water to the plant can be traced along the edge of the canyon behind the powerhouse.
G. Haven Bishop Photo, from the Edison Collection

IX
Raising Huntington Lake Dams

THE USE OF ELECTRICITY was increasing rapidly, and to meet the load demands, additional water for power had to be provided. The decision was made to enlarge Huntington Lake by increasing the height of the three dams by thirty-five feet, this being in accord with the United States Government permit under which the project was being developed. The storage capacity would be increased to almost 89,000 acre feet.

To ensure such a major job being completed the following year—it was now early in 1916—everything had to be in readiness to proceed as early as spring conditions would allow. Final approval was given to start as of September 1, and immediately everything was shifted into high gear. A huge supply of lumber had to be provided, and quickly, as camps had to be built, the sawmill reconditioned, a large rock-crushing plant constructed, power lines extended, railroad tracks laid, air compressors installed, cement stored, and material of many kinds obtained.

The responsibility for the job in the field was given to Rex Starr, who brought Bill Whitmire from Isabella as general foreman. I came along as resident engineer. Hospital facilities were one of the first things to be provided, under Dr. O. I. Bemis, and were established at old Camp 1D below Huntington Lake Lodge, at the same location where John Eastwood had built a log cabin in earlier years, while carrying on his surveys in the area.

A logging camp was set up on the south side of the lake. Huge logs were soon sliding down the long skidways, with such terrific speed that they would leave streamers of smoke behind from friction. As they hit the water there would be a splash like a small Niagara Falls in reverse.

Work got under way on Dam 3, the smallest of the three Huntington Lake dams, and by the time winter prevented further progress, a parapet wall seven feet high had been completed along the top of the structure. A rock quarry was opened a short distance east of Dam No. 2, and construction of a large crushing plant started nearby. A smaller plant was built near the main entrance to Huntington Lake Lodge. Work trains soon were shuttling back and forth from the top of the main incline, up which all material and equip-

The project to raise the height of the three dams impounding Huntington Lake called Dave Redinger back to Big Creek in September 1916. This view of the work at Dam No. 3 shows how, literally, a new dam had to be built on the downstream face, and on top of the older dam.
Photographer unknown, from the Edison Collection

ment coming into Big Creek by rail was handled. The shrieking of locomotive whistles and the clanging of bells made the area sound like a mainline railroad yard. Much of the work was carried on around the clock. Progress was halted when the operator of the large incline hoist went to sleep while the car was on its way up from Big Creek—it took half an hour for the ascent—and was awakened when the car came crashing through the hoist house and over the top of the hoist. He barely had time to shut off the power; otherwise, he would have been pinned beneath the car. He did not wait for his time check.

Thanksgiving came along and an excellent dinner was served in each camp. On the tables in Camp lE, serving the Dam No. 3 job, the waiters—"flunkies" in construction parlance—had arranged attractive and appropriate decorations. Don Morgan and Ned Woodbury, both from the Los Angeles office, were much intrigued with the display of mountain holly, peculiar to the Huntington Lake area—so they were told by the flunkies. Don was tipped off and saw a chance for some "foul" play—being very good at such—at the expense of Woodbury. The latter was quite anxious to get some of the "holly" to take back to Los Angeles, and with encouragement from Morgan, it was arranged for the head flunkie to escort Woodbury down the rugged and brushy Big Creek Canyon so he could select and pick his own. Naturally, such a rare bush grew in places difficult of access. When the head flunkie decided Woodbury had had enough scrambling through the brush, getting scratched and his clothes torn, he stopped at an unusually attractive manzanita bush. He broke off several small branches, stripped some leaves, then took some cranberries from his pocket and gently stuck them on the ends of the branches—at the same time saying, "Mr. Woodbury, there is your mountain holly. In the meantime, Don Morgan had disappeared.

We were able to continue work, with minor interruptions from storms, until Christmas Day, when we had to dig out of four feet of snow. The major activity for the remainder of the winter was centered at Big Creek, where a small crew was stationed to unload cement and place it in storage in preparation for the following spring, when work would be resumed at Huntington Lake. This routine was upset about 4:00 p.m. on February 19, 1917. A few of us in the office heard a heavy thump, followed shortly by an excited call from R. B. Lawton, in charge of operation. A break had occurred in one of the penstocks (pipelines) halfway up the mountain. They could not close, from the plant, the 42-inch gate at the top of the penstock-and could I send some men up there at once to close it. That was a tough order—the break could not have occurred at a worse time, as the snow even at Big Creek was deep enough to require travel by sled, and it was still snowing hard. Three of us left at once with three horses, hitched tandem to a long, narrow sled called a "snow boat." We were unable to proceed beyond Huntington Lake Lodge, as no trail had been broken and the snow was too deep for the horses. We loaded the heavy-duty jacks and other tools onto a large toboggan. Wearing snowshoes, we started for the gate house, about a mile distant, pulling the load. After much floundering, and fighting a blizzard all the way, with only a kerosene lantern for light, we reached the gate house about 2:00 a.m., eventually getting the gate jacked shut. It is disconcerting to note the

The picture opposite was taken in the summer of 1917. It shows the complex system of railroads and chuting employed to pour the concrete for the raising of the dams at Huntington Lake. Steam locomotives ran trains of three-yard dump cars over a standard-gauge remnant of the old "Basin Railroad," bringing concrete from the mixing plant to each dam site. At the dam, the standard-gauge trains dumped their concrete into smaller, one-yard dump cars. These cars, which ran on three-foot narrow-gauge track, were formed into three- or four-car trains and pulled out over the dam by gasoline-powered locomotives. In the middle of the picture, the narrow-gauge cars can be seen dumping their concrete into hoppers to be chuted down to the work face. *Photographer unknown, from the Edison Collection*

only item appearing in the powerhouse's log book is, "Gate was jacked down"—nothing to indicate the unusual difficulties experienced by those closing it.

Whenever a powerhouse generator is idle because of breakdown, all hands concentrate their efforts on restoring it to service. One was idle now. A special heavy laminated steel bulkhead was quickly designed and made in Los Angeles to blank off the broken branch of the penstock pipe. Upon arrival, it was manhandled by sled to the site of the break, well up the mountain, and bolted in place. It was then possible for water to flow through the other branch and operate the affected unit at reduced output with one water wheel. With men working day and night, repairs were completed and normal service restored on March 1.

Starr thought I needed a change, and suggested I take advantage of the opportunity of a slack period, for a month or so. He knew I was planning to be married. His suggestion made the step definite, and I left at once for the Middle West. One of the many jobs completed the previous fall at Huntington Lake, preparatory to raising the dams, was the building of five cottages. I had hinted at the time I would appreciate having one.

In spite of precautions on my part, the local espionage system worked to perfection as to the arrival of the newlyweds at Big Creek a month later. No better advertising was ever accomplished. When the S. J. & E. train was within half a mile of the Big Creek depot, "Spike" Meehan at the throttle, all hell broke loose—the fireman had a full head of steam ready for the occasion. The locomotive whistle was the signal for the other engines in the area to join in, as well as the machine shop. They kept it up until we alighted at the station, when bedlam broke out there. The entire school had been dismissed so all could be on hand to add to the noise. All available employees were present to do their part. Washtubs, wash basins, tin cans—anything and

This view of a narrow-gauge gasoline locomotive with empty dump cars was taken from the adjacent standard-gauge railroad trestle. The gas locomotives were primitive in the extreme: an automobile accelerator, a lever to change direction and a simple hand brake were the only controls. An unsprung pine board was the only seat for the engineer!
Photographer unknown, from the Edison Collection

everything that could be used to advantage for noise-making—had been commandeered. We were escorted to a much-decorated conveyance—one of the huge Shaver lumber wagons. Six shiny black mules, their harness wrapped with white cloth, were hitched to the outfit. Perched on the high driver's seat, black-faced, and in livery attire, was General Foreman Bill Whitmire. He even had on white gloves. A canopied seat for the bridal couple was arranged far below the driver, in the center of the long wagon bed. Hanging all around the wagon were dozens of tin cans, more dragged on the ground behind, and dozens of old shoes completed the decorations. The parade started—we were driven around Big Creek to the accompaniment of the noisy throng that followed, finally being allowed to alight at one of A. O. Smith's hotel tents, which was to be our home for about a month. About 10:00 p.m., as soon as the lights were out, rocks began to rattle over the corrugated iron roof. The stove began to smoke, as a cover had been placed over the chimney. Visitors had arrived—we had to have fresh air, so they were invited to come in. One carried a Victrola, another a coffee percolator, others brought food, and although the tent was crowded, the party made themselves at home until morning. Taken altogether, it was a reception we have never forgotten.

The latter part of April brought signs of life again in the Huntington Lake area, and by the middle of May a beehive in blossom time could not have been busier.

On April 30, Mrs. Redinger and I entered our new cottage, but to do so, much shovel work was necessary as the snow extended above the top of the front door.

Special quarters had been built the previous fall in one corner of the lodge grounds for the department of auditor C. P. Staal, whose representative on the job was C. R. Duncan. Not only did men have to be paid, but the amount of accounting for such a job naturally was large. It was more practical to handle all such work locally rather than in Los Angeles. Starr's office was also in the accounting department building.

Crews got busy, concentrating on Dam No. 3, where their work had been abandoned the previous fall. New excavation had to be made along the downstream toe of each dam for the new concrete section. Pneumatic drills started pounding away on the back of the dam, drilling holes for the steel rails to be used as reinforcements to bond the new concrete to the old. Carpenters were as thick as flies, building forms and long chutes to carry the concrete. One might think of the new concrete slab as a huge blanket covering the entire lower side and top of each structure. Bill Whitmire called the attention of Tom O'Connor, one of the carpenter foremen, to the wasted motion in keeping ahead with the concrete forms. O'Connor had an alibi when he pointed to one of his men carrying a two-by-four, emphasizing that the carpenter was not waiting for the helper. Just then the carpenter set the two-by-four down to gaze around. Whitmire inquired as to the need for such relaxation, whereupon O'Connor quickly countered with, "He's thinkin' now and plannin' his next move."

An unusually large gyratory rock crusher was being installed in the main aggregate plant between Dam No. 2 and the quarry. After climbing through a regular forest of trestle timbers one morning, I introduced myself to the

Early in the summer of 1917, as the dam-raising project went into high gear, a large new crushing plant was built near Dam No. 2. Trainloads of granite were crushed and washed in this facility, then mixed with cement to make concrete.
Photographer unknown, from the Edison Collection

man handling the installation. He said his name was Smith—a most uncommon one, I remarked. This was the way I first met T. A. Smith, who became one of our best foremen, with many years of service at the time of his early death. He was best known as "T.A." and was also called "Hard-Boiled" Smith, but all a man had to do to get along with him was put out a day's work—and "T.A." knew what constituted such.

As the Dam No. 3 job progressed, men moved to Dam No. 2 to make it ready for its share of the program. From Dam No. 2 the move would be to Dam No. 1, the-last of the large dams to be raised in height. The excavation at the toe of Dam No. 1 was considerable, since much loose material had accumulated since completion of the original structure. The derricks were repaired as necessary and used for the excavation required for the raising program. In the removal of all the material at the toe of Dam No. 1, a concrete mixer was uncovered, as well as a number of kegs of rusted nails.

The intake tower at Dam No. 1 had to be increased in height also. This structure stands in the lake high above the portal of the tunnel through which water flows to the plants below. Its purpose is to house the controls for operating the nine-foot tunnel gate. In addition to raising the tower, the machinery to operate the gate had to be installed and enclosed. Since the construction of the dams in 1913, the tower had functioned with a windlass arrangement, unhoused, and operated by manpower.

One of the many important details of any construction job involves material—its availability when and where wanted, whether it be 100,000 board feet of lumber, a keg of nails or whatever. It was the duty of Harold Fox (in later years builder of the Pacific Gas and Electric Company's Balch plant) to see that no phase of the job suffered for lack of anything. He probably covered more territory daily, expediting the needs of the various jobs, than any other individual. What he did not have in his head about things available, he carried as notes in a little canvas bag suspended from his shoulder.

The arrival of summer brought guests to the lodge, which was in the center of all the construction. Blasting in the quarry, a short half-mile away, occurred at all hours, especially at night. Guests who did not enjoy being severely shaken while in bed would check out, while others would complain to Manager Babb, who would ask Starr if something could not be done about it. An irate guest might even suggest firing the foreman. Starr was crowding everybody, especially the quarry crews, and I usually knew when to expect the heavy blasts. They were most likely to occur shortly after a special complaint had been made, just go give that "blankety-blank guest something to really squawk about."

The crushing and screening plant, built to serve the Dam No. 3 job, was only about 200 feet across the track from five new cottages, one of which I occupied. Starr had the one between mine and the office building. He always slept with at least one ear open and the crushing plant could not stop during the night but what he would be out to learn the reason. Actually, I saw him climb to the top of the plant in his pajamas at times. As I lived next door, I would hear him when he got out, or he would see that I was awake. A large stump was blasted about two o'clock one morning. The jolt was heavy, the center of the disturbance being nearby. My phone rang, as I was sure it

In addition to raising the dams at Huntington Lake, the intake tower had to be raised. It is located adjacent to Dam No. 1. When this picture was taken in August of 1917, pouring of the new portion of the intake was just under way. This location was the eastern end of the standard-gauge railroad that came up Incline No. 1 from the San Joaquin and Eastern Railroad at Cascada.
Photographer unknown, from the Edison Collection

would. Starr wanted to know "what in hell" that was, since it was not near the quarry. After being told, he remarked that the quarry was bad enough, but if we were moving other blasting into the lodge grounds, he would be accused of closing down the place.

An incident most unusual in those days occurred early one morning during the summer, of interest when compared to present-day customs. The mother of one of the timekeepers created a furor when she walked through the camp wearing trousers. Unfortunately for me, I happened to be near the office. Starr called me in excitedly, and wanted to know if I had seen what he saw. Of course I had—the outfit was really good-looking, too. He wanted to know who the woman was. I found out—and it then became my job to see that the mother and son were duly impressed with the "seriousness" of such an appearance, followed by instruction that it must not occur again. How times have changed! I don't think it is any exaggeration to say that today in the mountains, at the resorts especially, it is rather unusual to see a woman in a dress.

Last to be constructed was the much smaller structure called Dam 3A, which spans the saddle between Dams 2 and 3. The end of October saw the completion of all that had been done to make Huntington Lake ready to hold nearly twice as much water the following year as previously.

The Greater Edison

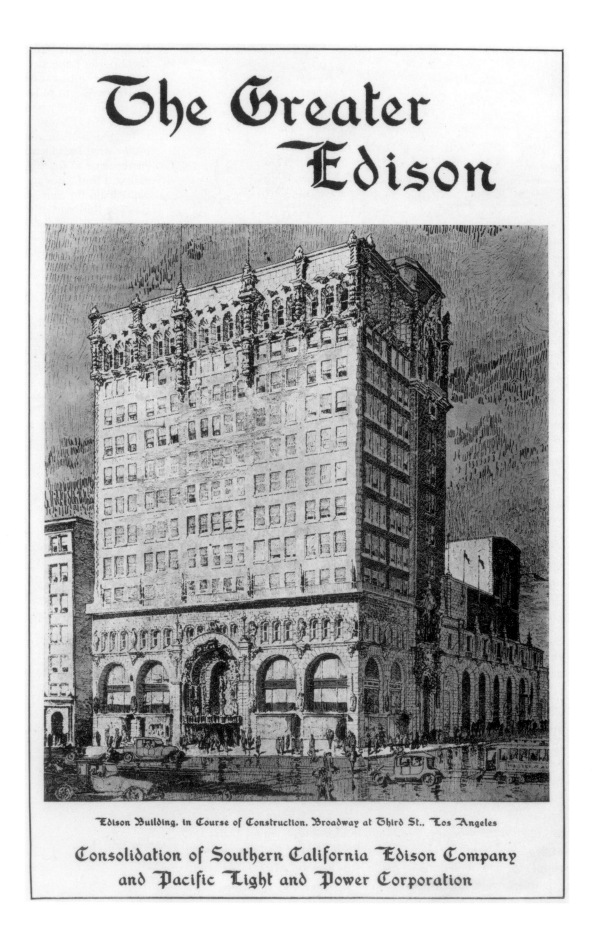

Edison Building, in Course of Construction, Broadway at Third St., Los Angeles

Consolidation of Southern California Edison Company and Pacific Light and Power Corporation

X
The Merger Takes Place

THE CONSOLIDATION of the Pacific Light & Power Corporation and Southern California Edison Company was completed in June 1917 when the rights of the former were transferred by government permit to the latter. Although this change took place in the midst of the raising of the Huntington Lake dams, those of us engaged on that work were practically unaware of any such move. The Pacific Light & Power Corporation did not really lose its identity in this area until the Huntington Lake job was finished.

Along with this consolidation, the Mt. Whitney Power & Electric Company was also taken over. John Hays Hammond was responsible for financing the parent company. While visiting his nephew, Col. William H. Hammond, in Honolulu just before World War II, I learned of his uncle's autobiography, in which the story is told about the raising of the money.

In 1898, John Hays Hammond was in London and received a visit from his brother Bill, to interest him in organizing the Mt. Whitney Power Company, since San Francisco bankers displayed no desire to invest. Mr. Hammond writes about A. G. Wishon and Ben M. Maddox being associated with his brother in the project of pumping water by electricity for that part of the San Joaquin Valley. There was much concern on the part of Mr. Hammond as to the feasibility of sending electricity so far--a distance of thirty-five miles--and he commented that it had never been done before for irrigation.Since he was a man of unusually keen vision, the capital for launching the project was quickly supplied by him and a London banker friend, whose interest Mr. Hammond bought shortly after returning to the United States, leaving Mr. Hammond as the sole backer.

To produce kilowatts, water is necessary. To get it, these men of real vision set out to enlarge four small lakes, fifty-five to sixty miles distant from Visalia and at elevations up to 11,000 feet. Just to explore the possibilities in such remote regions would be no small undertaking even today. Four small dams were built, utilizing local material and cement packed in on mules, and involving difficulties which would have discouraged less deter-

The consolidation of Pacific Light & Power into the Edison Company resulted in the formation of the nation's fifth largest electric utility. "The Greater Edison" combined the best talents from among both companies, so that while the Edison management team took charge of many of the enlarged company's operations, Pacific Light & Power men remained in charge of the Big Creek Project. Henry Huntington became a director of the Edison Company, and his longtime associate George C. Ward became Edison's Vice President of Engineering and Construction.
Photographer unknown, from the Edison Collection

mined individuals. Silver, Eagle, Monarch and Franklin Lakes, high above Mineral King, functioning today as the result of superhuman efforts, attest to the pioneering spirit of these men who deserve unusual credit as the originators of electric power in Visalia and vicinity.

The parent company, reincorporated in 1909 as the Mt. Whitney Power and Electric Company, started in business with a connected load of approximately 700 horsepower.

It is my good fortune to have known Mr. Wishon and Mr. Maddox in later years, while the former was president of the San Joaquin Light & Power Corporation, Fresno, and Mr. Maddox headed the Mt. Whitney Power and Electric Company in Visalia. I shall never forget their unusual experiences as pioneers in the field of electric power. Mr. Wishon, when in a reminiscing mood, enjoyed describing his efforts as a salesman to promote the use of a single light bulb at fifty cents to one dollar a month in the Visalia, Tulare, Lindsay, Exeter and Porterville areas.

By 1912, the Mt. Whitney Power and Electric Company had four plants in operation--Kaweah 1, 2, 3, and Tule, the rights of the latter having been

The original Kaweah No. 1 hydroelectric plant went into operation in June 1899, providing energy to several Tulare County communities. This was the beginning of the Mount Whitney Power Company, which was acquired by Edison in the merger with Pacific Light & Power in 1917.
Photographer unknown, from the Edison Collection

purchased from the Globe Light & Power Company in 1904 and placed in service five years later. Kaweah No. 3 and Tule plants are in operation today as originally constructed. Old Kaweah No. 1 has been replaced with a single unit in a new building. Kaweah No. 2 has been modernized with a new unit in place of the old one. The original buckets on the waterwheels of the two Tule plant units have been in use continuously to date, and only now are about ready for replacement. One of the original units of the old Kaweah No. 1 plant now stands as a monument on the site where it turned out kilowatts for so many years. A bronze plaque attests to that fact in these words:

Ben M. Maddox was one of the pioneers who brought hydro-electric power to Tulare County at the beginning of the Twentieth Century.
Courtesy Carl M. Ferguson

ON THIS SITE STOOD
POWER PLANT OF MT. WHITNEY POWER CO.

THIS GENERATOR, ONE OF THREE, WAS
THE FIRST TO DELIVER ELECTRIC POWER
TO TULARE COUNTY. IT WAS IN CONTINUOUS
SERVICE JUNE, 1899, TO MAY, 1929.
SOUTHERN CALIFORNIA EDISON COMPANY

Incidentally, I know of no book more inspiring and fascinating than the autobiography of John Hays Hammond, a California mining engineer who became an international figure.

One of the original Kaweah generators still stands in front of the modernized Kaweah No. 1 hydro-electric plant.
Greg O'Loughlin Photo, from the Edison Collection

XI
Building a
Transmission Line

D AM NO. 3A WAS ABOUT COMPLETED when Starr asked me to
move to the San Joaquin Valley and complete the east Big Creek transmission line. The two lines, each 150,000 volts, were to have been completed between Big Creek and Los Angeles in 1913. Partly for financial reasons,
the east line was left with a 10-mile gap between Bakersfield and Kings
River. The necessary tower steel, aluminum conductors, insulators, etc., had
been purchased and delivered to the nearest railroad stations through the valley in 1913.

Although I had no experience, I set out to get four camps established—
one to excavate for tower footings, one to set them, the third to erect the towers, the fourth to hang insulators, string the conductors and ground wire. The
last one also functioned as headquarters for the job. The first headquarters
camp was established near Richgrove.

The headaches were many—truck drivers, delivering material along the
line, would leave gates open; horses, cattle, pigs and what not would get out;
sometimes a horse, colt, cow or calf would get cut by barbed wire. Before I
knew a gate had been left open, an irate rancher would be on my neck. A
field or crop would suffer from our trucks. Sometimes damage would be
imaginary, but all complaints were not only listened to but followed up. One
frequent source of trouble was right-of-way problems. All property owners
were notified of our intentions, and their permission asked before we
entered. Many were surprised to learn, because of change of ownership, that
the right-of-way for two lines had been obtained originally. Trips were made
with a number of them to the courthouse in each county where our lines
were involved to show them the record. Mr. Sheridan, of Orange Cove,
appeared one day to show me something that made him most angry. In a far
corner of a very nice young olive orchard, he pointed to a sick-looking tree.
Then, calling my attention to truck tracks, he reached over and lifted the tree
out of the ground. The truck driver, in delivering steel for a tower nearby,

**The transmission lines that
carried Big Creek power into
Southern California were the
longest and highest-voltage lines
in the world in 1913. This photo
shows the lines very near to their
starting point at Big Creek
Powerhouse No. 1, some 243
miles from the terminal
substation at Eagle Rock.**
*G. Haven Bishop Photo, from the
Edison Collection*

had backed his vehicle over the tree, breaking it off. Instead of reporting it, he stood the tree up and heaped enough dirt around to keep it upright. By the time the tree attracted the owner's attention, the truck driver had left the job.

Ben Maddox was called on many times. Whenever I met up with a "rabid" rancher—one whom I could not reconcile—I would make a trip to Visalia. Mr. Maddox not only knew every individual in the entire area, but was highly respected by all. There was never a case involving a third party in which he was not able to help make an amicable settlement. Not infrequently, he would accompany me to the home of someone who felt he had a serious complaint. Eventually, Mr. Maddox, whenever I appeared at his office, would throw his head back and exclaim, with his hearty laugh, "Well, Dave, who is chasing you out of the country now?"

In those days, the conductors were pulled to tension with a four-up team of mules. While the crew members was working near Visalia they experienced some trouble with some small boys, who were vitally interested in such operations. One particular group was warned several times to keep its distance. Before the crew was aware of it, one youngster had taken hold of the conductor being raised and was too far above the ground to let loose, or he would have been seriously injured by the fall. By the time the team could be stopped, the boy was twenty-five feet in the air. Men began yelling at him to drop, which he finally had to do, being saved from injury by being caught.

This photograph of the construction of the Big Creek transmission line dates from the original construction phase in 1913, and shows the lifting of towers just south for Magunden, near Bakersfield. When Dave Redinger came into the San Joaquin Valley in 1918 to close the 100-mile gap in the East Line, the technology had not changed very much.
Pacific Light & Power Photo, from the Edison Collection

When the kid was turned loose, he hit the ground running—he had had enough.

During the summer the tower steel would get so hot it could not be handled without gloves. It was not unusual for pieces to be found missing. Piles of tower steel had been stored in railroad yards along the way for several years and some pieces were hidden by heavy growths of weeds. Now and then a station agent, new at the location, would know nothing of their presence. The heavy tower legs topped the list of shortages. Such pieces made excellent material for fence repairs. A trip around the local ranches always resulted in our finding missing members; small pieces were found around chicken yards. Identification was not difficult as the original stenciling was legible, and property owners never voiced any objection about removal. Having noticed the material for several years covered with weeds, they took for granted that it could not be of much importance. Because of World War I, aluminum was valuable; consequently, the reels of cable were never left unguarded along the line while waiting to be strung.

In taking over this job, it was necessary that I learn to drive a car. Being furnished a Ford pick-up with Waiter Bauermeister as instructor, I took the thing out along a little-used dirt road. Ever since, I can fully appreciate the feelings of anyone learning to drive, and especially how narrow a really wide highway can appear to be. Later, Jack Wheeler sent me a car which, even

Erecting a transmission tower in an orchard, exact location unknown.
G. Haven Bishop Photo, from the Edison Collection

today, I recall as a most wonderful automobile. The Stevens-Duryea roadster, Edison No. 3, more familiarly called the "3 Spot," was a real car even though it was nine years old at the time it was passed along to me. Cranked by hand, it was the only car I have ever driven that would start when warm merely by my turning on the ignition, provided it hadn't stood for more than fifteen or twenty minutes.

Mrs. Redinger was the only woman in the four camps. We had a twelve-by-fourteen tent. It is amazing what she accomplished in making our "rag house" comfortable—even when the time came for a Christmas tree. We moved every month or six weeks, camping in pastures, cut-over wheat or barley fields, some of which were newly plowed; one site was a stream bed. It was nothing unusual for interested cows or hogs to become tangled in the tent ropes, and their curiosity seemed to reach its peak at night. In general, our whole outfit was more or less frowned upon by the populace as we moved through the country. We seemed to be shunned as though we were gypsies. Mrs. Redinger, in her daytime loneliness, struck up a conversation one afternoon with a young woman who was working in an adjoining field, driving a team hitched to a harrow. Always fond of horses, she indicated that fact, and also mentioned a desire to do her part for the wartime effort. The stranger was interested, and I took Mrs. Redinger to the distant ranch house at six o'clock the following morning. Imagine her dismay, after anticipating a grand time driving the team, when she was informed by the ranch woman that the washing was ready, water was hot, etc. Rising to the occasion, and not to be outdone, she pitched into a stack of dirty clothes such as she had never seen outside a laundry. I returned between five and six o'clock that evening and found her just finishing. The premises reminded me of a circus—everything in the yard on all sides of the house, including the fences,

Increasing the voltage of the Big Creek transmission lines to a new world's record of 220,000 volts was a difficult task. In addition to replacing all of the insulators, most of the towers along the route had to be raised in height. The tower raising was accomplished by the use of winch-operated lifting devices, which enabled new bases to be placed beneath each tower.
G. Haven Bishop Photo, from the Edison Collection

was covered with drying clothes. The ranch woman was much chagrined the following day to learn from Mrs. Redinger that she had no intention of charging for the work, would accept nothing—and would have enjoyed the harrowing much more.

We experienced the usual difficulty in obtaining and keeping cookhouse help. This was particularly true of cooks. They were, perhaps, more temperamental than is usual because of the nature of the work, since the camps moved frequently. One winter morning before daylight, the camp foreman walked over to our tent to report that the chef had gone and there was no one to get breakfast. Mrs. Redinger heard the conversation and came to the rescue, saying that if she could have some help she would get up and do the cooking until another chef could be found. The men went to work at their usual hour, and the meals were reported to be most satisfactory. In fact, there was much reluctance on the part of the large crew to make a change. However, a chef was secured late the following day, and another of the episodes common to the cookhouses was at an end.

In the beginning, I tried to discourage Mrs. Redinger from joining me under the conditions as I knew they would be. In spite of this, she looked forward with deep anticipation to living in a tent. She has always held the viewpoint that a wife's place is with her husband and her duty is to make him as comfortable as possible regardless of where he has to be located. Not only was the isolation difficult for her—I was gone all day almost every day, week after week, month in and month out—but the summer heat in the valley was almost unbearable at times, in spite of our having a large canvas fly over the tent. In most of our camp locations there was not a shade tree within miles. On more than one occasion, when I returned in the afternoon I would find her wrapped in a wet sheet, and one suspended at either end of the tent. I am sure I will be pardoned when I say she deserves a world of credit for the part she has played, not only under conditions as she found them on the transmission line, but all through the construction camp life in which she has lived during our married years.

By September we had reached Kings River, and we were about ready to break camp. E. R. Davis, retired senior vice president of the Southern California Edison Company, in company with Don Morgan and Bob Lawton, arrived early one morning to inform me that Arthur Blight needed help to complete some surveys in the Big Creek country before bad winter-weather set in.

XII
Jackass Meadows and Vermilion Valley

THE MOUNTAINS HAVE MANY so-called "Jackass Meadows," and the Sierra is no exception. H. B. Howard had a survey party working in Upper Jackass Meadow, on the South Fork of the San Joaquin River a few miles below Blaney Meadows. At the time we were there, in 1918, the duck pond at the upper end of the meadow was known as "Florence Lake," having been so named about 1900 by a camper, Starr, for his daughter. The surveys we were making played their part in the later development of Florence Lake reservoir, dam and tunnel.

We had the whole back country pretty much to ourselves in those days. The road did not extend beyond the lower end of Huntington Lake, and packing concessions were few. Occasionally, we would see a cattleman or forest ranger, but seldom a tourist. A camp could be left indefinitely without being molested by humans. What a contrast with conditions as they are today! Cabins that have been built and stocked for use of hydrographers during winter months now are not safe even though padlocked. "Private Property" signs mean nothing to some who now come to the mountains. Formerly, if a prospector, cattleman, or such had any occasion to help himself to a food cache, or use a cabin, he was welcome—a note would always be left, or word passed along in some manner to the owner. Such was the law of the mountains. Today, locks are broken, windows smashed, chains cut, and property taken or destroyed, without any regard for anything or anybody. As the result of automobiles and extended roads, a new breed of people has found its way into the mountains.

The latter part of September we moved to the central part of Vermilion Valley for reconnaissance, establishing our camp on Mono Creek. The valley is reported to have been given its name by Theodore S. Solomons in 1894. We came across the name of this party frequently, as having visited these parts during the later years of the 1800s and the first of the 1900s. The color of the cliffs at the upper end of the valley, no doubt, is the reason for the name.

We were investigating the feasibility of water storage, which, of course,

94

would include a suitable site for a dam. These surveys were, in part, the fore-runners of the Mono-Bear development which came along ten years later.

In those days, fishing in some of the mountain streams, and particularly Mono Creek, was what the "Ike Waltons" really dream about. Although a limit of fifty trout had been established in 1905, it was seldom reached, as we caught no more than would be eaten. There were few fishing licenses in evidence in those days, although the first, according to the Division of Fish and Game, were issued at one dollar in 1913, the fee being increased to two dollars in 1927. For the type of people frequenting the mountains in the years about which I am writing, there was not much need for licenses or limits—certainly not the latter.

September changed to October, then November—and not only were the days growing shorter, but the nights colder. For a while after our move we could enjoy a bath in Mono Creek, or thought we did by kidding ourselves. Even in midsummer, the temperatures of such mountain streams seldom rise much above sixty degrees, and when ice started forming at night we thought it was time to think about the hot springs as a more appropriate place for a bath. Located on the South Fork of the San Joaquin River about three miles below Vermilion Valley, Mono Hot Springs was a favorite stopover to break a hot and dusty trail trip. Long before present-day facilities, the U. S. Forest Service had installed a large concrete tub at the principal spring, sheltered by a roughly constructed shake cabin. A sign cautioned all users not to remain in the bath more than twenty minutes—to stay longer would result in a devitalizing effect, and impair one's health. Through the years, the old tub was enjoyed by many passersby. As usual, one found many names, initials, and wisecracks as are found in public places. I recall seeing one somewhat unusual. Two Big Creek couples, one chaperoning the other, had enjoyed restful baths. Each had registered his or her name in a group on the wall, with the comment, "What a wonderful bath." Some jokester, taking advantage of the opportunity, had penciled beneath, "Ye Gods, what a tub-full."

The morning of November 11 arrived—the year, of course, was 1918. Being the first to arise after the cook, and having observed the weather, I noticed that the sky was overcast and snow was starting to fall. Our pack

Dave Redinger's pack train in Long Valley, 1918.
Photographer unknown, from the Edison Collection

train had just arrived from Huntington Lake the night before—with Dave Qualls in charge. Such an arrival was indeed timely. Word was passed around that everybody had better "shake a leg" and get going, as the weather was acting as if it meant business. Breakfast was quickly eaten, beds rolled, tents taken down, and everything made ready for the packers. By 8:30, the whole outfit started for Huntington Lake. It should be mentioned again that there were no roads above the lower end of the lake. The snowflakes grew in size and frequency, and the ground was soon covered with a white blanket. The trail became increasingly difficult for the pack animals. The mules appeared to sense the necessity of getting over Kaiser Pass as quickly as possible and did not lose very much time in their observations as they moved along. Pack mules have always entertained me. There was an unusually wise one on this trip. He was carrying an extra-wide load of bedrolls, with the camp cook stove on top. Frequently, I would notice him size up the clearance between trees, and if he decided it was too narrow, he would back up and go around. That particular mule, during his many trips that fall, never had an accident in losing or damaging a pack. We did not want to stop for lunch, but ate our hurriedly prepared sandwiches on the fly. We thought we did not even dare take the time to stop at the hot springs for a much-needed bath. Travel over the trail was growing more difficult for the pack animals, all of which had been loaded more heavily than usual in order to allow each man one animal to ride. Three o'clock in the afternoon found us on Kaiser Pass, elevation 9,305 feet. The snow was up to the animals' bellies, and we had to raise our feet in the stirrups to clear. We reached the upper end of Huntington Lake about six o'clock. Ever since five it had been dark. We had been hearing whistles blowing at Big Creek, and an occasional heavy report of a powder blast. We were so cold we did not pay much attention to the noise, but did wonder finally what the ruckus was all about. It suddenly dawned on us that maybe the war was over. No one ever traveled a trail that seemed so long as from the upper end of Huntington Lake around the lower end, past the lodge and on to Camp 1A, near Dam No. 1—a distance of about eight trail miles.

As soon as we arrived in camp I tried to call Big Creek. Nobody would

This panoramic view of the area surrounding Florence Lake was taken during Walter Sohier's 1917 survey trip. The original Florence Lake was a small alpine lake, now much enlarged by the construction of a reservoir.
Walter Sohier Photo, from the Edison Collection

Opposite page: This color photo is an aerial view of the town of Big Creek. Powerhouse No. 1 can be seen at lower right. Dam No. 4 is near the center.
Southern California Edison Company Photo Library

answer a telephone for quite a while. In the meantime, the noise appeared to be on the increase. After much ringing, someone at the other end yelled, "Hell's bells, we haven't time to talk—the war's over."

The next two months I spent with a crew, increasing clearances of conductors in the spans of the Big Creek transmission lines that cross some of the highways in the vicinity of Visalia.

Then, after a trip to Independence, California, to search through the old files of the U. S. Government Land Office for information relative to original surveys of land occupied by the Edison Company, I went to the Kern River No. 3 Project as assistant to Resident Engineer Capt. F. J. Mills. The Edison Company had decided to speed up completion of that development, involving miles of tunnels, installation of a powerhouse, penstocks, etc. The powerhouse was well started when, in February 1920, after a very busy year, I returned to Big Creek as assistant to Resident Engineer Arthur Blight.

This view of the future site of Florence Lake Dam was also taken by Walter Sohier during his 1917 survey of the area.
Walter Sohier Photo, from the Edison Collection

Right: Workers on the catwalk of Dam No. 4A.

Below: Florence Watershed.

Opposite page
An aerial view of Huntington Lake.

A waterfall near Big Creek.

All photos in this color section are from the Southern California Edison Company photo library

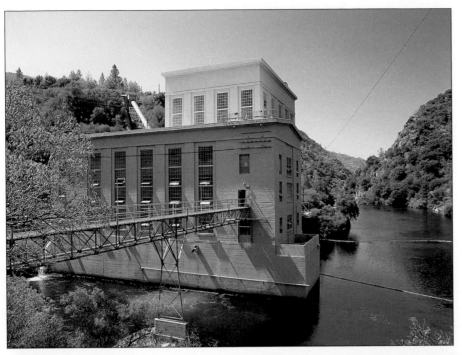

Powerhouse No. 8 is located at an elevation of 4,819 feet at the town of Big Creek. It was the first powerhouse on the Big Creek Project to be placed into commercial operation.

Powerhouse No. 1 is dramatic in this nighttime view.

Opposite page
Big Creek Powerhouse No. 1, in background, with Dam No. 4A.

Previous pages: The Florence Dam Spillway.

Right: A Pelton wheel, a type of impulse waterwheel, was often used as a prime mover in older hydroelectric plants. A stream of water under high pressure spins the wheel by hitting each bucket in turn.

Below: The Balsam Meadow Forebay at winter.

Opposite page Powerhouse No. 3.

Left: The John Eastwood Power Station Generator.

Below: Entrance to the John Eastwood Power Station. This facility generates electricity from water carried through the Huntington-Pitman-Shaver Conduit. After passing through the plant, the water is discharged into Shaver Lake.

Opposite page
Jackass bridge over the south fork of the San Joaquin River. Water is flowing from the Florence Dam spillway. (See photo, pages 103-104.)

Right: streamside plant life, in the Big Creek region.

Below: A bird's-eye view of the Thomas Edison Lake watershed.

Opposite page
Top: Snowpack from Rosemarie Meadows.

Bottom: Huntington Lake reservoir, with a drainage area of 80 square miles, was the first reservoir built as part of the initial development at Big Creek, 1911 to 1913.

Dam No. 5 is built across the watercourse of Big Creek, just below Powerhouse No. 2 and Powerhouse 2A.

Shaver Dam is a concrete gravity arch dam across Stevenson Creek. This dam has an overall length of 2,169 feet, and rises 185 feet from its foundation. 281,300 cubic yards of concrete were used in its construction.

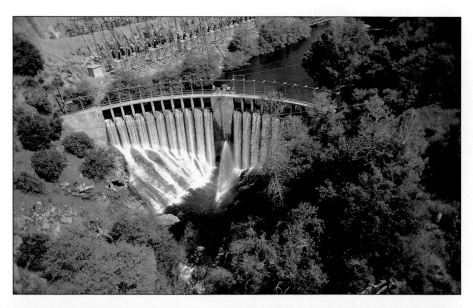

Edison hydrographers measure snowpack in the back country.

Water rushes through the Portal Powerhouse at the end of Ward Tunnel.

415-The Mill at Shaver, Calif. October, 1920.

XIII
Shaver Tunnel

THERE HAS BEEN considerable activity for many years in the lumber industry throughout the area extending from Tollhouse to Dinkey Creek. The first sawmill above Tollhouse was built by Moses Mack and John W. Humphries in 1867 near Pine Ridge. Another one was set up in 1881 at Ockenden, a few miles below Shaver Lake.

The lake got its name from C. B. Shaver, a Michigan lumberman who came to California and was a cofounder of the Fresno Flume & Irrigation Company, incorporated October 31, 1891, to make and deal in lumber. To have large storage space for logs and to float them to the sawmill, a sizable body of water was required. The site selected for the mill and pond was formerly known as Stevenson Basin and Meadows. To create the pond, a rock-fill dam, forty feet high and about 300 feet long, was built across Stevenson Creek at the mill site, thus forming the original Shaver Lake, elevation 5,275 feet, with a capacity of around 5,000 acre feet. Mrs. Shaver, whom I knew very well, told me the dam was built in 1893. When she first arrived to join her husband on July 4th of that year, riding behind a team of oxen, she found him busy with a crew of men on its construction.

Lumber was delivered to the San Joaquin Valley in a unique manner, since it was floated through a flume from the mill to Clovis, sixty flume miles distant. Abandoned in 1917, the flume has almost disappeared, except for one long trestle which can be seen today clinging to the cliff high on Mt. Stevenson, also called "Flume Point." The water in which the lumber floated was released for irrigation after reaching Clovis. During the heyday of the San Joaquin & Eastern Railroad, trainmen frequently would create merriment at the expense of some timid passenger, by telling him or her, "You haven't seen anything yet—wait until we get up there," pointing to the old flume trestle two or three thousand feet above.

By court decree, the firm's name was changed on September 8, 1908, to Fresno Flume & Lumber Company. On July 30, 1919, the company conveyed to the Southern California Edison Company by deed certain lands for the present reservoir site. Adjoining properties were conveyed as of

This view of the old lumber mill at Shaver Lake was taken in October 1920. By this time, it was owned by the Edison Company, and was nearing the end of its operations. Prior to being dismantled to make way for the new Shaver Lake reservoir, the mill cut much of the form lumber used to construct Powerhouse No. 8.
Murphy's Studio Photo, from the Edison Collection

This rare photo shows the 1893 construction of the original, timber-faced, rock-filled dam that impounded the millpond for C.B. Shaver's pioneer lumbering venture at Shaver Lake.
Courtesy United States Forest Service, Shaver Lake

August 1, 1919, to the Shaver Lake Lumber Company, which had been incorporated for that purpose. Including the reservoir site, a total of some 32,000 acres was involved, a large portion of which had been logged during the previous twenty-five years.

When the year 1920 came along, it found the Edison Company operating the sawmill, and a heavy construction program getting under way, with every indication of its continuing for some years. Involved were quite a number of powerhouses, dams, tunnels, roads, etc. Lumber was needed for such a vast program. Scattered trees were being put through the mill, and

The Fresno Flume and Lumber Company was the successor to C. B. Shaver's original Fresno Flume and Irrigation Company. The company owned timber land and a reservoir site around today's Shaver Lake, as well as land near Clovis.
Edison Collection

they not only provided lumber, but also cleared the area destined to become the enlarged Shaver Lake reservoir.

At Big Creek, cottages, shops, a mess hall, warehouses, and quarters for a large clerical force had to be built. Provided for the latter was a three-story building adjacent to the new headquarters office. Facilities had to be made available for supplying medical attention, and a hospital was constructed— Dr. H. M. McNeil taking charge on February 1, 1920. This was the first of three base hospitals, the other two coming along a year or so later. The lumber had to be hauled from the Shaver mill by heavy wagons to the San Joaquin & Eastern Railroad at Shaver Crossing. The main highway was not oiled, and winter storms made it almost impassable. An eight-up team at times would literally drag the huge wagons through mud hub-deep. On one occasion a wagon, upon arrival at the railroad, carried only four remaining 4 by 4s, all that was left of the original load, which had to be lightened along the way.

My house, like all other new structures, was built of green lumber, which did not dry very fast in such wet weather. A large heating stove was kept going day and night, not only for warmth but to dry the house inside. In spite of the heat and good care, we found our clothes would mildew. As the boards dried, they would crack here and there, accompanied by a loud noise comparable to the shooting of a heavy rifle. There were no complaints—others had the same experience. Everybody was happy about his job and "raring to go."

Our house was built on a sandy slope, mostly barren except for a manzanita bush here and there. Mrs. Redinger wanted to set out some fruit trees immediately. I told her it was foolish, as we would not be here long enough to enjoy any of the fruit—that no construction job lasts more than two, three or four years at the most. She went ahead and got her fruit trees—twenty-five to thirty of them. That was in 1920 and we enjoyed the apples for more than twenty years. We also gave hundreds of boxes to local families, the cookhouses, and friends outside.

Several camps were built to serve the tunnel to be driven from Shaver Lake towards Powerhouse No.2, beneath Musick Mountain, named for Henry or Charles Musick, both of whom were connected with the sawmill at Shaver. The tunnel would carry water to powerhouse No. 2 and, subsequently, to Powerhouse No. 2A. Large air compressors were skidded over snow and through mud to the Camp 19 site—the adit about midway along the tunnel.

At Camp 29, the north portal, we had our first experience with portable frame bunkhouses. They were shipped in sections ready for assembly, and under the circumstances served very well. A large number were also set up for family use at Big Creek headquarters.

The word had been given to get the tunnel started, and when such instructions are turned loose in construction, the "dirt must fly" right now—and what's more, it usually does. The Shaver Tunnel, 14,300 feet long, eight by eleven feet in cross-section, actually got under way with respect to driving, on February 5, 1920, and was completed May 6, 1921. An average crew of ninety men for each of the four headings worked continuously throughout

Shaver's lumber company depended upon a 60-mile-long flume to float cut lumber to the finishing mill and drying yards at Clovis. Portions of the flume traversed some spectacular scenery, such as at Rocky Point, on the flanks of Musick Mountain. Although abandoned as long ago as 1917, one section of flume still survives today!
Courtesy United States Forest Service, Shaver Lake

Early in April 1921, with lumbering operations at Shaver Lake virtually abandoned, Edison crews were at work building a temporary flume to carry water from the original Shaver Lake millpond into the portal of the new Shaver Tunnel. This tunnel carried the water to be used at Powerhouse No. 2. This work was temporary, pending the completion of the higher Shaver Dam and Powerhouse No. 2A several years later.
Photographer unknown, from the Edison Collection

the job. At that time we considered the progress to be excellent. In one heading, an advance of 522 feet was made in a thirty-day period. Equipment included air-operated "Shuveloaders," or mucking machines, "Leyner" drills, pneumatic drill sharpeners, storage battery locomotives, and huge blowers for supplying fresh air. The experience with this equipment served as a valuable guide for driving other large tunnels during the next ten years.

Because the outflow from the original lake did not justify higher head units in Powerhouse No. 2, with an increasingly longer penstock, water from the lake was to be carried into Tunnel No. 2 through a temporary diversion tunnel and pipeline at the north portal. This water would be used in Powerhouse No. 2 under a head of 1,860 feet, together with water coming through Tunnel No. 2 from Big Creek No. 1, until Powerhouse No. 2A would be built, some years hence.

Arthur Blight and I were paid our first visit by President John B. Miller with Mrs. Miller, Medical Director Dr. E. A. Bryant and Mrs. Bryant, late in the summer of 1920. We met the party, piloted by George C. Ward, at Shaver Crossing. For small groups, the San Joaquin & Eastern had a White truck chassis equipped with a special body and car wheels, adapted for travel over

The "Sierra" was a Boston Shay-type geared locomotive, operated by the Shaver Lake Railroad. The railroad was operated in conjunction with the lumbering activities at Shaver Lake, and had no rail connection to the outside world. After the logging operations were closed down in 1921, this locomotive went to the San Joaquin and Eastern Railroad, which used it occasionally for switching, until abandonment in 1933.
Collection of William A. Myers

the rails. Instead of the regular train, our guests chose to make the trip in the White bus (also known locally as "White Elephant"). The visitors were shown, among other things, the Commissary, or store, at Camp 19. Mr. Ward reflected embarrassment when Mrs. Miller, looking over the stores, inquired about there being no Borden's milk on the shelves at the time. This went over my head, but I learned afterwards that Mrs. Miller was a Borden. It was not long until that brand put in its appearance.

In August of that same year, we received word from our Los Angeles office to check up on the whereabouts of one of the Edison Company attorneys, who was making an investigation of a quarter section of land within the Shaver Lake area, all of which, covered with dense brush and thickets of small trees, made searching difficult. Eventually I found him wandering and stumbling around, his shirt open, bareheaded, perspiration rolling off his face. How glad he was to see me, even though I was a stranger! Such was my introduction to George E. Trowbridge, a member of the Edison Company legal staff.

Coincident with completion of the tunnel, a large wooden flume, about one-half mile in length, was ready to carry Shaver Lake water from the old rockfill dam to the tunnel intake until construction of the present dam. To utilize the additional water thus to be made available, a third unit was installed at Powerhouse No. 2 during 1920, increasing its capacity from 45,000 to 66,000 horsepower.

None of the Big Creek tunnels is lined with concrete except where it is required to support bad ground. Several places required such treatment, but less than 1,000 feet of the Shaver Tunnel is lined.

After the Shaver property was purchased by the Southern California Edison Company for reservoir purposes, the company dismantled, moved from the lake area and reassembled in what is known as "Rockhaven," adjoining the lake, the house that had been occupied by the Shaver family during the preceding summers.

A new device tried out on the construction of the Shaver Tunnel was the "Armstrong Mucker" (referred to in the text as a Shuveloader), a mechanical shovel that speeded up the removal of "tunnel muck." Muck is the name miners give to the broken rock and debris that results from the excavation of a tunnel.
Photographer unknown, from the Edison Collection

XIV
Powerhouse No. 8 Is Built

I N A PRECEDING CHAPTER, reference was made to the tunnel which was started in 1914 on a slow schedule towards Powerhouse No. 3, yet to be built. Prior to June i, 1920, the proposed plant was intended to operate under a head of about 1,400 feet. Progress on the 14-foot by 17-foot tunnel was slow, as is obvious from the fact that a distance of only 2,050 feet was driven between July 1914 and February 1920. Late in 1919, the job was speeded up, and extension of the road was started below Powerhouse No. 2 to serve the adits to be located along the tunnel.

On May 1, 1920, with a total of 8,400 feet of the extension completed, the road building was suddenly halted. Because of the urgent need for more power, drastic steps had to be taken. It was decided to abandon plans, temporarily, for Plant No. 3 and concentrate on one having a head of 700 feet, half that intended for the former. Such a plant, provided it was built quickly, would relieve the critical load situation until Powerhouse No. 3 could be completed.

World War I is credited with playing a large part in the rapidly increasing load demand. Another important factor favoring the sudden change of plans was the perfection of the vertical reaction turbine to greater efficiency.

A site for the new plant was selected at the mouth of Big Creek, on the San Joaquin River. The change in plans reduced the length of the tunnel to approximately 6,000 feet, making it unnecessary to extend the road further on tunnel grade, but requiring a new location for it, the forebay, penstock and powerhouse. The designating number "8" was assigned to the proposed plant. It has been something of a puzzle to many why a powerhouse called No. 8 is located between numbers 2 and 3. It is because the other numbers up to eight had already been assigned in other filings with the U. S. Government.

To expedite tunnel driving, Adit No. 1 was started on February 20, 1920, and by May 17 a 20-foot by 20-foot section, 193 feet long, had been driven. From this point the crews could turn in opposite directions and work two additional headings in the main tunnel—one towards the intake, the other

When the decision was made to speed up work on the water tunnel below Powerhouse No. 2, the new tunnel sections were drilled by the "pioneer tunnel method," where a tunnel of smaller diameter is driven ahead of the larger bore. This method has the advantage in that it takes less time to drill a smaller tunnel, so drilling can proceed far ahead of the widening work. This photo, taken in September, 1920, shows the multiple-drill setups used for enlarging the pioneer bore to full-size dimensions.
Photographer unknown, from the Edison Collection

To enlarge the pioneer tunnel to its full size, a standard Marion Model 40 steam shovel was employed to remove the muck. The Marion was mounted on standard-gauge railroad wheelsets, but was operated by compressed air instead of steam. This 1920 photo also shows the battery-powered electric locomotives that pulled the muck trains out of the tunnel.
Photographer unknown, from the Edison Collection

Previous pages: Camp 33 housed the men working on Powerhouse No. 8. The new plant was built at the confluence of Big Creek and the South Fork of the San Joaquin River.
G. Haven Bishop Photo, from the Edison Collection

towards the outlet. It was then decided to enlarge it to the adit size and use standard steam shovels, Marion 40s, operated with compressed air, for loading the muck or blasted rock. Up to May 5, 1920, there had been 2,415 feet of the original 14-foot by 17-foot size driven; the remainder was finished to the adit size.

Instead of the usual type of surge chamber at the outlet of a pressure tunnel, the one provided for Big Creek No. 8 is a large steel tank, 35 feet in diameter and 95 feet in height. At the bottom, outlets are provided for three penstocks, of which there are now two, one for each unit.

Camp No. 31 had been built near the mouth of the adit, and No. 32 established near the outlet. The "30" series of numbers had been assigned for use on the Big Creek 3 construction, but because of the change in plans, that plant had to share them with No. 8.

The number of camps was increasing rapidly, and with prospects for many more we decided to go into the hog business. Garbage disposal is an important item, especially for large construction camps. Instead of burning it every day, the fattening of hogs seemed a more satisfactory solution, besides offering some promise of being profitable. If we should break even, it would be worthwhile. Several hundred pigs were placed in locations readily accessible from one or more camps, a tender put in charge, and the pork project was launched. We also had a real veterinarian, "Doc" Dwight, who not only watched over the hogs but took care of the many horses and mules scattered over the job.

The first track-laying Caterpillar-type steam shovel, a revolving Marion 21, to appear on the Big Creek Project went to work on November 1, 1920. It served as prime mover in excavating the present road to the site where Camp 33, for powerhouse workmen, was to be built. Construction of the camp was begun before completion of the road to it; in fact, it was ready for occupancy by 300 men shortly before Christmas. The "rag houses," with floors, sprang up like mushrooms. Almost before the shovel crew had time to wash up after reaching the site, the sound of the steel triangle, so familiar in construction camps, was calling men to the first meal.

The two-mile incline to serve No. 8, longest on the San Joaquin & Eastern Railroad, was built to Camp 42, also known as Feeney, after its first foreman.

General foreman Bill Whitmire was crowding the various phases of the work, getting excavation under way for the powerhouse and the penstock. A short tunnel was built to bypass Big Creek water around the powerhouse site during the excavation and construction. Dam No. 5 was being built across Big Creek just below Powerhouse No. 2, to form the Powerhouse No. 8 forebay at the intake of its tunnel.

The penstock pipes for Powerhouse No. 8 were anchored to the mountainside by large concrete blocks. This July 1921 picture shows one anchor under construction, and also shows a long stretch of the inclined railway that led from the San Joaquin and Eastern Railroad on the mountainside above, down to the power plant site. All construction materials needed at Powerhouse No. 8, including all of the pipe, were lowered to the point of use via this incline. *Photographer unknown, from the Edison Collection*

This August 1921 picture shows Powerhouse No. 8 under construction. The waterfall at the left shows discharge from a temporary diversion tunnel built to detour the waters of Big Creek around the site while the power-house was under construction.
Photographer unknown, from the Edison Collection

The large generator was shipped for assembly in the field, including "stacking the iron." Load limitation on the incline was the main reason for such field work. Not to lose any time on installation of the turbine and generator, an unusual procedure was followed for assembly of the latter. A tower of heavy timbers was built to support a large platform twenty feet above the turbine. While the 30,000-horsepower Francis-Pelton turbine was being installed, the 22,500-kilowatt General Electric generator was being assembled on the platform, both being fenced in gradually by the powerhouse. As the building grew in height, so did the foundation beneath the generator, which did not have to be disturbed except to be lowered slightly to its permanent position after assembly.

While on a trip to New York in January and February 1921, I visited the I. P. Morris Department of William Cramp & Sons, Philadelphia, where the hydraulic part of the unit for No. 8 was being made. There I received a telegram from construction engineer Harry Dennis in Los Angeles. It contained the sad news that Arthur Blight had been seriously injured at Big Creek on February 14, as the result of being dragged by his horse. I was to return at once.

Besides regular pick-and-shovel work, the excavation for the powerhouse was carried on by hydraulic sluicing and a revolving steam shovel, using oil for fuel. This shovel was replaced shortly by a larger Marion 40 to speed up the work. The small one was moved to a higher level to pass material down to the larger, which loaded the dump cars for final disposal. Air hammers were used extensively, since much blasting was required for breaking the hard gray granite throughout the lower foundation area. Ten and one-half tons of forty-percent gelatin powder were used for the blasting. Besides the area for the foundation of one unit, an additional area was excavated for future installation, to avoid damaging the first unit at such a time. The first concrete was poured on May 12, 1921, and exactly ninety days later, on August 10, water flowed through the penstock and the unit rolled. Three days later it was generating power, establishing a record for such construction, made possible by working two shifts on the building and three on the equipment installation.

The plant had been in operation only a few days when the penstock broke at 5:39 a.m., August 20, 1921, not far above the building. The tear in the huge pipe occurred in such a way as to direct the water, rushing out under full pressure, against the east side of the generator room, where a temporary covering of corrugated iron had been placed, with an eye to future extension of the building. Such a cover served as no barrier for the water, which tore through it as though the wall were tissue paper, and into the generator room and transformer bay, carrying with it timbers, concrete and debris. The 150,000-volt leads were grounded, and about 500 feet of penstock at the upper end collapsed. With all hands working around the clock we were able to have service restored on September 13.

Big Creek No. 8, Big Creek No. 1 and Big Creek No. 2 operated at 150,000 volts each for transmission until May 1923, when the entire Big Creek system was changed to 220,000 volts, the first commercial use of such high voltage in the world.

About the first of September 1921 a sizable pack party was arranged by Harry Dennis, with Fred Fowler, district engineer of the U. S. Forest Service. To obtain stream-flow data, gauging stations had to be installed, and this party was to select the locations. The two-week trip would also allow each member of the party, particularly Mr. Fowler, to visit the places under investigation for possible power development. Mr. W. A. Brackenridge, senior vice president of the Edison Company, started with us, but turned back after our first night at Mono Hot Springs, since he did not feel equal to the trip. We visited Blaney Meadows and Vermilion Valley, went over Silver Pass and down through Fish Creek where the mosquitoes hadn't had a square meal for weeks. We selected several sites for gauging stations, looked over many places along the west side of the San Joaquin River, and finally reached Miller's Bridge and Mammoth Pool. Each morning we were up early, had breakfast, and were in the saddle before six o'clock. In the afternoon we

Lower left: Powerhouse No. 8 had been in use only a few days when, on August 20, 1921, the penstock pipe carrying water to Unit No. 1 failed due to a flaw in the steel. Such is the force of the water falling down these penstock pipes, that the 1-1/8-inch-thick steel tore like paper! The penstock for the original Big Creek plants had been made in Germany before the war, because no American manufacturer could build pipe strong enough. When Powerhouse No. 8 was built right after the war, political considerations forced the Edison Company to go to American pipe makers, and this was the result.
Photographer unknown, from the Edison Collection

Below: When the penstock pipe to Powerhouse No. 8's Unit No. 1 failed, the escaping water created a vacuum in the upper portion of the pipe, causing five hundred feet to collapse. Despite this damage, the plant was restored to operation by September 13th.
Photographer unknown, from the Edison Collection

would stop early enough for the fishermen in the party to provide enough trout for supper. Harry Dennis, always allergic to onions, was involved in the only incident to mar the trip for him, when some culprit placed one in his bedroll. The effect was about the same as having limburger put in the finger of one's glove.

On August 13, 1922, Edison president John B. Miller; Mrs. Miller; their son and daughter, Morris and Carrita, accompanied by Mr. George C. Ward, arrived for their first camping trip in the Sierra. Mr. Miller inspected the various jobs under way, as the party proceeded by automobile from Hairpin over the Lower Road. Messrs. Davis and Blight and I escorted the party next day from Huntington Lake Lodge as far as Ward Lake. The road had not yet been completed beyond that point. We put the visitors on their horses in the care of H. B. Howard, one of our engineers. They left for their camp, which had been set up near the river at the lower end of Upper Jackass Meadow, the reservoir site for Florence Lake.

The most active member of the party was Mike, the wire-haired terrier. Such wide-open spaces presented an entirely new world for him-so much so that he jumped out of the kayak to chase a chipmunk. He did not catch up with the pack train, and consequently there was much concern when he didn't show up in camp that night. The lost dog was well advertised in the various camps, and diligent search was made, but without results. On the fourth day after his disappearance, the foreman of the road crew appeared in the Miller camp with the bedraggled and footsore pooch, barely able to wag his stubby tail. Just to have him back was ample cause for rejoicing. There was no cause for further worry during the remainder of the stay in camp, as Mike never left its site.

During his ten-day outing, Mr. Miller took full advantage of this opportunity and, steered by Howard, saw much of the country, some of which was then being prepared to furnish water for more kilowatts for the people of California.

A second failure at Big Creek No. 8 occurred at 8:40 a.m. on New Year's Day, 1924, taking two lives, when a section of the penstock broke, some distance above the powerhouse. The rush of water down the steep hillside destroyed a cottage in which an employee's wife and his sister were sleeping. The upper end of the penstock collapsed again.

Although the necessary repairs constituted a major job, they were made and service resumed on January 16. I happened to be returning from another trip to New York, and at Kansas City my attention was attracted to a press report of the disaster. In 1924 and 1925, steel reinforcing bands were placed around the penstock pipe—which was American-made—and lap-welded to prevent further failures.

Powerhouse No. 8, so numbered because it was not a part of the original projected chain of plants, was the first on the Big Creek Project to use the "Francis vertical reaction turbine" in place of the more traditional Pelton wheel. This interior view of the plant, taken in 1930, shows the huge units, one of which was built by William Cramp & Sons of Philadelphia, more famous as the builder of World War I "Four Stacker" destroyers for the Navy.
G. Haven Bishop Photo, from the Edison Collection

After a second failure of the penstock pipe to Powerhouse No. 8, reinforcing bands were installed to prevent further occurrences. Installed during 1924 and 1925, the bands consist of two halves bolted together, and are made of progressively thicker material towards the bottom of the pipeline.
Photographer unknown, from the Edison Collection

XV
Big Creek No. 3 Development

BEFORE THE COMPLETION of Powerhouse No. 8, plans had been revised to extend the road down the San Joaquin River Canyon to serve the Big Creek No. 3 development. The road was favored instead of three cable-operated inclines, each one of which would serve the adits proposed for the large No. 3 tunnel. The inclines would have served only during construction of the tunnel, whereas the road would always be necessary for use between plants. There was little difference in the cost of the two methods.

On August 10, 1921, construction was started to extend the road down the canyon below Powerhouse No. 8. W. A. (Bill) Whitmire continued as general foreman on this and the entire development of Project No. 3.

Manager of construction E. R. Davis and I decided to look at Stevenson Creek, which the road would have to cross. That creek is the natural outlet for Shaver Lake, and at times carries a considerable amount of water. We left the trail high up on the mountain and worked our way down to a saddle near the river, about two miles below the creek, where we tied our horses. We could not have picked a hotter day, and we were in prime rattlesnake country. We crawled through and under thick brush. We slipped and slid all over rock ledges along the steep mountainside, all the way to Stevenson Creek and back to our horses, which had enjoyed the four hours' rest in the shade. We made a good guess on the location of the bridge, as the spot where we reached the creek was the one hit exactly by the road crew several months later. We had no hand level and no survey had been made—it was a case of estimating elevations.

We had several railroad steam shovels. The Caterpillar type in such a size was not yet in general use. The former were equipped to operate on a standard-gauge railroad track. One of these was eating its way down the canyon, using compressed air furnished by a four-inch pipeline which followed closely. Another crew started from Hairpin, the opposite end of the road, on December 1. This latter crew made more rapid progress, as there was less rock encountered than on the upper portion of the road.

As each of the three different adit locations was reached by either crew, camp would be built and preparations would proceed for tunnel driving. Cuts in solid granite, fifty to one hundred feet high, were not uncommon. One section, about a quarter of a mile long, was blasted through hardest granite. The 45-degree slope presented a problem, as there were no footholds from which to start work, and these had to be made by men hanging on ropes anchored to trees or rocks as much as 500 feet above.

Between August 10, 1921, and May 30, 1922, the "Lower Road," eleven miles in length between Powerhouse No. 8 and Hairpin, on the San Joaquin & Eastern Railroad, was completed by three crews working continuously. Shortly thereafter, the one and one-half mile branch to the site for Powerhouse No. 3 was built. Preference was given the road to serve the tunnel, which had to be ready a year and one-half hence to coincide with completion of the powerhouse.

A portent of things to come was the use of this Mack "Bulldog" truck to carry pipe sections into Tunnel No. 3. Sections of the lower end of the tunnel had to be lined to prevent leakage, and the pipe was hauled by truck, rather than by rail.
Photographer unknown, from the Edison Collection

During the road construction a certain route was desirable in the vicinity of Mill Creek. By purchasing an eighty-acre homestead which had been unoccupied for years, we could have the more favorable route. The property had stood at $250 for years unsold, but when it came time to buy it, the price had risen to $2,500. Even so, several times that figure was saved by being able to build over the more direct and easier route.

Tunnel No. 3, even without allowing for over-break in driving, is larger in cross-section, 21 feet by 21 feet, than any other on the Big Creek Project. At the time it was driven it was advantageous to provide for future installation of units in the powerhouse; that is why the present capacity of 3,000 feet is double what is now required.

Railroad-type Marion steam shovels, operated by compressed air, with 16-foot boom and 11-foot dipper sticks, were used in the headings.

The faithful Marion Model 40 steam shovel had been the workhorse of the Big Creek Project since the beginning. Mounted on a railroad chassis, and powered by steam or compressed air, depending upon the work location, the Marion could go anywhere railroad track could be built. This picture of a Marion was taken inside Tunnel No. 3. Few then realized that this was the last big job for the railroad-mounted units. Soon, Caterpillar-tracked shovels would replace the older shovels.
Photographer unknown, from the Edison Collection

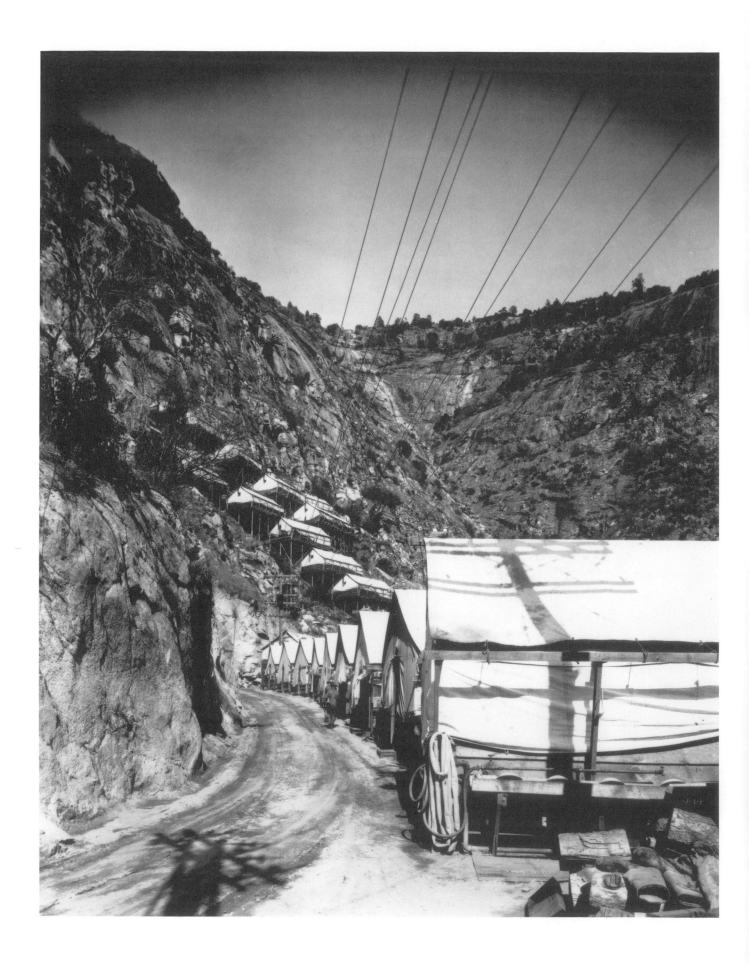

Eight-ton combination battery and trolley locomotives hauled the muck from the shovels in cars of ten cubic yards capacity, which were built on the job. Under average conditions, a shovel would clean up a 15-foot round, about 450 cubic yards, of loose material, in seven to ten hours. The best progress made in a heading in any one month was 476 feet, a record at that time for a hard rock tunnel of that size. The Ingersoll-Rand Company developed a special type of drill, known as Model X-70, for handling steel of sixteen-foot to twenty-four-foot lengths. One of these was tried in the tunnel, with results good enough to justify its adoption.

The shortage of experienced machine men, a situation attributed to World War 1, made it necessary for us to train them, in view of the large amount of tunnel work we had under way. Beginners would start as "chuck tenders," changing drill steel in the machines at a tunnel heading. Occasionally it has been necessary to explain that this was their duty instead of waiting on tables in mess halls.

Prior to completion of the Lower Road, a diamond drill was skidded down the mountainside from Hairpin to explore foundation possibilities at the site selected for Powerhouse No. 3, and it continued drilling until early the following year. Actual excavation for the powerhouse was started on June 5, 1922, and completed on January 10, 1923. During the excavation, made with one of the larger size railroad steam shovels, three human skeletons were uncovered at a depth of twenty feet. They were taken to be those of Indians, as an unusually good specimen of a stone axe was found nearby. Presumably they had been covered that deep with material washed in by the river through the years.

During the latter part of 1922, Mill Creek, which empties into the river at the powerhouse site, went on a rampage. The water broke over into the site being excavated, and shortly all that could be seen of the huge steam shovel was twelve inches of the smokestack.

A large camp for the powerhouse construction had to be built, and was known as No. 38. One of the principal buildings was a base hospital, the second to be provided on the Big Creek Project, with Dr. G. K. Nider in charge.

It was not always easy to pick out desirable campsites, which had to be placed where the job would be served to the best advantage. Visitors seeing some of our former camp locations today are reluctant to believe we had such camps. One example is the site where Camp 35 clung to the slick rock in Stevenson Creek Canyon. The floored tents, placed on the extremely steep and rocky slope, required posts twenty to thirty feet in height on the lower side. The occupants of this camp were referred to as "cliff dwellers." Camp 34, at Adit 1, was a good runner-up for No. 35, as it hugged the cliff above the river. Camps 36 and 37, for Adit 3 and the tunnel outlet, respectively, fared much better in location.

On August 1, 1923, the last section of the tunnel was "holed through," after which the effort was concentrated towards making ready for a huge flushing of the upper half. The side walls and roof were given a good washing with a fire hose before turning the river through for the final washing. All such bathing was to remove finely crushed rock, sand, rock dust, etc., as such material causes damage if allowed to go through the powerhouse

Opposite page: Tunnel Camp 35 was located on the steep cliffs at the junction of Stevenson Creek and the San Joaquin River. It housed one of the crews digging the tunnel to Powerhouse No. 3. Perhaps the most remote of any camp below Huntington Lake, its tent-cabins were built on stilts and lashed by cables pegged into the cliff.
G. Haven Bishop Photo, from the Edison Collection

High above the location of Powerhouse No. 3 at Camp 38 was Camp 37, which housed the tunnel crews working on the lower end of the water tunnel. This August 1922 view shows the tunnel portal and the curious metal portable bunkhouses that were tried out here.
Photographer unknown, from the Edison Collection

These "portable" metal bunkhouses used at Camp 37 must be ranked as one of the less successful innovations on the Big Creek Project. One can only wonder what it must have been like to try to sleep inside one of them during hot summer nights!
Photographer unknown, from the Edison Collection

turbines. August 14 arrived—the day for the river to be turned in at the intake. A heavy bulkhead had been built across the main tunnel just below Adit 2, to divert the water and debris into Stevenson Creek, and thence to the San Joaquin River. John B. Miller, president of the company, his daughter, Carrita, and some guests, accompanied by George C. Ward, were on hand at the adit portal, besides local personnel, to see the tunnel given its first bath. The roar of the water could be heard long before its arrival. All spectators were tense and time passed slowly. Finally, through the adit rushed the dirtiest river, carrying pieces of broken ties, odds and ends of lumber, wire, rocks, sand—everything left in the tunnel—in spite of a previous general clean-up. Mr. Miller, deeply impressed, remarked he had never in all his life witnessed such a spectacle. After extending congratulations to all of us, he and his party proceeded to Huntington Lake Lodge to stay overnight, prior to leaving on their second camping trip in this area.

The following morning, forest supervisor M. A. Benedict and Frank Bonner, district engineer of the U. S. Forest Service, joined us at the lodge to help escort the party to Florence Lake. On the way, stops were made to inspect the work above Huntington Lake, and a call was made on Jerry and his dog team. (See pages 149 to 153.) Having enjoyed a bounteous lunch beneath the pines at Florence Lake, the campers left by pack train for Blaney Meadows, where a comfortable camp had been established. Messrs. Ward and Howard accompanied the party, as Mr. Miller wished to have them remain with him during his ten-day stay.

On Sunday the 19th, piloted by Mr. Ward, who had returned to Huntington Lake for the purpose, Mr. Miller had as visitors executive vice president R. H. Ballard, Capt. John Fredericks, Shannon Crandall, H. A. Barre, E. R. Davis and myself. A horse equal to the carrying of Mr. Ballard's substantial size had been provided. On the trip, this particular rider allowed his steed to wander off the trail as he pleased. Much to the surprise of both, they ran into a large hornets' nest. Apparently, all the occupants were at home and vigorously resented being molested. The resulting disturbance through the aspen thickets was proportionate to the size of the nest. Needless to say, there were no more wanderings away from the trail.

Mah jong, which was sweeping over the country, was a favorite pastime in the Miller camp, and the expert players saw to it that all visiting money remained there. Never do I hear "Parade of the Wooden Soldiers" without being taken back to the delightful atmosphere around those Blaney Meadow campfires, where I heard it for the first time on Carrita's portable Victrola. She had just returned from school at Dobb's Ferry, and had brought along the record which was then so popular in the East. Carrita loved the mountains—even her dad said so. In later years, as Mrs. Nobles, she returned numerous times, bringing her own children, hoping they would acquire their mother's taste for the big outdoors.

One important feature of pressure tunnels, and, of course, of Tunnel No. 3, is the surge chamber constructed at the lower end. Its chief function is to act as a cushion for the water column. Any surge caused by the sudden shutdown of machines in the powerhouse will be relieved by the waters being allowed to rise and fall in such a chamber. The one under discussion has a shape similar to an hourglass's large section at the top and bottom, with a smaller diameter connecting shaft. The reason for such a shape is to permit small and unexpected demands to be taken care of easily by the water available in the enlarged section, without the need for carrying the chamber, full size, all the way to the surface, a distance of 200 feet. It was located off to the side of the tunnel for construction purposes, since it was easier to proceed with excavation than it would have been had the chamber been placed directly over the tunnel.

At the tunnel outlet, to provide takeoff for each of the seven-foot, six inch penstocks (three to be for future use) an unusual manifold was located. It consisted of two spheres twenty-four feet in diameter, four penstock outlets from one, and two from the other nearest the tunnel outlet. In the spheres, hoop tension is the force to provide against and this is taken care of by the addition of several steel plate collars around the penstock outlets.

As another part of the No. 3 development, a dam was required in the San Joaquin River gorge for impounding water to be passed through the tunnel for use at the powerhouse. Diamond drill borings were made at three separate sites before a suitable foundation for Dam No. 6 was found. The dam is of simple arch type, having an upstream radius of 108 feet. The base had a maximum thickness of 37 feet 9 inches, and a spillway crest 8.0 feet in width. Late in 1937, 58,600 second feet of water passed over the dam, the greatest amount the dam has ever discharged.

The construction of this dam was about the most difficult job

By January 1923, the concrete gravity arch dam that was to become Dam No. 6 was beginning to take shape just below the confluence of Big Creek and the South Fork of the San Joaquin River. This view looks upstream, and shows the concrete-mixing plant at right, and a small part of the narrow-gauge railway network that carried the concrete to the working locations.
Photographer unknown, from the Edison Collection

encountered in the development of the entire Big Creek Project. While the dam was being built, the flow of the river had to be carried around the site through a flume hanging on the slick canyon side. A wooden flume was constructed, having a capacity of 5,000 second-feet. The size was adopted after careful study of the hydrographic records showed this to be the maximum flow to be expected during the period when diversion would be necessary. Two cofferdams were required—one at the intake of the flume and the other at the outlet-to keep the excavation in the riverbed clear. Fifty-six thousand sacks of earth were required for these two cofferdams, and once during the critical part of excavation, the flume was taxed to the limit. It would have been disastrous had it overflowed and flooded the three shovels working deep below in the riverbed. We removed a large, waterlogged tree, which probably had been covered at such a depth for hundreds of years. It was heavy as lead and in an excellent state of preservation. The excavation was completed on November 15, 1922, and placing of concrete began on November 20. By December 6 it was possible to abandon the flume, much to the relief of all concerned, and to carry the river through the sluice gates in the bottom of the dam. The placing of concrete was completed on February 8, 1923, except for the closing of the temporary openings above the sluice gates, the last one of which was closed on March 18, just a few days before the first spring flood came down the river.

While the dam was being built, progress was under way on the concrete

Camp 38 was the main camp for the construction of Powerhouse No. 3, and several of its buildings became part of the permanent company housing for the operating staff. In 1986, there remained a community of Edison employees and their families living at this location. This view was taken in 1923.

Photographer unknown, from the Edison Collection

Safety practices prevalent during the early years of the Big Creek Project might seem primitive by today's standards. Compared to other contemporary projects, however, the project had an admirable safety record. Here, the hospital staff at Camp 38 pose beside their ambulance.
Photographer unknown, from the Edison Collection

The lineup for the mess hall was second in importance only to the lineup for payday! Here the workers at Camp 38 await their "chow" in June 1923.
Photographer unknown, from the Edison Collection

intake for the tunnel, since it was imperative that it, too, be completed before high water. It was designed to control the flow into the tunnel from the forebay created by Dam No. 6. The structure rises 100 feet from the lowest point of the foundation, and the control gate is a single cylinder, 22 feet in diameter, and 771/2 feet in height. Standing inside this immense structure at its base, one might be reminded—or at least I was—of one of the larger movie theaters in Hollywood.

A railroad needs dispatchers to handle its trains, which must go through. A company in the power business needs them to see that the electricity reaches the places where and when it is needed, as it, too, must go through. The dispatchers who control the output of all the Big Creek plants, as well

136

This view down the inclined railway shows Powerhouse No. 3 nearing completion in September of 1923.
Photographer unknown, from the Edison Collection

The gigantic, snail shell-like scroll case is the heart of the Francis-style water turbine. Water under great pressure scrolls around the casing and leaves through the center, in the process spinning a massive "impeller," which turns the generator shaft to produce electricity. Although small by today's standards, the three original units at Big Creek No. 3 were the largest water reaction turbines in the world when built.
Photographer unknown, from the Edison Collection

Powerhouse No. 3 utilized the efficient Francis vertical reaction turbines in place of the older Pelton wheels. The generators at this plant were the first Westinghouse units ever purchased by the Edison Company. This September 1923 view of the interior of the plant shows the rotor for Unit No. 3 about to be installed. One month later, the plant was in operation. *Photographer unknown, from the Edison Collection*

as the allocation of water from the reservoirs, are located in a separate building at Big Creek No. 3, and operate under the chief system dispatcher at Alhambra. The dispatcher's load chart, or graphic record, is interesting to study. From it one can see what is happening in the evening as the load decreases—with stores, shops, factories closing, cities going to bed. As early morning activities begin, the increase in load is reflected in the upswing of the graph. In other words, it is possible to observe the comings and goings of cities pretty well from these charts. For instance, at the time of Franklin D. Roosevelt's funeral, a total of 85,000 kilowatts was dropped on the Edison system for one minute.

Much switching is as necessary in the handling of electricity, as of trains, but the switches, of course, are of a different type. A large outdoor switching station was built near Big Creek No. 3 Powerhouse. The main transmission lines from all the Big Creek plants are looped into this "switch garden." It consists of many huge switches called "oil circuit breakers" which are operated by remote control from the powerhouse, and other necessary appurtenances. This arrangement is quite flexible—a main line in trouble can be taken out of service, a plant may be isolated, and many situations handled by using various combinations obtainable in the switch garden.

Unit No. 2, the first in the Big Creek No. 3 Plant, went in service on September 30, 1923, at 7:09 p.m., in time to replace the load being supplied to the system from an outside source, the agreement for which expired at midnight. Unit I followed on October 2, Unit 3 on the morning of October 5, and the plant was turned over to the Operating Department on October 29.

A most unfortunate accident occurred at the plant on the afternoon of March 14, 1924—the worst ever to happen there. Two men were working on

Big Creek Powerhouse No. 3 was the first generating plant designed to accommodate the new 220,000-volt transmission voltage that had been developed by the Edison Company. The massive, water-cooled transformers at Powerhouse No. 3 dwarf the men standing beside them. It is easy to understand from this photo why the trade press referred to this powerhouse as the "Electrical Giant of the West."
Photographer unknown, from the Edison Collection

the plunger valve inside the No. 3 penstock, a short distance above the turbine. For some cause unknown to this day, the butterfly valve at the top of the penstock opened, letting in a full head of water. One man was literally blown out the manhole, unhurt, onto the turbine floor, but the other was forced through the eight-inch relief valve opening. The geyser from the penstock manhole tore through the powerhouse roof about 100 feet overhead, and attracted the attention of the crew of a passing train on the San Joaquin & Eastern, several miles above.

In May 1923 a radical departure was made in connection with a practice common to most construction jobs. Prior to that date, men following construction work furnished and carried their own bedding. It was now optional with those on the job whether they continued to do so, or availed themselves of beds furnished by the company. Many, but not all, took advantage of the company bedding; however, it wasn't long until all did so.

At this same time, a program was adopted of showing movies in the various camps at least once a week, and sometimes twice. Another feature which also proved to be popular was boxing bouts. Much talent along this line was found in one camp or another, and it was a common sight during summer to see several hundred men sitting around an outside arena in the evening, watching their favorites in bouts of almost any number of rounds. A referee was always in attendance.

A job such as ours during the 1920s was most unusual from any standpoint, and was a mecca for large numbers of salesmen, representing many companies throughout the country. Seldom was there a day when at least one, two, or several did not visit us. We did a large amount of pioneering in the use of various materials and equipment, and close collaboration between salesmen and ourselves resulted in mutual benefit.

XVI
Florence Lake Development
PREPARATIONS

A MAJOR UNDERTAKING, as well as the most conspicuous and spectacular one of the entire Big Creek Project, was the driving of Florence Lake Tunnel.

Preparations on a large scale had to be made. Full advantage had to be taken of the summer months—not only during 1920, the beginning, but through the years until completion of the tunnel. Underground work could proceed, of course, regardless of the weather.

The "60" series of numbers was allocated to the camps which would be constructed for the Florence Lake development. Camp 60, the first, was established for the tunnel outlet at the upper end of Huntington Lake. Men, equipment and material for building the camp were transported that summer by boat and barge across Huntington Lake to Chipmunk Landing. The name was given the place by the men because it appeared to be the favorite hangout for all Huntington Lake chipmunks. The following year we established a regular landing a short distance to the west, calling it Camp 59.

Horses and mules traveled around the lake by trail. Late that summer, and as work on the camp progressed, the road over Kaiser Pass was started by our own forces under the direct supervision of Harry M. Allen, general foreman. Men, mules, plows, scrapers, and a donkey engine constituted the outfit. Although a preliminary survey had been made, the actual location took place as the men, mules and scrapers pushed ahead. The wood-burning donkey engine, with its long reels of cable, pulled itself along and was used to remove boulders, trees, etc., that were too much for the mules.

When the engine reached Kaiser Pass, at an elevation of 9,305 feet, the black smoke was responsible for much excitement on the part of the Forest Service lookouts. Since there was nothing much to catch fire on the summit, the incident was all the more puzzling until the fire guards learned of the road crew's arrival at that point. Our objective was to reach the Camp 61 site in time to establish a permanent base before winter. It was to be an adit location from which to drive that section of the tunnel towards Huntington Lake. The road crew continued pushing down on the far side of Kaiser Pass,

The winter snows of the Sierras were the entire reason for the Big Creek Project. As the heavy snowpack melted, the runoff water was stored in reservoirs, then used to generate electricity before going down to irrigate crops in the San Joaquin Valley below. Unfortunately, the heavy snowfalls at higher altitudes made construction of portions of the project very difficult, shortening the working season and impeding transportation.
G. Haven Bishop Photo, from the Edison Collection

142

dodging huge boulders and removing many others. Spared wherever possible were the junipers—those sturdy denizens of the High Sierra which have withstood the elements through so many centuries. Though smaller in stature, they are comparable in age to the *Sequoia gigantea*. The nature of their environment and their general appearance indicate a struggle for existence.

Beyond the Pass about two miles, a scraper exposed some thinly covered fragments of a human skeleton. The mule skinners carefully collected the pieces, fragile from many years of exposure. A large cross, carved on a lodgepole pine, marks the tree at the base of which they were placed.

Temporary "fly" camps were made as the road moved along. Not to cause confusion later with a permanent camp number, they were designated 61A, B, C, etc.; there being five in all between Camps 60 and 61. The only one retaining its identity today is 61C on Kaiser Pass.

Following the road closely was a line crew, cutting and setting native poles for the construction of a 30,000-volt transmission line from Big Creek, since power was one of the most important items to have available as soon as the Camp 61 site was reached.

In about two months, eleven and one-half miles of fairly good road had been completed, connecting Camps 60 and 61. During the same summer, and as described in an earlier chapter, the government was building, and completed, the present road along the north side of Huntington Lake. Connecting with ours at Camp 60, it completed the length from Big Creek through to Camp 61.

Workmen were busy as bees, constructing facilities not only at Camp 60 but also at Camp 61, now that the road was through. Mess halls, bunkhouses, warehouses, etc., common to both camps, had to be ready before the snow started to fly—and that wasn't far off. Enough supplies had to be provided to see several hundred men through the winter months, as the road

This horse-drawn sledge was one method used to transport materials over rugged Kaiser Pass while the road was under construction in 1920.
Photographer unknown, from the Edison Collection

would then be closed to ordinary transportation. We built a log cabin on the northerly side of Kaiser Pass, large enough to care for several men if it were necessary for them to remain overnight while passing back and forth between camps. A cook was stationed there to serve meals. Although lumber for the Camp 60 buildings had been taken across Huntington Lake by barge, none could reach Camp 61 until the road was completed—and it was getting late. Shakes were made, which, together with logs and saplings cut nearby, constituted material for beginning construction of enough buildings for the first winter's use until an adequate supply of lumber was available.

Arthur Blight and I showed president Miller, Dr. Bryant, and Mr. Ward over the newly constructed road during Mr. Miller's visit in September 1920, as far as we could drive by automobile. We took Mr. Ward the two or three remaining miles to Camp 61 by wagon. The other visitors preferred to remain with the cars.

Lower left: "Double jack drillers" (two men hitting, and one man holding the drill) prepare a rock for blasting during the construction of Kaiser Pass road on August 25, 1920.
Photographer unknown, from the Edison Collection

Below: Harry M. Allen, the foreman in charge of building the road over Kaiser Pass to the site of Camp 61, drove the first car over the new road on September 8, 1920.
Photographer unknown, from the Edison Collection

The remoteness of Camp 63 required it to be virtually self-sufficient for nearly half the year. The cold storage locker was just one of the facilities designed to provision the camp for the long winters.
Murphy's Studio Photo, from the Edison Collection

As it took two months to build the road between Camp 60 and 61, there remained a scant two months more for equipping the latter camp for the winter. At its elevation, 7,100 feet, there are only about six months in the year when the ground is free of snow. The new road which had just been completed around the north side of the lake allowed us to transport supplies by truck from the lake all the way to both camps. During the years that there has been a road over Kaiser Pass, we have always hoped to get "just one more job done" before snow called a halt. This was especially true late in 1920, when Old Man Winter stepped in and closed the road just before Christmas.

Whenever weather permitted, during the first winter at Camp 61, everything possible was accomplished outside. As soon as the road over the Pass was opened in 1921, there were many jobs to be done in the way of further preparation- even at Camp 61. It seemed we never really finished preparations. In fact, up to and including the last year of construction, we were doing things preparatory to completion beyond the pass. Each camp had to have its own cold storage plant for meat, butter, poultry, etc., and they would have done credit to any large packing concern. A central laundry was built and operated at Camp 61, at which attempts were made to handle work for employees, in addition to the company items. Such efforts were usually accompanied by many headaches, and we were always glad when we could limit orders to company material, of which there was a great deal. Our experience was much more satisfactory at the large laundry operated at Big Creek headquarters, where women were available as help.

To cut down on distance for hauling lumber, the old sawmill at Shaver was moved and installed near Camp 61 in the summer of 1921. A million board-feet did not go far in the midst of so many needs both outside and underground.

This hospital was located at Camp 61, 11 miles east of Huntington Lake, on the far side of Kaiser Pass. It served as the base hospital for the tunnel project.
Photographer unknown, from the Edison Collection

A large recreation hall was built at each camp for the movies and all sorts of gatherings. In summer months there were many boxing bouts, which were popular just as at our lower camps. Of course, there was gambling of a sort in spite of attempts to discourage it. The main concerns were the fleecing of the men by "card sharks"—and the games reaching the nuisance stage.

Mono Base Hospital was built at Camp 61 to serve all camps on that side of Kaiser Pass. Dr. W. N. Carter, formerly located at Kern River No. 3, assumed charge, with Mrs. Carter as head nurse. The large new building had just been completed, and was all in readiness for patients when, on December 17, 1921, at 5:30 a.m., it caught fire and was completely destroyed. Besides that serious loss, four bunkhouses, the timekeeper's office, the detention ward, and the doctor's residence—suffered damage. It was too late-winter was upon us—to undertake building a new structure. We had to get along with a makeshift arrangement until the following summer, when a duplicate structure was built. First-aid stations at the other camps, each managed by a competent nurse, completed the medical facilities.

Work got under way in the early summer of 1922 to extend the road from Camp 61 to Florence Lake. To expedite completion of the tunnel, it was desirable to have another adit. Camp 62 was chosen as the location, not quite halfway between Camp 61 and Florence Lake. Before adoption of the final location for the present road beyond Camp 61, it was considered advisable

Camp 62 was established on the far side of Kaiser Ridge, between Huntington Lake and the future site of Florence Lake. At this location, a second "adit," or side tunnel, was dug into the ridge to provide access to the line of the tunnel for additional working faces. The camp was pleasant enough in summer, but the snow-sheds over the railroad tracks leading out of the tunnel give an idea of winter conditions.
Murphy's Studio Photo, from the Edison Collection

146

Ward Lake, a small natural alpine lake, was located along the Kaiser Pass road. In 1922, it was named for George C. Ward, then Edison's vice president of engineering and construction.
G. Haven Bishop Photo, from the Edison Collection

to make one more inspection. After a road is once built, it costs money to make changes.

A party consisting of Messrs. Ward, Barre, Davis, Dennis, and Howard and myself, on horseback, spent an entire day reconnoitering along the ridges to the south high above the road as it is today. The trip was difficult; the steep cliffs we encountered confirmed our judgment on the location already adopted. Numerous places over slick rock were so dangerous to cross that each rider led his horse. During the last crossing, Mr. Ward's horse slipped and slid about fifteen feet, landing upside down at the bottom of a large hole. Slick rock on all sides prevented the animal from getting a foothold; consequently, he couldn't right himself. The poor fellow tried until exhausted, the saddle on his back making it more difficult. We had to wait for a rest period between his efforts, or risk being injured by flying hoofs. Finally, he must have realized the futility of further attempts on his part, and welcomed our assistance. With head, foot and tail holds, we maneuvered the animal into various positions. With the help of all, plus his remaining energy, he was able to turn right side up; fortunately, he was unhurt. It does not take much imagination to picture what the consequences might have been had the rider been aboard. The trip was treacherous in any direction, so we decided to lead our horses down and out as best we could. We came out upon the shore of a lovely pond which we could not identify on any government map. Then and there we named it "Ward Lake" and such it has appeared ever since upon maps. We built our road along its shore.

By the summer's end, one could drive all the way to the site where Camp 63 was built—the intake for the Florence Lake Tunnel. All facilities previously provided at Camp 61 had to be practically duplicated at the two new camps, 62 and 63, the lumber being cut in the mill then in operation at Camp 61.

Camp 63 was established at the site of the upper end of the Florence Lake Tunnel, near the future site of Florence Dam. Although the dam was built only during the short summer seasons, work on the tunnel went on year-round. Once again, this picture of the camp in mild summer weather belies the harsh winters experienced here.
Vic Stahl Photo, from the Edison Collection

XVII
Florence Lake Development
ALASKA DOG TEAM

W E WERE FACED WITH the problem during winter months, of getting mail and light supplies of various kinds, particularly medicine, over Kaiser Pass with the road impassable on account of deep snow. Equipment for snow removal such as we have today had not been perfected. The decision was made to secure a dog team, the question being how to get one which was trained, with a driver, in time to be of use during the winter which was then upon us. With the assistance of Ingersoll-Rand Company, we obtained a team of seven dogs and a driver from Alaska.

Jerry Dwyer, the dogs (Babe, the leader, Patsy, Dooley, Trim, Riley, Whiskey and Barney), and complete equipment arrived, going into service on December 16, 1920. The team operated between Camp 60 at the upper end of Huntington Lake where it was based, and Camp 61, beyond Kaiser Pass. The normal schedule consisted of a trip over the pass one day and back the next. During the summer months of the first two years, the team was quartered at Camp 61C on Kaiser Pass, where it was cooler because of the elevation—9,305 feet.

The dogs received careful attention from Jerry, who cared for them as though they were children. They were fond of fresh fish, especially salmon, which they were fed when it was obtainable. They always had to be tied and kept far enough apart to prevent their fighting with one another. Along the trail, under some conditions, the snow would cause trouble by balling-up on their feet. To prevent this, Jerry had leather shoes made. The dogs were not too keen about wearing them and when the shoes were put on would jump around for a while as if they were walking over hot coals. Frequently, a trail had to be broken in the deep snow, and this would be accomplished by several men walking ahead, as there was always some traveling back and forth.

Before the first heavy snow, road markers—short wood blocks painted red—were nailed on trees fifteen feet above the ground, and spaced about 100 yards apart. Where there were no trees, a sapling was cut and set in a mound of rocks along the roadside. These markers were for the guidance of men on foot, as well as for the dog team. It does not take long in these

Previous pages: Jerry Dwyer, the famous Alaskan "sourdough," with his dog team on the Kaiser Pass Road in March 1922. Babe is the lead dog.
Photographer unknown, from the Edison Collection

mountains for a blizzard to completely obliterate a road. After nearly thirty years, many of these markers remain in place, arousing the curiosity of visitors.

The dog team had not been working long before it was called into action on an errand of mercy, but too late. An employee located at Camp 61, six miles beyond Kaiser Pass, was determined to get home to spend Christmas with his family in the San Joaquin Valley. Against the advice of his superiors and contemporaries, he reached Camp 61C on Kaiser Pass, where quarters were available for anyone who might need shelter during storms. After a short stopover, he insisted on going ahead. It was six and one-half miles to Camp 60, at the upper end of Huntington Lake, and the snow at the pass was more than waist deep. Three men volunteered to accompany him, not wanting to see him go on alone. The party had not gone far when his exhaustion made it necessary for the others to place their companion at the foot of a large juniper tree—the snow is always light around the bases of large trees—and return to camp for Jerry and his dogs. When the rescue party finally reached the juniper tree, the man was dead.

Jerry Dwyer holds Patsy, who became lead dog after the death of Babe.
G. Haven Bishop Photo from the Edison Collection

Several of our men thought the Alaska dogs should have some competition. Besides, they needed some help as the sled loads were increasing. Seven camp mongrels were pressed into service, to alternate on trips with their more favored competitors. The mongrels presented no problem whatsoever, even though none had ever been harnessed. The new outfit started off like old-timers, and on the first trip the two teams met on Kaiser Pass. It was anticipated there might be trouble, and to prevent this, the teams were kept at a distance in passing. The Alaska dogs paid no particular attention, merely giving a few glances off to the side, as much as to say, "Huh, where did you punks come from?" The mongrel team, however, really had a fit. Each dog growled or snarled, some barked, and the hair on their backs stood straight up; but both teams kept moving. The mongrel team acted in much the same manner each time the other team came in sight during the few weeks, as if saying, "You guys are not so hot."

In September 1922, Babe, the leader of the Alaskan dogs, died. Jerry buried her on Kaiser Pass, where Whiskey and Trim found a resting place subsequently. Their graves have been marked with an appropriate redwood slab, made and erected by the United States Forest Service. Before the marker was erected there was no identification other than a border of stones around each grave. Since they are alongside the main road, they have become a center of attraction for passing motorists. On numerous occasions I have stopped to join a group—out of curiosity—as it has always been interesting to hear the conjectures. Once when there was only a single grave, one member of such a group, after a long powwow, opined, "Some poor old prospector, I suppose."

After Babe's death, the leadership of the team fell to the black dog, Patsy, a most likable and friendly creature. Mrs. Redinger extended her sympathy to Jerry, and his reaction to the loss of Babe can be described more easily by quoting his letter to her, written at Camp 61C on September 20, 1922:

Dear Mrs. Redinger:
I received your letter this morning and wish to let you know that I am
sincerely grateful for your interest and sympathy.
Losing Babe hurt more than I thought possible. For a number of years
past I have thought that nothing mattered, but I was mistaken. I consoled
myself with the knowledge that I was always good to Babe, and I believe
it is better to have her die than to have me leave her. She did not suffer,
and died in the arms of the one she loved best in all the world, game to
the last. Her last effort was to snuggle up in my arms. That is more than I
expect myself when I pass out.
I thank you for the picture. It looks to me a great deal like the picture of
Maude Adams in 'Joan of Arc'—another great lover of dogs. Her favorite
was the dog of all dogs, the Irish wolfhound. I used to know Maude
Adams, the angel of the stage, and thought she was the loveliest ever.
With best wishes to you, Mrs. Redinger, I remain
                    Sincerely,

                    (Signed) Jerry Dwyer

With the letter, he enclosed, in his own handwriting, a copy of that much-publicized "A Tribute to the Dog," by Senator George Graham Vest. I do not see how anyone can read it without being deeply touched, causing one, perhaps, to have a more kindly feeling towards man's canine friends. In addition, Jerry also sent, in further tribute to Babe, a poem that had been sent to him, written by G. F. Rinehart, who, at that time, was editor of the *Covina Citizen*. This is the poem:

On the topmost reach of the Kaiser Crest
Where the clouds commune and weep,
In a granite tomb 'til the crack of doom,
Babe lies in her last long sleep.

Though born to the law of the tooth and fang
In the land of Alaskan Snow
Of the Savage pack that follows the track
In blood-lust for its foe.

The Wolf-Dog shatters genetic law
That each seeks kith or clan
For the Wolf-Dog mind will forsake its kind
To become the friend of Man.

At the word of command from her Friend and Pal
Past pinnacle, spire and dome
Through the blizzard's blast she was sure and fast
To mush with the mail from home.

For thirty miles to the snow bound lake
She was always willing to go
On a dangerous trail, with the daily mail
To the men marooned in snow.

When the Tourist conquers the tortuous steeps
With the Kaiser Pass as his goal
He will pause and rest on the wind-swept Crest
Where lies this Dog with a soul.

The author, during visits to the lodge and area at previous times, had become acquainted with Jerry and his dogs.

As he indicated in his letter, Jerry had thought of his leaving Babe at some future time, and had felt prior to Babe's death that nothing mattered insofar as he himself was concerned. He seldom talked about himself, his principal interest being his dogs—this being true at least during the several years he was here. We never knew much about his past, as there was not any inclination on his part to discuss it. He and his dog team received wide publicity and accomplished much in their line of work, especially during emergencies in storms. An inquiry came to me from Hartford, Connecticut, the writer being the editor of the *Hartford Courant*. By indirect questioning, all that could be learned was that Jerry was familiar with that part of the country. The Hartford editor replied, appreciating the information—even though what we learned was meager—stating that Jerry came from a high-ranking New England family.

Jerry liked Mrs. Redinger, probably because she displayed interest in him and his dogs. When he left here in 1927, he told her that he would send her a card from time to time but that she would never find any address on it. That proved to be the case with several which she did receive. The last one, received in 1931, was postmarked "Seattle, Washington," and nothing was known as to what happened to him after that date.

During the winter months, when the upper camps on the Florence Lake tunnel project were virtually isolated due to the snowpack, the arrival of Jerry Dwyer's dog team with a sled load of U. S. mail was a welcome event. Here, Jerry's team is seen between Camp 60 and Camp 61 on March 30, 1924. *Photographer unknown, from the Edison Collection*

Snow parties were important social events at Big Creek. One popular activity featured "snow boats" pulled by horses. Races between rival dog teams were another pastime. This group picture taken at Cascada (Big Creek) on February 2, 1922, includes operations superintendent E. R. Davis (left); Dave Redinger (second from left); and Dee (Edith) Redinger (second from right). *G. Haven Bishop Photo, from the Edison Collection*

XVIII
Florence Lake Development
RADIO COMMUNICATION

ONE OF THE MOST IMPORTANT factors of any construction job is a means of quick and dependable communication. We realized the uncertainty of reliable service from a telephone line over Kaiser Pass and besides, maintenance would be expensive. Previously, the Edison Company had used satisfactorily a telegraph circuit between Los Angeles and the Kern River No. 3 project. A similar hookup had already been made between Los Angeles and Big Creek.

It was decided to make some tests in the Big Creek area as to the practicability of radio-telegraph for the upper camps. The late Messrs. Roy Ashbrook and Ralph Henry were encouraged sufficiently by the tests to proceed with the installation of such communication between Big Creek and all the upper camps to be established. Ashbrook was furnished a small, pine, slab-covered structure about eight by ten feet, from which he made the necessary tests at the Big Creek end. After it had served its purpose, I had it moved into my back yard. Called "the little brown house," it continued through the years to render valuable service, sometimes as guests' quarters.

What with the telephone and telegraph circuits to Los Angeles, supplemented by the radio, communication traffic was seen as a major item of the construction program; consequently, we constructed a special building here at headquarters to accommodate the facilities and operators, there being three shifts—telephone and radio—on duty during the heavy construction years.

Radio operations really started in November 1920. En route to Camp 61 on foot early in 1922, 1 heard my first radio broadcast. While lying on a cot in the attic of Camp 61C's log cabin overnight, I listened with headphones to an alumni address by Dr. Suzzalo, president of the University of Washington. In those years, the Camp 61C radio station was reported to be the highest in the world.

Knowing my interest in radio, operator "Red" Fordham would always hand me items of interest whenever I stopped at his station. I recall several messages passing between Ashbrook and Henry, in which Ashbrook was try-

In the evening of February 18, 1925, word was sent by radio telegraph to the station at Camp 62 to fire the last round of explosives to complete the Florence Lake Tunnel. The operator is seen receiving the message at his spartan "radio shack."
Murphy's Studio Photo, from the Edison Collection

Previous pages: This picture of the radio-telegraph base station at Big Creek shows operator "Red" Fordham at the key (right). It was taken in September of 1923, during which month the office handled more radio traffic than any other station on the West Coast.
Photographer unknown, from the Edison Collection

ing to locate his "Church Warden." As I was not familiar with the name, and since there were no churches in the vicinity, my curiosity was aroused—hence, my message, "What is all this church warden stuff?" Had I recalled James Whitcomb Riley's "That Old Sweetheart of Mine," I would have known it was also Ashbrook's favorite smoking tobacco.

The communication traffic flourished, especially via radio and telegraph circuits. Our reports indicated that for the month of November 1923 more than a half-million words were handled. By that time the service had been extended to Camp 63 at Florence Lake.

Typical radiogram sent from the Big Creek Base Station, 1927.
Redinger Family Album

MESSAGE RECEIVED

'81 Avenue dubail, Shanghai.

VIA AMATER RADIO   AC-1CRS.   AERL.

From 6CQ via OP-1HR   No. 1   No. of words ...   date and Time handed in   Feb 12   *1927* M

Service Instructions Mail Olvy   Date and time rcvd. Feb 16 7.40p   M   By

To   D.M. Redinger, Oriental Hotel Kobe Japan.

Greetings and best wishes for a pleasant trip herewith sent by radio from Big Creek amateur station -

Sign:- Big Creek,
Construction Dept.

With Compliments
R SHEKURY

A letter was received from a man in Idaho. Being an amateur, he had been picking up some of our messages and was concerned about a special type of bolt a camp foreman was having trouble locating. He offered to send down one he happened to have.

The operators at Big Creek Headquarters were discussing the possibility of reaching the Redingers, who were in Japan on a trip in the Orient. They decided to try, and their message, picked up by an amateur in Shanghai, was received by mail at Kobe. The $10 for the three-word acknowledgement by cable was considered well spent.

Milton Kempt, foreman at Camp 61, in sending radio messages to Big Creek Headquarters, always ended with the words, "Everything else O.K.," regardless of the contents. As we went aboard ship at Honolulu to continue across the Pacific after a two-week stopover, I found in my mail a message from Big Creek sent by George C. Heckman which was a takeoff on those by Kempt. Typewritten on the standard form used for radio was the following:

CAMP 61C, JANUARY 15, 1927.

SNOWING HARD STOP SNOW ON LEVEL TWELVE FEET STOP DOG TEAM COMING UP FROM CAMP SIXTY WITH FRESH FISH AND ORANGES FOR THE MEN ISOLATED IN THE CAMPS STOP TRUCK NO. 1313 LOST ITS ENGINE BETWEEN CAMP 60 AND CAMP 61C. THIS WAS NOT NOTICED UNTIL TRUCK ARRIVED. SHALL WE SEND THE DOG TEAM BACK TO LOOK FOR THE ENGINE STOP THE ROSES AND CARNATIONS DID NOT ARRIVE ON THE TRUCK. THOUGHT THE COOK AT CAMP 60 MIGHT HAVE MADE A MISTAKE AND USED THEM FOR SALAD. PLEASE ADVISE STOP HAVE FOUND ONLY ONE POTATO FROZEN OUT OF THE TEN MILLION STOP CARETAKER AT CAMP 63 TURNING THE EGGS OVER FINDS THERE A MILLION OR MORE AND WILL TAKE HIM SEVERAL YEARS TO DO THE JOB HOWEVER HAVE ADVISED HIM NOT TO TURN ONE AT A TIME BUT ONE CRATE INSTEAD. THIS METHOD WILL TAKE ONLY A FEW HOURS STOP THE ELECTRIC LOCOMOTIVES ARE STILL LOCO STOP HECKMAN, PESTERFIELD AND THE GOODWILL MAN JUST LEFT HERE IN A BOB SLED FOR A VISIT TO THE OTHER CAMPS. EVERYTHING ELSE O.K.

(SIGNED) CAMP FOREMAN

The radio operators were able to keep the various camps quite well posted on current news items gleaned from various sources, and the men looked forward each day to such information.

As far as is known, our radio-telegraph was the first to be used on such a large construction job. It was very satisfactory through the years—most of the 1920s—that it served the upper camps. Today, at Florence Lake we are using as a mess hall the steel building which formerly served as the radio building. It is still referred to and better known as "the old radio shack." Here at Big Creek, Boy Scouts make use of the tile-roofed concrete structure which for years was the headquarters for all our heavy telephone, telegraph and radio traffic.

XIX
Florence Lake Tunnel

QUARTERS FOR THE WINTER had been made ready at Camp 60, the tunnel outlet, by October. The big job for which there had been so much preparation was ready to be tackled. The distance through the mountain beneath Kaiser Pass to Camp 61 is six and one-half miles, and it was a mammoth undertaking to blast a hole that length, in hard granite most of the way. Tunnel men refer to any kind of tunnel material as "ground."

A short open cut to establish the outlet portal was necessary. This done, the first set of timbers was placed on October 15, 1920, marking the start to go underground.

A big factor to be expected in most tunnel work is water. It constitutes a problem by itself, and conditions are aggravated if boulders, sand and mud are encountered with it. To start with, we struck all four at the outlet. Progress was slow the first winter. Much timbering was required, and hand labor was all that could be used. The open cut to the adit portal at Camp 61 was started in November, the same year. Progress underground was also slow and discouraging due to running sand, always difficult to handle. Many bales of straw were stuffed behind the timbers to combat the sand effectively.

By April 1921, the adit was less than one-third the distance to the point where tunnel driving could start towards Camp 60 and Florence Lake. A glance at the progress chart was sufficient to realize the seriousness of the situation, in looking ahead to final completion and ultimate expenditures. The decision was made to sink a shaft to the main tunnel grade west of the adit, toward Camp 60, to speed progress. Started on April 15, it was finished to tunnel grade on July 23, a depth of 247 feet through hard granite.

Excavation started at once on the tunnel, one crew working toward the outlet, six miles away, the other toward the Camp 61 adit intersection.

To speed up excavation still further, another shaft was started on June 25, the same year, near the Camp 61 adit intersection, to permit driving toward the adit portal and also towards the first shaft. Of great importance was the completion of this adit, which allowed the muck trains to operate over a level

160

This was the original lower portal of the Florence Lake Tunnel as it appeared in October 1920, before the work was speeded up. In April, 1921, the decision was made to accelerate the work on this tunnel, which led to the decision to drill several adits to provide additional working faces. At this time, the existing tunnel was expanded to 15- by 15-foot dimensions, to accommodate standard-gauge railway tracks. This lower portal gave much trouble during the early stages of construction, due to the soft ground encountered.
Photographer unknown, from the Edison Collection

Previous pages: The inlet to the Florence Lake Tunnel was this hole blasted from the granite of Kaiser Ridge at Camp 63. This camp had an extensive system of standard electric railway tracks to haul "muck" out of the tunnel to various rock dumps. This site was later inundated by the enlarged Florence Lake.
Photographer unknown, from the Edison Collection

grade to and from the tunnel. The 87-foot depth to tunnel grade, through very hard granite, was completed in forty-nine days—very good progress for a large two-compartment shaft.

By the middle of February 1922, the adit was completed, and the muck trains could operate to and from the outside. On April 6, the section of tunnel between the two shafts holed through, and the total progress at Camp 61 amounted to 2,900 feet of main tunnel in addition to the 1,086 feet of adit. In the meantime, more than half a mile had been driven at Camp 60. Things were now set for straightaway tunnel driving from both Camps 60 and 61—the long section, the one towards the outlet at Camp 60, where efforts were now concentrated.

A natural question that has been asked frequently is, "Why were two angles made in the tunnel, thereby increasing its length?" A straight tunnel would have been two miles shorter. The longer one could be driven in two years' less time because it allowed two adits, whereas the topography on a straight line would not. Each adit provided two more headings, or working faces, a total of six including the intake and outlet. On a straight line there would have been only two. Moreover, shafts on a straight line tunnel would have been impractical because of the great depth.

By the latter part of 1922, Adit Camp 62 had been established, as had Camp 63 at the intake portal. The job had reached a stage at which close supervision was required, and Herman Kruger assumed direct charge through to completion, after which time he became general superintendent on field construction. Equipment to suit the 15- by 15-foot tunnel was provided, and with better organization all around, we looked forward to improvement in progress.

Tunnel crews commenced to vie with one another in making footage. Three eight-hour shifts seemed to work best. The small Armstrong "Shoveloders" were replaced with special Marion steam shovels, operated by compressed air. Combination storage battery and trolley locomotives, Baldwin-Westinghouse eight-ton type, hauled trains of muck cars of four to six cubic feet capacity. The trolley was used to within 800 to 1,000 feet of a heading, after which the storage battery took over. The trolley could not go closer, as it would be shot down or damaged each time a round of holes was fired.

Our payroll and the number of camps were not the only things increasing rapidly with the expanding program along the sixty-mile front from Auberry to Camp 63. Uptown Big Creek was enjoying a boom during the '20s, such as it never knew before or has known since. Our 5,000 to 5,200 men, spread over thirty-two camps, kept three barber shops and six dentists busy. In the larger camps, especially those isolated in winter, there were always those amongst the employees with enough barber experience to cater to tonsorial needs until summer. Reardon's movie theater provided good films and current newsreels. Busiest of all was Murphy's Art Shop. If he didn't have what you wanted, he would order it—whether it was a penny article or a grand piano. *Murphy's Art Shop News,* printed by him and distributed free of charge over the project, served as an excellent advertising medium, besides carrying local items of interest. The unique publication attracted attention far and near. W. L. Murphy came to Big Creek as a stenographer for R. V. Haslett, our storekeeper. He recognized and took advantage of an opportunity which would have proved even more profitable if fire had not destroyed the enterprise in 1930.

During all the years of construction, the Florence Lake road above Camp 60 was closed to the general public in summer months. The gate between the upper end of Huntington Lake and Camp 60 was attended twenty-four hours a day, entrance being restricted to Edison Company and U. S. Forest Service vehicles. It took something most extraordinary to justify a special pass. This restriction was necessary because travel by the general public would have seriously interfered with the operation of all equipment, to say nothing of endangering the cars of campers, sightseers, fishermen, etc. No restriction was placed on hikers or horseback riders, of which there were few. Because of our heavy traffic, and in order to keep the road in good condition, we kept the road wet with tank sprinklers which worked at night, when evaporation and travel were less. Today we would probably use oil.

The results we were getting elsewhere with the faster and more powerful Ingersoll-Rand X-70 rock drills—or "machines," as the men called them— justified their use in the Florence Lake Tunnel, so we replaced the lighter and smaller 248s with them.

Good ventilation must be provided in tunnel work. We started with a positive type of blower, Root No. 3, but as the working faces were pushed ahead, we naturally required more capacity. The smaller blowers were replaced with the larger Root No. 7, which was ample for distances varying from 11,000 to 12,000 feet. Beyond that distance another one would be installed along the 24-inch ventilation pipeline to act as a booster, in the same capacity as a booster pump in a large oil line. Woodstave pipe had two advantages over iron; less chance of collapse from blasting concussion, and, if a rock fragment punched a hole, it could readily be patched, whereas iron pipe, if crushed, requires renewal of the section.

In spite of these advantages we found after two years woodstave pipe had become unsatisfactory, having dried and shrunk from the air and powder smoke passing through, and extensive maintenance was necessary, such as putting on bands to squeeze the staves together. Tests with 24-inch corrugated iron pipe proved quite satisfactory, provided a smooth liner was placed inside to reduce friction caused by the corrugation. The ventilating pipe, or blower pipe, was carried along near the roof and kept within about 300 feet of a working face. This allowed more space along the tunnel wall on the floor for storing various kinds of material. Another advantage of this practice was that it was easier to remove gases generated from blasting, which ordinarily rise. After a round was fired, the blowers would be reversed to withdraw the powder smoke.

To assist in clearing the heading as quickly as possible, it was effective to use an air curtain. Perforated one-inch pipe was laid transversely to the tunnel, on the floor, a short distance toward the portal from the end of the 24-inch blower pipe. The last man to leave the heading before the round was fired would open the air valve feeding the one-inch pipe. The released air, directed towards the roof, would retard the smoke until it was withdrawn by the blower. Somewhat more effective was the use of a water spray instead of air. No one was allowed to return to the heading until a half hour after blasting; this was a safety measure against delayed holes. The heading and bench method was used in driving, the blasting being done electrically from a 440-volt circuit. The various powder companies endeavored to provide a product that would generate the smallest amounts of objectionable gases, and a means to that end was a special kind of paper wrapper. Much improvement was made in that respect with the explosives then used exclusively, 40-60 percent gelatin powder, known to the layman as *dynamite*.

Our hog business was extended to Camp 61, where it thrived as it had in locations below Big Creek. We did have some problems, which were caused by such diseases as cholera. One of the tenders at Camp 61 was a character. He admitted frankly that he had known nothing about shoes until he reached the age of twenty—so why should he bother with socks, which had to be changed every two or three weeks? The garbage was hauled in the camp "candy" wagon, and this tender attracted attention because of a washtub in front of the seat, in which he always kept his feet when he was driving. The men's curiosity was satisfied only when they learned he was keeping his feet warm on cool mornings by submerging them in leftover cooked cereal, still warm. He was forced to occupy isolated quarters, as the men objected to his brand of "perfume," which was anything but My Sin or Chanel No. 5!

A winter spent in any of the Florence Lake camps was an excellent way for a man to accumulate a good stake. Some made good use of their savings; others, when they went out for a time, did not fare too well. I recall one who had twenty-five paychecks in his pocket, and who was back at work, broke, within ten days. In Fresno the train would be met by men waiting for "live ones" from Big Creek, who were ready and willing to help relieve the workers of their "wads" across the tracks. It did not take long to get "rolled" or "hijacked" in various other places. Back they would come for another "sentence," as some workers termed it.

Many times I have wondered how many millions of Big Creek dollars were spent through the years in Fresno alone. During the big years, the Edison Company maintained offices in Fresno. Fred Henry, as purchasing agent, kept R. V. Haslett busy at the Big Creek end, and vice versa, both handling millions of dollars' worth of material and equipment. The Los Angeles office was in there "pitching" also. George Campbell, in Fresno, kept the men coming. The accounting department at Big Creek, under the field supervision of C. R. Duncan, representing C. P. Staal, was kept busy, too. Not only did invoices have to be paid, but there were paydays for the thousands of employees, who were divided into three groups—one working, one coming and one going. In those days we could give jobs to all comers.

As soon as the road over Kaiser Pass was open each spring, everyone would go all out during the summer to stock the upper camps for another winter. One of the major items of food for any camp was fresh meat. There were about 2,000 men in the Florence Lake Camps when all six tunnel headings were being worked. During the four and one-half years of tunnel construction, 2,000,000 pounds of fresh meat were consumed, and served with it were 1,770,000 pounds of potatoes. The latter, some of the finest in the land, were bought several carloads at a time. Fred Henry would send a man

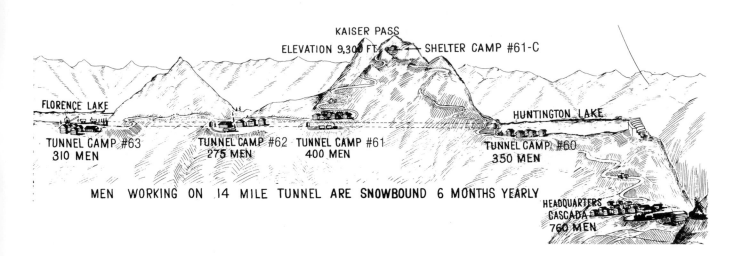

This sketch shows the relative locations of the four tunnel camps located along the Florence Lake Tunnel construction project.
Drawing from the Edison Collection

to Idaho into the field while the crop was being harvested. Such spuds! The Northern Pacific and the Great Northern dining cars featuring those tubers had nothing on the camps. An ideal arrangement was made with a local cattleman to supply our meat and deliver it to each cold storage plant. The cattle would be driven into the back country as early as the season would allow, grazing under a Forest Service permit until fall, when they were slaughtered nearby. The rows upon rows of halves of choicest beef hanging in each plant would have given Paul Bunyan a thrill. Mr. Ward, vice president of the Edison Company in charge of all construction and operation, was a connoisseur who, on his many visits, never missed an opportunity to look in on the sight that would have made an avowed vegetarian drool. What's more, we always saw to it that he enjoyed a choice cut at any of the upper camps. He was an early riser and liked to leave Big Creek early enough to have breakfast at Camp 61C, where we had a chef renowned for his golden brown hotcakes, the size of a breakfast plate and really "out of this world."

On numerous occasions, Mr. Ward had discussed the Kaiser Crest junipers, in which he displayed unusual interest, especially when observing them in their habitat. On one trip, he and a guest, also interested in trees, stopped to study closely one we could not dodge when building the road. During luncheon at Camp 61, comments were made about the age of the grizzled monarchs, the conclusion being there was no question but that they were at least 2,500 years old. The conversation, carried on extensively, attracted the attention of several tunnel men at an adjoining table, who listened in silence. On my next trip to the camp one of the timekeepers, reminding me of the previous discussion, related what took place after we had left. The tunnel men took up the subject, and reached some conclusions themselves—at least one man did. He remarked, "You fellows can let those guys stuff that kind of bunk down your necks, but they can't make me believe anything like those trees being two or three thousand years old. Hell, this is only 1922 now."

A sizable job was the proper coordination of the numerous mess halls, meals, proper supplies, help, etc. A. F. McCarthy, chief steward of the upper camps, did not find time heavy on his hands. Neither did C. A. McDonald,

164

As the headings extended longer distances beneath Kaiser Ridge, it would have seriously slowed down the work to bring out crews for their mid-shift meal. The commissaries at each camp devised these special "hot lunch trains" to bring meals right to the working faces. Although not as elegant as the trappings of a railroad dining car, the food was hearty, hot, and available in huge quantities. This particular electric train is at the work face in one of the headings extending from the adit at Camp 62.

Photographer unknown, from the Edison Collection

who supervised the Big Creek headquarters camp along with some others. Under each were chief cooks, day cooks, night cooks, bakers, waiters ("flunkies" in construction), vegetable men, dishwashers and roustabouts. A mess hall crew "raised hob" occasionally when they tapped a keg of home brew which had been "working" beneath the kitchen floor or in an obscure closet. Sometimes such festivities would be delayed when the thing blew up without warning. Eternal vigilance by the chief steward did not prevent such occurrences. It was no cure to discharge the culprits and get a new gang; everything would be serene for a while, then would usually end in a blow-up, again disrupting the meal situation temporarily.

"Daddy" Grabner was head baker at Big Creek headquarters, where a huge bakery was operated for years. The upper camps had to do their own baking, especially during the winters. When the whole project was going full blast, a month's consumption required 55,000 loaves of bread, 5,000 cakes and 36,000 pies. Mess halls—the larger ones, of course—were operating around the clock.

As the Florence Lake tunnel headings in the longer sections progressed, they were so far underground that it was impracticable to transport the men in and out for meals. To do so would have taken about two hours for a three to six-mile round trip. For the midshift meal, a unique dining car service was established, which took the food to the men and served it near the heading.

These trains consisted of five electric-lighted flatcars—three equipped with tables and benches, the other two with racks holding the food in hot containers. Help from the mess hall served as if it were a regular dining room. One of those underground meals was a novel experience, and I do not recall ever hearing a complaint. It was much more comfortable inside the tunnel than out, being that it was cool in summer and warm in winter.

For several summers we operated courtesy cars, taking as guests people who were interested in seeing the work being done in the back country. Regular schedules starting from the lodge accommodated hundreds. Special groups were handled in large buses, like those used to transport our men to and from the upper camps. One particular party sponsored by the Edison Company was being escorted by D. A. Munger, the usual genial host on such occasions. Having been shown over the Florence Lake work, the guests were returning to the lodge, when from the black smoke darkening the sky it was evident that there was a bad forest fire some miles distant. The grave consequences of such fires were purposely called to the guests' attention, for reasons shortly to become obvious. The subject under discussion, according to hurriedly made plans unknown to Munger, was that forest rangers, in dire need of firefighters, can commandeer anyone in the vicinity. By the time the group had conceived such a possibility in its own case, the buses reached the gate at Camp 60. Two rangers "happened" to be with the gate attendant. Approaching the buses, they proceeded to enlighten the occupants further, stressing the seriousness of the fire and the urgent need for help. Herb Barre, executive engineer of the Edison Company—good at playing pranks, and one of the instigators of the plot—was accompanying the party. He was chuckling to himself at the expense of the innocent visitors, some of whom were now literally shaking in their shoes. All kinds of excuses were made to the rangers—important business engagements elsewhere, no suitable clothes or shoes, poor physical condition, even such excuses as heart ailments. By this time Barre was about to explode, and Munger, for once, was at his wit's end. The situation was tense for a long five minutes while Munger was looking for me, being sure I knew the rangers. Pretending innocence, I had difficulty maintaining a straight face. He came running, and asked frantically, "Dave, for God's sake, can't you call off the dogs? These men are in no condition to fight fires!" Someone "in the know" giggled at this most opportune time and the jig was up. That evening relief was evident in the guests' unusually high spirits and good humor as they sat around the fireplace in the lodge lobby.

As the tunnel was pushed ahead, we ran into bad ground from time to time. Such places always retard progress. The worst condition was encountered where we least expected to find it—beneath Kaiser Meadow, which is close to Kaiser Pass. The half-mile depth of cover is greater there than anywhere else along the tunnel. Extra-heavy timbers, closely spaced, were required to hold the "swelling ground"—boulders, broken rock, sand, mud and much water—all were present for several hundred feet. Water is a problem any time. Pumping is required when the water is on the wrong side of a heading and cannot drain out. The slope, or grade, of the tunnel is about three feet in one thousand. We flattened it for several hundred feet in one section to ease the water difficulties. An eminent geologist on the staff of the

It came as an unpleasant surprise when tunnelers broke into several sections of "bad ground" during the excavation of the Florence Lake Tunnel. These pockets of sand and fissured rock required extensive timbering, which slowed the progress of construction. This picture shows the timbering required to pass through one section of soft ground encountered in the western heading from the adit at Camp 61.
Murphy's Studio Photo, from the Edison Collection

Before each new "round" is drilled, the drillers must carefully measure the location of each hole, as the placement of dynamite charges is crucial to the straight boring of the tunnel.
Both photos: Photographer unknown, from the Edison Collection

U. S. Geological Survey, Francois E. Matthes, displayed great interest in our tunnel excavation. He had studied the formations of the Grand Canyon and Yosemite Valley. I spent considerable time with him beneath Kaiser Meadow, while he was making observations. To explain the "swelling ground" in such a location, he applied the geological term "roof pendant," a former canyon filled during the Glacial Age with the material we encountered. When the bad section was concreted later, the heaviest reinforcement in the tunnel was provided in the form of steel rails placed close together, supplementing the regular reinforcing bars.

Each camp had to be self-sustaining in practically all respects. Each had its own compressor plant to furnish the large amounts of compressed air required for the respective tunnel headings. A machine shop, sufficient for mechanical maintenance, was busy continuously. Machine "doctors" for keeping their X-70 "patients" in drilling condition had their work benches inside the tunnel and out. Day and night the heavy thump of the pneumatic drill sharpeners could be heard, as if they were playing bass to the pound of

Drilling through hard ground in Florence Lake Tunnel was done by the "bench" or "step" method, where a bench was cut along the top half of the tunnel, and then excavated down to floor level. This picture clearly shows this technique, and also shows the dozens of sharp drill rods required to cut holes into the hard Sierra granite. Sharpening drill steel was a full-time job for several men at each camp.
Photographer unknown, from the Edison Collection

This October 1922 photo shows the drills arranged to cut vertical holes for the powder charges needed to blast the bench down to floor level.
Photographer unknown, from the Edison Collection

After the round of dynamite charges is blasted, miners re-enter the tunnel and check for unexploded charges, after which roof "scale" is pried down. The "scale" is composed of fragments of rock, some weighing several tons, that have been loosened by the blast, but which have not fallen down. For the safety of the working miners, it is essential to "bar down" these rocks right away.
Photographer unknown, from the Edison Collection

Each of the tunnel camps had a system of electric railways to haul out "muck" from the tunnels and, when necessary, to carry concrete in to working faces in soft ground.

This picture shows an electric train at Camp 62, carrying a load of concrete from the batch plant in the background into the tunnel.

The concrete was used to grout and seal fissures in the rock walls of the tunnel to keep it watertight in the future.

Photographer unknown, from the Edison Collection

the huge compressors before the pressure was relieved by the unloader valves. "Nippers" shuttled in and out of the tunnel, bringing drill steel to be sharpened, and hurrying back with a load ready to go into the machines at the heading. The miles of track required the continuous attention of maintenance crews, or "gandy dancers," as they were later called.

We experimented at Camp 60 with the first detachable bit for hard-rock drilling. Being something new, it did not take with the tunnel men. Today, an improved bit in all sizes and shapes is used universally. However, tunnel men on large jobs where much steel is used prefer the orthodox type with the bit an integral part of the drill steel.

Electricians were "on the go" like everyone else, the electric locomotives requiring not only their attention but also that of mechanics. Storage batteries were on the racks continuously, especially for recharging. Our electric railway system was rather unique, although its use was not peculiar to the Florence Lake Tunnel. Ours had, for safety in operation, quite an elaborate, but not complicated, block signal system. Extra precautions were necessary where long stretches of single track were involved. Tunnels are usually more or less smoky or hazy. Switches were operated automatically—with red lights indicating oncoming trains, and white, a clear track.

Somewhat electrical-minded myself, I wanted to satisfy a desire to observe a real electric locomotive at work. Thanks to D. A. Munger, Edison Company traffic manager, I was able to ride over a division in a huge one, pulling the Olympian of the Chicago, Milwaukee and St. Paul on a trip east. Without a bobble or an indication of wanting to catch its breath, the giant pulled a long train through the Cascades and headed for the wide-open spaces like a race horse given full rein after having been held back. The cab was spic and span; there was no coal or oil to cause smoke. Seated behind the engineer, I felt as if I were enjoying a ride in a parlor car. His hair being white, I assumed he had had a steam locomotive previously, and inquired how he liked the electric in comparison. His face lit up, and with no desire

This building housed the electric locomotive repair facility at Camp 60. The electric locomotives used on the tunnel project were powered by a combination of batteries and side-mounted trolley wire. The trolley wire ran only to within a few hundred feet of the work face. From that point to the end of track, the locomotives operated on their batteries.
Photographer unknown, from the Edison Collection

to cast any reflection on his first love, he explained the difference. When something went wrong with the steam locomotive only a few minutes were necessary to locate the trouble but all day to fix it; whereas, it took all day to find trouble in the electric, and only a few minutes to fix it.

The upper camps enjoyed the services of the County Library, supervised by Lila Lofberg, who subsequently wrote a book of her own, *Sierra Outpost,* in which she gives an excellent picture of the unusual experiences of herself and her husband, Ted, during the nine years they lived year-round at Florence Lake.

Any description of our tunnel work would not be complete without something about Milton Kempt, the camp foreman who always ended his radio messages, "Everything else O.K." He had added the "t" to his surname because he thought there were "too damn many people as Kemp." Often referred to as a "human mole," he had spent his thirty years underground in every large tunnel in the western hemisphere. He was a large man and a hard worker—it seemed as if he were always in the tunnel. His command of "cuss" words on occasion would have shocked Ingersoll, but a man more tenderhearted and kind never lived. His one objective was tunnel progress, and he did not spare himself to achieve it. Previously, he had been engaged on the Edison Company's Kern River No. 3 Project. Occasionally, he rendered a discourse on the stage of degradation reached by any man who would wear a wristwatch, so Harry Dennis not only presented him with one at a mess hall dinner in his honor, but actually put it on his wrist. His contemporaries, asking the time of day, made life miserable for him until the novelty wore off. Kempt was a confirmed bachelor—or so we thought, until he fell for an attractive lady known to many of us. He would not return to camp with her, but preferred to return alone, planning to have her follow shortly. The "reception committee" took care of him when he arrived by train at Big Creek. He was given a ride in the bottom of a dump wagon, which stopped in front of the main office. Before the crowd, the driver

The library at Camp 61 was a popular place during the long winter months, not least because it afforded the workmen the rare sight of a woman. For much of the tunnel project, the librarian at Camp 61 was Lila Lofberg.
Photographer unknown, from the Edison Collection

released the trip, dumping the bridegroom through the bottom onto the ground, much to his embarrassment. The joke might have had serious consequences had the mules taken a notion to run at that moment. On my trips to Camp 61, after he had forsaken bachelor quarters, I enjoyed the hospitality of his home. Always, as soon as the evening meal was over, he would have something out in camp or in the tunnel to show me. After one experience I knew the reason and expected such an invitation. He had been for too many years a devotee of "Lady Nicotine," which was objectionable to his wife in the form he used it—chewing—and how! He could not get out of the house fast enough. We always visited the tunnel because of the special cache where he kept his "chawin'." Several times on the way out, I had to remind him to remove the eight- to ten-inch plug sticking out of his hip pocket. Such a reminder would be an excuse for biting off a hunk big enough to last until he made a return trip.

An item that received special attention, and was common to the upper camp commissary particularly, was "snoose." To allow the supply to run out would have caused worse repercussions than would dynamite. A "snoose eater" will turn Heaven and earth upside down if he runs out and finds none on hand. The black stuff is removed from around the inside edge of the small circular cardboard box by a simple twist of the forefinger. The ultimate in the art of its use has been reached when the proper amount for a good gob can be judged and tenderly placed between the cheek and lower gums.

During most of the winter, the road over Kaiser Pass was virtually impassable, except to Jerry Dwyer's dog team. Occasionally, however, the road could still be used for a while after the first snowfall. This picture taken on October 22, 1924, shows two Caterpillar tractors struggling to move a heavy rock crusher to Camp 63 to enable concreting work to begin on Florence Dam as early as possible the following season.
Photographer unknown, from the Edison Collection

The transportation of material and supplies to the upper camps during the summer months for the following winter was always a big job for many, especially the transportation department. As many as twenty-five large dump trucks at a time were hauling between Camp 10, near the top of the main incline to Huntington Lake, and the camps. Grover Blades kept the fleet moving in both directions, besides looking after vehicles traveling here, there, and elsewhere.

There was so much mail we had to establish our own facilities for handling it after we received it from the local U. S. Post Office. During the years 1923, '24 and '25 alone, we received a total of 1,463,352 pounds by actual weight. During the same period, there was a total of 168,879 pieces of registered and insured mail handled, without the loss of a single one.

Edison Company's vice president and general manager, R. H. Ballard, paid us an occasional visit. He might accompany some special group from Los Angeles, in which case, he would usually address them during the evening in the Huntington Lodge lobby, giving a general description of the development under way, and its magnitude. On one occasion, telling about the Florence Lake tunnel, he referred to the crews, two or three years hence, looking for each other deep beneath Kaiser Pass. Herb Barre, sitting next to me in a far corner, leaned over at that moment and said, "Dave, there'll certainly be hell to pay if they don't find each other."

It was always a thrill, especially for tunnel crews that had been working towards each other for several years, when the first faintest "peck-peck" of the drills was heard in the opposite heading. The sound, of course, grows louder as the distance between headings decreases. In hard rock the sound can be heard for a long distance. The harder the rock, the farther it carries.

We were using an enormous amount of powder. I recall one order for

On October 15, 1924, the 4 p.m. shift at Camp 60 established three records for hard-rock tunneling. This hard-working crew drilled 30 feet in one shift, 174 feet in one (six-day) week, and amassed 692 feet for one entire month. These records stood until 1986 when they were surpassed by workers at Edison's Balsam Meadow Project. This photo shows Edison officials, including vice president George C. Ward (fifth from left) at the tunnel portal at Camp 60, reviewing the crew's progress.
Murphy's Studio Photo, from the Edison Collection

thirty-two carloads. During the period from 1921 to 1925, inclusive, for the entire Big Creek project we used twelve million pounds—which would have filled 200 flatcars. Had the sticks been placed end to end, they would have extended from the Edison Building in Los Angeles to the Hawaiian Islands. Although in most of our tunnel shooting the exploders were detonated from an electric circuit, there were many uses for fuse. The 5,750,000 feet in one piece would have been over 1,000 miles long, and if ignited would have required ten years for the spark to travel from one end to the other.

After the final holing through, a rail-mounted Marion Model 40 steam shovel, operating on compressed air, cleared away the last piles of "muck," and Florence Lake Tunnel was complete.
Murphy's Studio Photo, from the Edison Collection

Besides the food supplies consumed in the mess halls, there was food purchased for resale to the hundreds of families scattered over many camps. During the five-year period previously mentioned, 12,750,000 pounds of ham and bacon were purchased. The 11,100,000 eggs, if distributed among the people of Los Angeles at that time, would have provided each person with not less than one dozen. The food purchased for the mess halls alone, during the period, would have sustained 1,000 people for fourteen years. Items of special interest today are the 36,750 bales of hay and 33,500 sacks of barley for horses and mules, enough to feed 100 head for ten years. The 25,000,000 board feet of lumber, with the 1,000,000 pounds of nails, were sufficient to build 4,000 Southern California five-room bungalows, with enough left over for a fence around each.

It is not unusual for someone to ask, because of the name, if all the Edison companies in the country are under the same management. The only connection is in the name "Edison," which is symbolic of electricity. This reminds me of the man employed at Camp 61 who had something on his mind. He addressed a letter to "Thomas A. Edison" stating that he was a firm believer in always taking unusual matters up with the "top management." He certainly went all out in this case. The letter, making the rounds, must have been the source of many chuckles in the various Edison plants and offices, judging from the initials, comments, etc., when it finally found its way to Big Creek, having been forwarded from New Jersey.

The "breakthrough," awaited with utmost anxiety as its time drew near, was the last one in the stretch between Camp 62 and the upper portal. Everyone watched the progress charts, from which the time could be estimated closely. During the early part of the night of February 18, 1925, it happened. The last shot was fired, and a number of us in addition to the crews were on hand to peer through the hole which completed the tunnel excavation nearly two years ahead of schedule. For such a hard-rock tunnel, and for those days, some excellent progress had been made: 30 feet in one day, 174 feet in one week, and 692 feet in one month. Being the longest water tunnel of its size ever constructed up to that time, it was famous among the big tunnels of the world.

Before the track was removed, full advantage was taken of the opportunity to haul material all the way through from Huntington Lake. Going through Kaiser Crest instead of over was indeed a new experience for all of us, besides expediting the start of construction on the Florence Lake Dam.

To permit steam diversion to the tunnel, and to serve as a cofferdam during construction of the big dam, a low timber-crib dam, rock-filled, was built several hundred feet upstream. The permanent intake for regulating the flow into the tunnel consists of two cylinder gates, each six feet in diameter and about 100 feet long, placed in an open shaft 500 feet downstream from the upper portal—freedom from ice being an important factor in selecting the location and type of structure.

The first water release through the tunnel is officially recorded as having taken place on April 13, 1925. In passing through, the water drops 220 feet from the floor of the upper portal to the outlet, fifty feet above the high-water level of Huntington Lake. The total natural seepage into the tunnel throughout its length was five cubic feet per second at the time it was placed

The last section of the Florence Lake Tunnel to be completed was between Camps 62 and 63. Crews from the two camps could hear each other through the rock, and raced to complete the work. The final round of dynamite was fired on February 18, 1925. As the air cleared, miners raced through the hole to shake hands with men from the other camp. Here, the foreman of Camp 62 shakes hands with his counterpart from Camp 63.
Murphy's Studio Photo, from the Edison Collection

Water was first turned through Florence Lake Tunnel on April 13, 1925, from the still-incomplete reservoir above. A temporary timber flume carried the water from the outlet of the tunnel to the shore of Huntington Lake. A baffle made of rails salvaged from the tunnel project dissipated the force of the water discharge to prevent erosion of the lakeshore. Thirty years later, a power plant was built on this site.

Photographer unknown, from the Edison Collection

in service. About ten percent of its length is lined with concrete, most of which was placed concurrently with tunnel excavation.

The enormous amount of material and equipment placed in the tunnel during the four and one-half years of construction was in direct contrast to the short time required for its removal after the last round was fired. Regardless of how interesting a big job may have been, men usually delight in tearing down and clearing out everything they have built up for purposes of construction. One reason, perhaps, is the excitement created by that "extra burst of speed" as the main job is finished.

There was much concern about possible undercutting due to backlash of the water discharging at the tunnel outlet, which is surrounded by a deep layer of glacial-like material. To determine what the action would be, we built a lumber flume about 1,000 feet in length to discharge onto a rail mat near the high water line of Huntington Lake. Observations over a period of two years, with flows as high as 2,300 second feet, were such as to justify the flume's abandonment and subsequent replacement with the present 300 feet of twelve-foot-diameter riveted pipe on a steeper grade, sealed into the tunnel outlet. The water, rushing madly as it left the big pipe, quickly made its own pool, with no tendency to encroach beyond the banks. The pool, which is twenty to twenty-five feet deep and 100 feet across, is a favorite spot for trout which wander upstream from the lake. Depending upon the amount of water coming through the tunnel, its velocity as it leaves the large pipe may be as high as forty to fifty feet per second, knocking the trout end over end in their attempts to move upstream through it.

Day and night, month after month, year after year, the electric locomotives rolled out their trains of muck cars to be dumped on the ever-widening "spoil" banks along the hillside in front of each tunnel and adit portal. Long snow sheds kept the main entrance tracks clear in winter. Several hundred thousand cubic yards of broken granite will long remain as silent markers of the former camps where men labored, not only for their livelihood, but to help provide more electric power for the comfort and progress of humanity.

Mr. Ward became president of the company in 1932, and served as such until his death in 1933. As our large construction program drew to a close, he was the recipient of many honors. The Edison Company paid him further honor, posthumously, when it arranged for the name of Florence Lake Tunnel to be changed to Ward Tunnel, and for the erection of an appropriate monument. The latter, built of bluish-grey blocks of tunnel granite laid in mortar, stands over the big pipe at the tunnel outlet. Imbedded in the granite is a copper tablet, bearing the following inscription:

These are the Edison men who oversaw the Big Creek Project and its power plants during the busy years of the 1920s
Left to right: Edwin R. Davis, Superintendent of Hydro-Generation; David H. Redinger, Resident Engineer, Big Creek Project; Russell H. Ballard, Vice President and General Manager; George C. Ward, Vice President of Operation and Construction; and Herbert A. Barre, Executive Engineer.
G. Haven Bishop Photo, from the Edison Collection

OUTLET OF
WARD TUNNEL
NAMED BY THE
SOUTHERN CALIFORNIA EDISON COMPANY LTD.
HONORING
GEORGE CLINTON WARD
1863-1933
WHO DIRECTED CONSTRUCTION OF THE ENTIRE
HYDRO ELECTRIC DEVELOPMENT OF THE COMPANY
ON THE SAN JOAQUIN RIVER AND ITS TRIBUTARIES.
THIS TUNNEL DIVERTS THE WATERS OF
MONO CREEK, BEAR CREEK AND THE SOUTH FORK
OF THE SAN JOAQUIN RIVER UNDER THE
KAISER EDGE INTO HUNTINGTON LAKE.
CONSTRUCTED IN 1920-1925
LENGTH 67620 FEET
DIAMETER 15 FEET
CAPACITY 2500 CUBIC FEET PER SECOND

Mrs. Ward and their daughter, Louise Ward Watkins, were among those present on August 26, 1936, to hear W. C. Mullendore, executive vice president at the time, deliver the principal dedicatory address.

XX
Florence Lake Dam

ALTHOUGH THERE WAS stream diversion—the South Fork of the San Joaquin River into Florence Lake Tunnel in 1925—there was no storage at the site of the Florence Lake Dam, as the dam had not been constructed, and some legal matters were pending.

The site for the dam had been selected after extensive field studies beginning in 1923, which were supplemented by those in the office, dealing with quantities and costs. Various types of dams were investigated to find one suitable for the site. Several estimates of cost were made with respect to selecting the most suitable and economical design. A rockfill structure using material from the Florence Lake Tunnel, faced with either earth or asphalt-covered planking to make it impervious, was given extensive study, with the facing to be replaced by concrete after settlement. Various disadvantages were foreseen with such a design, and test pits in nearby meadows indicated a possible shortage of material for the earth covering. Adopted finally was the multiple arch, which estimates showed to be about ten percent lower in cost than any other type. John S. Eastwood is credited with having originated and developed the first designs for a dam of that type.

In support of this selection were numerous important factors. The transportation of material from the railhead at Big Creek was a major item, and less cement would be required than for a gravity or part-gravity structure—hence, less tonnage; the large amount of the steel needed for reinforcing could be supplied by using rail removed from the tunnel; concrete aggregate could be made by crushing the tunnel granite, examinations having shown it to be suitable; and, although more lumber for forms would be required, it could be supplied by our mill in the vicinity.

Full consideration was given to the possible effect of freezing temperatures on the concrete at that high elevation. It was felt that protection would be afforded by making concrete of highest quality, placed under the best methods known at the time. Furthermore, with Florence Lake empty, under normal operating conditions the concrete would be comparatively dry by the time freezing temperatures occurred.

Previous pages: The reason for the drilling of Florence Lake Tunnel was to carry water from a proposed new reservoir down to Huntington Lake. The new reservoir was to be located in Florence Meadows, where a small natural lake already existed. This view of the site of the new reservoir was taken on December 20, 1923, and shows the clearing then taking place. The absence of heavy snow on the ground was an omen of the mild winter that led to the serious drought of 1924.

Photographer unknown, from the Edison Collection

A large rock-crushing and screening plant was installed at the dam site for making the various sizes of rock and the sand. To distribute the concrete an appropriate chuting system was constructed—the Insley chutes being suspended from two Insley steel towers several hundred feet in height-and the job was off to a good start, under the direct supervision of E. C. Panton, assisted by T. A. Smith, Anton Wellman, O. N. Kulberg, and other capable men.

The first concrete was poured on March 4, 1925. To ensure the best concrete possible, rigid inspection was provided which covered all phases—cement testing, batching, mixing, placing, testing concrete samples, etc. A well-equipped laboratory was built near the dam, including a temperature-controlled moist-air curing room. The latter permitted concrete tests to be made unaffected by outside temperature. Some idea may be had of the extent of the tests from the number made—over 800 field samples and 1,200 laboratory cylinders. The opinion is general, even today, that we went farther than was the usual practice to get a uniform concrete of highest quality.

The use of powder was generally avoided in the footing excavation for the arches, the "plug and feather" method being used largely to prevent shattering of the foundation granite. The forms for the concrete, difficult in some respects to make, were in panels on the upstream face, and were carried up in four-foot lifts. A hinged truss design was used for forms on the downstream side, matching in height those on the upper.

Being the longest dam of the type ever built—3,200 feet, and made up of fifty-eight arches—it attracted considerable attention from engineers, the general public, and, of course, the Edison Company itself.

Mr. Ward was, as always during construction, a frequent visitor. If there were a steam shovel in the vicinity, that's where he would be found. He would stand and watch one work for hours at a time. Other members of the top management from Los Angeles would visit the job occasionally, the most convenient time being the summer months. Roy Reppy, general counsel for the Edison Company, paid us a visit whenever possible. On one trip he brought along Jack Healy, a mining engineer and friend of long standing, who lived in South Africa. Healy's strong English accent caused me to ask from what part of England he came. After sheepish glances between the two, Reppy said, "Don't let him fool you—he was born in Ventura!" Long residence in Johannesburg had had its effect. In looking over the work on the dam, Healy's use of the word "shutters" several times caused me to inquire as to what he was referring. I learned that in South Africa that is what concrete forms are called, and "fitters" are the men who handle them, those whom we call "carpenters."

Once, en route across the Pacific, I was talking to a fellow passenger registered from Johannesburg. Somewhat apologetically—since it is a large city—I asked if by chance she had ever heard of a mining engineer there by the name of Healy. Quick as a flash, she said, "Do you mean Jack Healy?" He was her next-door neighbor for twenty-five years. What a small world!

Mr. Reppy, besides his interest in the job, loved the outdoors, and enjoyed getting into khaki, high boots, an old hat, and a red bandana around his neck. In such regalia he was in his element, and there was none better as a companion on a camping trip. I found President Story, of the Santa Fe, an excellent runner-up for him. Both men, gentlemen in every sense of the word, loved the mountains. It has been my experience that men, without exception, who like the wide-open spaces, are very much worthwhile. Also, I know of no better way for men to really become acquainted than on a camping trip. If they cannot click after sitting around a campfire together, there is not much hope.

We saw a great deal of H. A. Barre, who had much to do with the general scheme of the Big Creek development. With his unusual sense of humor, he had the uncanny knack of being able to see through a knotty problem, and would come out quickly with the answer—frequently in a facetious manner. A chain cigarette smoker, he remarked at various times that he might tackle a cigar if given one. I happened to come across a perfect rubber imitation of a "Perfecto," so I bided my time. Barre touched a match to it—a puff or two, and then Messrs. Ward, Davis and I got the real lowdown on his opinion of the perpetrator of such a trick. I knew I was in for it sooner or later.

To enable him to carry out his "evil" design of revenge, he inveigled Mrs. Redinger into becoming his confederate. Two weeks or so later, I learned all about it, while I was all set to enjoy some wieners and sauerkraut, which he knew I liked. He had slipped into the kitchen a perfect rubber imitation of a nice juicy wiener, and certainly evened up the score.

This view of the western section of Florence Dam shows the deep foundations of arches 13 and 14 under construction in May 1925. This was the site of the first work on the dam, begun earlier, in March. Rail salvaged from the recently completed Florence Lake Tunnel was used to reinforce the lower portion of the dam's arches. In the background can be seen the concrete mixing plant, supplied by a railroad trestle, and the west chuting tower, used to place the concrete at the work site.
Murphy's Studio Photo, from the Edison Collection

The general design of the multiple-arch dam was carried out by Messrs. Pierce and Heywood, under the supervision of Harry Dennis, who, with Harold Doolittle and their respective competent men, had their hands full for years in Los Angeles, with the plans, designs, layouts, etc., for all the major jobs. Arthur Blight played a most important role as assistant manager of construction during the program of major activity, the larger portion of his time being spent in the Los Angeles office. F. J. Mills, representing the Los Angeles engineering office, called on us frequently, and rendered valuable assistance with our construction problems—particularly with the Florence Lake Dam. Many of the designs worked out by Harold Doolittle reflect to the highest degree his most extraordinary ability, as, like Barre, he could see through a tough problem and quickly arrive at the solution.

Besides building the dam, we had to clear the reservoir of trees and undergrowth preparatory for storage. Our sawmill at Camp 61, having served its purpose in that location, was moved in 1925 and installed in upper Jackass Meadow, which was to become the reservoir. Camp 65 was established as the base for the mill operations and the clearing of the whole area. All trees large enough were run through the mill, the lumber being used largely in construction of the dam. For logging, we purchased three 60 Best tractors, the first of such equipment to put in appearance on our work. It was amazing what jobs the "cat skinners" found besides logging, and we wondered how we had ever gotten along without tractors. When the time came to move the Camp 63 buildings to higher ground, preparatory to reservoir storage, one of these tractors could yank a two-story bunkhouse to the new location, Camp 64, in short order. In one such structure, supposedly empty, a lone man from the night crew was asleep—but not for long—as it started bumping over the rocks. Half awake, and not knowing whether the structure had been beset by an earthquake, he leaped out the window clad in his underwear, and hit the ground on the run. He had quickly decided he was not going places inside.

Looking for additional storage for the future, we sent a diamond drill to Blaney Meadows to make some exploratory borings for a dam site, having in mind possible storage there of 32,000 acre-feet, but the study was later abandoned. "Lost Valley" is said to have been the first and true name for Blaney Meadows as early as 1870. In later years, a man by the name of Blaney grazed sheep there and, no doubt, is responsible for the name we know today.

Our courtesy cars were bringing visitors daily to see the dam as it gradually rose in height. The concrete skips running up and down in the high steel towers absorbed their attention. In fact, they were fascinated by everything. The central portion of the dam was of less height than the others, and could not be reached by the chuting system of either tower, so two traveling cranes were used to pour the concrete in that section. Many of our visitors were curious about the holes in the vertical face of a rock ledge not far from the dam. During tunnel construction, it had served as an ideal proving ground for trying out the drilling speed of various new machines, resulting in the large number of holes which puzzled the visitors. It occurred to the engineers to have some fun by explaining how the holes were made by "rock swallows," peculiar to that locality.

The largest saddle-and-pack train ever seen in those parts appeared during the summer of 1925, when the Simpson party left from the area we were clearing for the reservoir. James Simpson, board chairman of Marshall Field, Chicago, arrived with his party by private car in Fresno. I was asked to meet them, accompany them over the project, extend the usual courtesies, and see that they contacted the pack train. Col. John R. White, superintendent of Sequoia National Park, joined in doing the honors, as he expected the party as guests at the end of their thirty-day pack trip. Even with Mr. Simpson's assistance, we had a tough time rounding up the scions of several prominent Chicago families after they had scattered in Fresno. From Big Creek, Mr. Simpson paid his respects by wire to Mr. John B. Miller, and eventually we met the huge pack outfit in upper Jackass Meadow. Getting the group on its way was as exciting as attending a big rodeo. After meals in our mess halls, the group would ask about gratuities to the help. I always told them this was not necessary. The party was well on its way, and excitement had died down somewhat, when I learned of the generous distribution of twenty-dollar gold pieces! In fact, that was the smallest denomination handed out. It was with some difficulty that the gang got back to earth.

The time had come to close down the work on the dam for the winter. Sixty percent of the concrete had been placed, the last for the season being poured on October 30, 1925. The cleared reservoir was ready to store water. The height to which the dam had been built would provide storage from the 1926 runoff for 35,000 acre-feet—more than half of the ultimate capacity of 64,400. Concrete operations were resumed on April 29, 1926, and complet-

This view of the western end of Florence Dam was taken on October 1, 1925, just a month before operations closed down for the winter. The picture shows the erection of forms for the graceful arches of the dam (left center), the placement of reinforcing steel (foreground), and the pouring of concrete on a buttress (upper right).
Murphy's Studio Photo, from the Edison Collection

ed on August 15. Work continued on the final clean-up, such as handrailing, backfill, gate mechanisms, grouting, etc., until November when the camp was closed.

Since water storage is of the utmost importance, it is highly desirable to know as definitely and as early as possible something about the water crop for each season. Irrigation needs are also important, besides those for power. If the latter are ample, the former will benefit, as the water is always returned to the river after passing through our Big Creek plants. Our storage reservoirs benefit the San Joaquin Valley by helping to prevent floods and regulating the runoff, distributing it over a longer period of time. To know what to expect in the way of a runoff from a watershed, precipitation during winter months is of much concern, and is becoming even more so as the years roll by; consequently, beginning in the fall, much attention is paid to the weather. By spring, especially if the winter has been light, water becomes a topic of serious discussion. Many companies have, for years, in cooperation with the state and each other, conducted snow surveys at intervals during winter months. The depth and water content data obtained by these snow surveys at various locations produce more accurate results than precipitation, in estimating the water crop expected from the 450 square miles of watershed upon which our reservoirs depend for runoff.

Weather prophets have been found to be quite unreliable—even the

This view of the Florence Lake dam site looks easterly from the west end, and shows the work just six weeks before it was completed. Concrete was hauled from the mixing plant by electric trains, and was poured in small batches by cranes and hoists.
Murphy's Studio Photo, from the Edison Collection

Indians, who have been looked upon by the white man as something of a guide. A heavy winter was indicated if the Indians were seen laying in an unusually large supply of acorns, etc. M. A. Benedict, for many years supervisor of the Sierra National Forest, is authority for a new version. When he asked an aged Indian who had lived near Forest Service headquarters for years what kind of a winter to expect, he received this reply: "Me think heap bad. White man, he get in much wood." Several years after hearing this from Benedict, I read the same story, but from another source, in the *Saturday Evening Post*.

The height of the arches in the dam, 147 feet, is greatest where they span the river. It is desirable to have some means for draining a reservoir below the level of its tunnel, which does not always take off from the lowest point. Two thirty-six-inch sluice pipes in the bottom of the river span, each equipped with a forty-six-inch square slide gate on its upstream end, hydraulically operated, permit drawing the water below the tunnel intake.

To provide for the release of water to sustain fish life in the river below the dam, a special eight-inch pipe and valve were installed near the main sluice pipes.

Reservoirs must also be equipped for safely releasing—that is, spilling—water above their capacity. In the Florence Lake Dam the spillway in the central section is 100 feet long, the water being controlled by two 50-foot drum gates. This type of spillway allows drift material to be carried over the gates with the excess water, and the lake level may be controlled by automatic or manual operation of the drum gates. Our practice has been mostly the latter, not taking any chances on faulty operation with the consequent loss of part of a full reservoir.

On the downstream side of the arches sufficient backfilling was done and drainage provided to keep water from standing against the concrete in freezing weather. Some backfill at the base of the arches on the upstream side was placed for the same reason when the lake would be empty. In spite of efforts to produce concrete of highest quality possible, it was not long after completion of the dam before the effects of freezing were recognized. The water from snow melting on the walkway would run down over the concrete in the daytime and was followed by low temperatures at night. No doubt some of the trouble was due, too, to the concrete being more or less wet as the lake level went down. Many theories have been advanced about this frost action on concrete that causes it to *spall*—flake off—or disintegrate. It has been a most puzzling problem for years to engineers who have tried to reach the root of the trouble and make concrete which would not be vulnerable to freezing temperatures. Is it due to some unfavorable characteristic of the aggregate, the cement, the water used for mixing, or some combination of all three? The method of distributing the concrete may have been a factor.

Attention was given to some means for waterproofing the upstream face of the dam. Studies resulted in the application of "Inertol," a German formula, in 1926, which did not prove very satisfactory. In the early '30s, a covering of emulsified asphalt was applied. Through the years to date, considerable maintenance has been necessary to retard the spalling, which has been greatest on the walkway, buttress heads, and upstream face of the arches and angle buttresses.

Florence Dam, as completed, September 11, 1926. This dam is a classic example of what John Eastwood intended when he originated the design for the multiple-arch dam. Built in just two short working seasons at a remote area difficult of access, the dam was built with a minimum of cement, yet achieves maximum strength. Florence Dam is a lasting tribute to John Eastwood's engineering genius!
G. Haven Bishop Photo, from the Edison Collection

During the war years, we were at a considerable disadvantage because of the limited field for waterproofing materials. The application of "Asbestile," with some yearly maintenance, has been on the whole more or less satisfactory, but it is not considered to be the final answer. Many different materials have been investigated in the laboratory, including the "Asbestile," which was selected as it had the advantage of being reasonable in cost, as well as in application, and was not a strategic war material. One arch has been covered with steel plates, welded together, and applications of gunite have been made on other arches, on the spillway, walkway, and buttress heads. As to what the final answer will be, time may tell.

A program of longtime study has been undertaken by the Portland Cement Association, in cooperation with many interested companies, including ours, the State of California, the U. S. Bureau of Reclamation, and others. Official inspections and tests are made at least once a year of specimen concrete bars, walkway sections made of different brands of cement, etc., on the Florence Lake Dam. Many cores have been cut from the arches for testing. Linseed oil as a protective coating is being tried on walkway sections. Light-reflecting paint, to hold down temperatures from the sun, has been applied on the arches. All such efforts may someday lead to the adoption of some material or method as the satisfactory solution for present concrete troubles. With intensive efforts, progress has been made in the past

fifteen years in the manufacture of cement, and more has been learned about the aggregate, proportioning, mixing, and placing of concrete.

Mr. John B. Miller made his last visit to Big Creek in 1926, bringing his daughter Carrita. They were the first visitors to enjoy a ride on Florence Lake. I can still see the expression of satisfaction on his face as he sat in the boat with Carrita and me, puffing on his pipe and scanning the body of water stored for the first time.

Stretching the imagination, one might have noticed an expression of approval from Mt. Shinn, overlooking the newly made lake. This prominent pyramid-shaped mountain was named by the U. S. Forest Service, honoring the memory of Charles Howard Shinn, first supervisor of the Sierra National Forest, which was established as "Sierra Forest Reserve" by proclamation of President Harrison on February 14, 1893. Additions were made under the present name by President Theodore Roosevelt, in his proclamation of April 20, 1908.

Keeping Mt. Shinn company is Ward Mountain, officially named for George Clinton Ward, by action of the Division of Geographic Names, Washington, D. C. The attractive bronze marker standing near the west end of Florence Lake Dam and pointing to Ward Mountain, was dedicated appropriately on August 26, 1936, following a similar ceremony for the monument at the outlet of Ward Tunnel.

Edison photographer G. Haven Bishop took this picture of Florence Lake Reservoir filled to capacity on June 1, 1930.
G. Haven Bishop Photo, from the Edison Collection

XXI
Diversion of Mono and Bear Creeks

WHILE THE Florence Lake Dam was being built, and even before that, extensive studies were being made for new sources of water for additional power. The rapid development of power resources in the Big Creek area came as a result of the remarkable growth in industry, business and population throughout the territory served by the Edison Company. This condition has continued up to the present, 1949. The opinion was general that a lull could be expected after the World War II years, but so far it has been just the opposite.

During the 1920s, our new plants and additional units in the existing plants were rushed to completion in an effort to keep pace with the power demand. Not previously mentioned are the following additional units that were installed: a third unit in Powerhouse No. 2 in November 1920, and a fourth during April 1925; in Powerhouse No. 1 a third unit was added in July 1923, followed by a fourth in June 1925. These four increased the installed capacity in the two plants by 110,500 horsepower.

The possibility of storage in Vermilion Valley was being explored, diamond-drill borings being made for a dam site. The lower end of the valley-the logical location for such a dam-is crossed by several terminal moraines left by the glacier as it receded.

F. J. Mills, with his usual philosophic outlook on things, opined that, apparently, the Creator had placed material for the toe of the dam on the wrong side of the site. This calls to mind another incident in which Mr. Mills played an important part. At the time we were building Plant No. 3 on Kern River, there were indications that the shale formation back of the location for that power house would require a retaining wall. Mr. Brackenridge, senior vice president then, Harry Dennis, Mr. Mills and I, besides a few others, met on the hillside to discuss the situation. Except for Mr. Mills, we thought we noticed a twinkle in Mr. Brackenridge's eyes as he turned and asked, "Mr. Mills, why did you put the powerhouse in this location?" After a few seconds of silence, Mr. Mills replied, "Because that is where you told us to put it." There was another short interval of silence before Mr. Brackenridge

The heavy, riveted pipe of the Mono-Bear Siphon stretches southward up the south side of the canyon of the San Joaquin River in this September 7, 1927, view taken from the river crossing. In the foreground can be seen an expansion joint housing, and at several places up the hill concrete anchors are in various stages of completion. When construction was completed, the entire pipeline was buried.
Photographer unknown, from the Edison Collection

asked him, "What would you do if I asked you to turn the flow of the river out there, upstream?" Without any hesitation, Mr. Mills replied, "Mr. Brackenridge, if you gave me such instructions, I certainly would do my damnedest."

Mr. Brackenridge was not as well known to our Big Creek personnel as others of the top management, since he made only a few visits to this area.

The decision ultimately reached favored a small concrete diversion dam on Mono Creek and one on Bear Creek, both streams to be carried across the South Fork of the San Joaquin River through a steel siphon, emptying into the Florence Lake Tunnel at the Camp 62 Adit. To accomplish this, the means had to be provided to get both streams into the siphon. One tunnel through hard granite had to be built from Bear Creek to converge with the shorter one from Mono Creek at the intake of the long siphon.

The "80" series of numbers was assigned for the camps established for the construction. Camp 80 was built near the site for the Mono Dam; 81 at the intake of the Mono Tunnel; 82 at the intersection of both tunnel outlets, where the siphon would connect; 83 and 84 along the siphon; 85 at Bear Creek tunnel adit; and 86 at the Bear Creek dam site.

Between six and seven miles of road had to be built through the worst terrain imaginable. Boulders the size of houses, and huge ledges of the hardest granite, were encountered. Steep grades and sharp turns resulted from dodging such obstacles. The routes appeared to be almost impossible, since many large trucks would have to be used for the delivery of material. It is amazing what men with determination, portable air compressors, jackhammers and powder can accomplish when once started. The "C. and N."—Cheap and Nasty—road was completed, camps made ready, and work on the conduit got under way in July 1926. Winter caused stoppage of activity on November 24, and it was resumed in the early spring of 1927.

A 1-1/4-cubic-yard Link-Belt gas-operated shovel was purchased for use largely as a crane for placing the siphon pipe sections. To reach the job early, we used it in May 1927 to dig its way over Kaiser Pass through snow six feet deep, and of course, in doing so, it opened the road for all traffic.

Many people have asked about the origin of the name "Kaiser," given to the Pass and Peak. In spite of efforts to find out, all I have been able to learn is that the name is very old and the correct spelling unknown. L. A. Winchell reports hearing miners speak of Kaiser Gulch in 1862—hence, perhaps, the name "Kaiser Diggings."

As one travels beyond Kaiser Pass towards Florence Lake and emerges from the timber one sees Mt. Ritter towering above others in the distance. It was named for the German geographer, Karl Ritter. This lofty peak, it is reported, was approached from the southwest by Clarence King about 1866, in an unsuccessful attempt to reach the summit.

The remote Mono-Bear camps were not without their virtues. There were excellent opportunities for fishing. The "Ike Waltons" enjoyed such advantages, and a trout dinner at any camp could be had on short notice. In season, there was venison for those desiring a change in meat diet. I recall having bear meat at one meal. Even though scarce, bears have always raised havoc with hydrographers' supplies stored for intermittent trips in remote

Camp 82, located at the outlet of the Mono and Bear tunnels, was one of seven remote camps that housed men working on the Mono-Bear Siphon. Due to severe winter conditions, work on this project was restricted to about six months of the year.
Photographer unknown, from the Edison Collection

cabins unless protection somewhat comparable to a bank vault is provided.

We were paid a visit by a special government representative named Welch, from Washington, D. C., who was sent out by the Secretary of the Interior to visit our national parks. During his visit here, and while being shown around by E. R. Davis and me, he related an interesting experience with some local cattlemen. I cannot vouch for his veracity in this respect, but he told it on himself. He had always wanted to get into some western cattle country and take a trip with cattlemen. After being out several days with them when they were taking a large herd into the back country for summer grazing, he was caught off his horse one afternoon by a large steer. Apparently, the steer had taken a dislike to this individual for some reason or other. Being unsuccessful in reaching his horse, Welch jumped into a hollow tree, the nearest place of safety. The steer ran around the opposite side and Welch came out—only to be chased in again. This performance occurred several times before the cattlemen came to the rescue. One suggested to their guest that he should have stayed in there until help came. Welch replied, "Stay in there, hell—there's a bear in there."

Two small concrete-arch dams, one on Mono Creek and the other on Bear, were built for stream diversion only. Sluice pipes and valves were installed as is customary, and means provided to release water for fish life below. The diversion conduit from Mono Dam to the head of the siphon consists of a ninety-two-inch steel pipeline, about three-quarters of a mile long, connecting into an eight-by-nine-foot tunnel of approximately the same length. The Bear Creek branch is also but one and one-half miles in length, but all tunnel, part being seven by seven feet, and part eight by nine feet— meeting the Mono Tunnel at the siphon intake. The siphon, three miles long, varying in diameter from seventy-five inches to 102 inches, has a capacity of 600 cubic feet per second, and carries the water across the South Fork of the San Joaquin River into the Florence Lake Tunnel.

190

This May 1927 view shows the outlet of the Mono Tunnel at left, and the Bear Tunnel outlet at right, at the north end of the future Mono-Bear Siphon pipeline. Notice the boxes of dynamite stacked at right. Trucks brought the "powder" up the Kaiser Pass Road to this point, where it was transferred to rail flatcars for final delivery to the powder magazine.
Photographer unknown, from the Edison Collection

The Mono-Bear tunnels were too small for the use of our regular mucking equipment. To facilitate the loading of the cars, tunnel foreman Ed McCabe, who had been on the Florence Lake Tunnel, improvised the "McCabe Mucker." This contraption elevated the muck and dumped it into the cars. The men had to shovel it onto the endless belt, but this method was easier and faster than hand-shoveling into the cars, as they would have had to raise the muck four or five feet.

The excavation for the siphon was made mostly through hardest granite, a sizable job in itself. The blasting echoes from the tunnels and siphon excavation reverberated through the canyon like the sound of huge guns on a terrific battlefront.

Russell Booth, one of the assistant engineers, was in direct charge of the job during the greatest activity, which was in 1927.

Big trucks, as many as twenty-five in service at one time, hauled the steel pipe sections from the top of the main incline at Huntington Lake to the site, where the Link-Belt shovel, as a crane, unloaded and placed each in the proper position in the trench. In general, things clicked like clockwork.

There was a big question as to whether or not the siphon, especially, and Mono flow line, should be backfilled—that is, covered. No precedent could be found to satisfy those concerned that there would be no trouble from ice

This view taken just below the site of Mono Creek Dam on August 5, 1927, shows the flowline pipes in the course of construction. The concrete-mixing plant for the dam project is on the hillside at upper left.
Photographer unknown, from the Edison Collection

in the pipe unless it were adequately covered; anchor ice forming on the inside could cause much trouble. The only safe thing to do was cover it—a huge job—but this was done to a minimum depth of three feet. Recording thermometers were installed at several locations along the siphon the first winter, and results indicated that satisfactory operation, free from ice trouble, could be expected. The intakes at Mono and Bear were submerged to eliminate trouble with ice at those points. Strange as it may seem, there has been nothing of consequence to develop on either of these small dams in the way of the concrete spalling, as has occurred on other structures at high elevation. Just why is a question.

The Mono-Bear job was completed on November 15, 1927, and diversion started into the Florence Lake Tunnel, ending another important unit in the development of power resources in this area.

The major activity beyond Kaiser Pass having come to a close, the Edison Company in 1929 turned over to the government, through the U. S. Forest Service, the Florence Lake Road, also abandoning the one to Mono-Bear. In recent years, the Forest Service has oiled the road from the upper end of Huntington Lake to Florence, and a flourishing concession, a motel, with store and cottages, has grown up at Mono Hot Springs. With mail service during summer months, and a public campground established by the Forest Service near Mono Dam, one appreciates the extent to which once-remote mountain areas are being made available to the motorist.

XXII
Shaver Dam
and Powerhouse 2A

EVEN THOUGH Florence Lake Dam had been completed, the reservoir would not provide storage for all the runoff of the South Fork of the San Joaquin River. Neither could Huntington Lake store the excess in addition to the runoff from its own watershed, plus that from Mono and Bear Creeks. This situation was fully understood and taken into consideration in planning.

During the period between purchase by the Edison Company of the Shaver property in 1917, described in a previous chapter, and 1925, careful studies were made involving that portion, 2,200 acres, that would be suitable for a reservoir, and its coordination with the entire Big Creek development. By 1925 the studies had resulted in final plans for storage of the excess water from the Florence and Huntington Lake watersheds, plus that from Shaver Lake, in the new reservoir to be provided by the construction of a large concrete, gravity-type dam at Shaver.

As is usually the case, several sites for a dam were explored before final selection. There are always many factors to be considered from the standpoint of economics, especially when it comes to deciding on the capacity of a reservoir and the type of dam to be built. The gravity type, stable because of its own weight against the water pressure, would have a maximum height of 183 feet above the bedrock, a thickness of about 125 feet at the base, and length of nearly 2,200 feet along the crest. Such a structure would provide storage for 135,000 acre-feet, plus, of water.

Much had to be done preparatory for construction of the dam—spitting on one's hands," as Herb Barre said. A huge amount of cement and lumber would be required, besides all other material common to a job of such magnitude—though in comparison to several dams built since, its 280,000 cubic yards of concrete are not so significant.

To serve the job, we built 4.6 miles of standard-gauge railroad from Dawn, where connection was made to the main line of the San Joaquin & Eastern (from which H. L. Wheeler was borrowed to supervise construction of the branch, and to open and handle the rock quarry). Early in May 1926 construction started on the large rock-crushing plant for making the concrete

194

This domed granite outcropping at the north end of Shaver Lake was quarried to produce aggregate for the concrete used in Shaver Dam. Today, this quarry site houses the temporary offices of the Balsam Meadow Project (see page 239), after the completion of which it will revert to public parking and a boat launching ramp.
Photographer unknown, from the Edison Collection

Previous pages: Early in the spring of 1926, work began on the construction of Shaver Dam. This picture of the new dam site, taken late in May, shows the remnants of the original Shaver lumber mill at left in the middle distance. Leading from the old rock-fill dam is the temporary flume that carried water from the former millpond into the Shaver Tunnel. At this time, the water was being temporarily added to the outflow from Tunnel No. 2 to operate the units at Powerhouse No. 2. In the right foreground, work has already begun to clear the ground down to bedrock for the foundations of the new dam.
Photographer unknown, from the Edison Collection

material, including sand, all of which was to come from the quarry to be opened on the side of a granite cliff a short mile distant. To keep the hungry crushers fed from the quarry was Hank Wheeler's job, the rock to be transported by trolley locomotives over a narrow-gauge track. Today the quarry "scar" is pointed out to visitors as "where the Shaver Dam used to be."

While stockpiles of the various sizes of crushed material grew in size, excavation to bedrock at the dam site was progressing. It was worked towards both ends from the center, and continued ultimately to the extent of about 150,000 cubic yards, half of it being in solid rock.

Two steel towers were rising high in the air to support the counterbalanced chutes of the concrete distributing system. The concrete mixing plant was taking shape, and finally the bank of three large Smith mixers was ready to perform. The last concrete in the Florence Lake Dam having been poured, the entire crew moved from there to Camp 21 at the Shaver Dam site. Everything was in readiness, and the first concrete was poured onto the foundation on September 21, 1926. Because of freezing weather, operations were discontinued on December 4 and resumed April 1, 1927.

The dam was built in fifty-foot blocks, with a construction joint between each. Besides the usual key-way at each joint, a thin copper sheet about thirty inches wide extends from top to bottom, spanning the joint to make it watertight. The sheets were placed in ten to twelve-foot lengths, lapped and brazed at the ends. Concrete expands and contracts with temperature changes. To allow the copper sheets to withstand the slight movement of the huge blocks without breaking, they were corrugated, or "V"-shaped in the center.

Another feature provided in the dam is the large gallery running through most of its length, a short distance above the foundation. Its twelve-foot height was to permit the later operation of a diamond drill for holes which would relieve pressure from possible seepage water. Water will find its way through crevices in the foundation rock in spite of precautions to seal them by grouting. It will also work its way, more or less, through a day's work joint and even around a construction joint.

Such a gallery provides the means for periodic inspections also. The one in the Shaver Dam is the only one among the dams on the Big Creek project. Several years later, another and shorter gallery was excavated along the contact of the concrete and bedrock for purposes of observation.

The largest mess hall on the project, seating several hundred men, took care of the "inner man," and sleeping quarters upstairs accommodated those who were not allocated to bunkhouses.

Another big job, clearing the reservoir site, was handled by Bretz Brothers, local men, who programmed their work to have the site ready for storage as the dam approached completion, which occurred on October 23, 1927. Between April and August 1 of that year, an average of 1,431 cubic yards of concrete per day was placed, the maximum for one day being 1,808.

The spillway elevation in the central portion of the dam—5,370 feet above sea level—sets the mark for high water. The reservoir has been full certain years, but no appreciable spill was allowed, the storage, diversion and use being controlled by operating conditions in the reservoirs above.

Some means had to be provided to control the flow of water from the

195

reservoir for use in the power house far below in the Big Creek Canyon. A vertical shaft, about 100 feet in depth, was excavated near the north end of the dam to tap the Shaver Tunnel, and a nine-foot gate was installed at the bottom, operated by an electric motor in the intake house on the surface, with a gas engine for emergency use.

With completion of the Shaver Dam and clearing of the reservoir, one of the last things to be done was the removal, by burning, from the reservoir area, of all structures that remained. This included the old sawmill, store, and surrounding buildings. In the final clean-up of the store and post office, we found a sizable box of gadgets which no one could identify until Mr. Ferguson, "Fergie," of Clovis, an old-time employee of the former lumber company, was called on for assistance. Apparently, the rest of us were too young to have recognized the contents of that box as oxen shoes. To fit the hoof of an ox, the shoes, of course, had to be in two halves, a right and left piece.

The county road—it had not yet been taken over by the state—had to be changed as it passed over the old rockfill dam and by the Shaver Store. We built the road as it is today, about two miles in length, winding below the dam and joining the old highway opposite the rock quarry.

Several years before the reservoir clearing started, the Sulphur Springs area served as a golf course for Edison employees. Early in 1923—spurred

This September 1927 view of Shaver Dam under construction looks south from the north abutment. Work on the dam had been under way for one year.
Photographer unknown, from the Edison Collection

After granite was quarried, it was crushed and stockpiled until needed to make concrete for the dam. This is one of four conveyor-belt systems used to transport the aggregate to the stockpile.
Photographer unknown, from the Edison Collection

on by O. J. Schieber and Vallery White—golf enthusiasts, practically every employee spent his days off helping clear fairways and making sand "greens" for a nine-hole course. The wives were just as much interested as the men, and did their part in the preparation of many picnic lunches and dinners. The employees built a clubhouse, and the finest in the land could not have furnished more pleasure. For those who needed lessons in the game—and most of us did—there was a "pro" available; and he was a busy "bird," too. Many of those who became proficient in handling the little white ball continue in the sport today elsewhere, crediting their beginnings to the Shaver golf course. It was with much regret that we dismantled the clubhouse and played our last games in 1926, to make way for what is today the greater Shaver Lake.

The expression of regret by others was even greater in the passing from the scene of an old landmark-the hallowed quarters of the Shaver Lake Fishing Club. The old building had for many years been the rendezvous—for two weeks each spring—of Fresno business and professional men. Each outing ended with an annual dinner and "Hi-Jinks." "Chef" Eddie Jones, known to many travelers as the popular "Redcap" at the Southern Pacific Station in Fresno, had for years prepared the annual dinners deluxe, and he did his stuff for the last one, which in some respects would have caused George Rector to sit up and take notice. The dinner lasted for hours, including stunts by the top "jinksters." General Mueller, a grand old gentleman and dean of the group, sat at the head of the table with his big sombrero on—a privilege enjoyed by him only. One guest, a bit tipsy, apparently felt sorry for the group lamenting the impending loss of the quarters, and poking his head through an open window, attempted to toast those at the long table, addressing them as members of the "Fisher Lake Shaving Club." The closing ceremony was impressive, as well as somewhat pathetic, when a torch was applied to the building while all sang "Auld Lang Syne." For several years thereafter the club held its meetings in quarters made available in the resort camp built by the Edison Company, and which was the forerunner of what became "Johnny's." The yearning for a building of their own was too great, and the club built its own quarters, which it now enjoys, on the southern shore of the lake.

The Shaver Lake area must have been frequented in times past by Indians, as many arrowheads, spearheads and countless beads have been found by members of our Big Creek personnel. Emery Morrison, who has become quite an authority on the Indian lore in this vicinity, has built up a huge collection from his annual searches after the lake has been drawn down.

During his last visit to Big Creek in 1926, Mr. John B. Miller, with his daughter Carrita, wished to camp out in the Shaver reservoir area. It was my pleasure to share their enjoyment for two days and nights in the special camp we had established. Before going to sleep, Mr. Miller would lie on his cot and talk about the wonderful progress he had seen through the years, how interesting it had been to watch his company grow to what it was at the time, and envisage even more greatness for the not-too-distant future.

To utilize the water to be stored in Shaver reservoir, and as a part of the general scheme of development, a new powerhouse called "2A" was started in June 1926, while we were getting ready to build the dam. It is located adjacent to Plant No. 2, both being operated as one. The water for the former plant is diverted through the Shaver Tunnel, previously described. The first unit of the new plant went into service during August 1928, followed by the second in December. The total head of 2,418 feet, under which both units operate, is one of the highest in the United States, and exerts a pressure on the water wheels of more than a thousand pounds per square inch. Each generator, with an operating capacity of 46,500 kilowatts, is driven by double overhung impulse wheels, or turbines—the largest of the type, 63, 000-horsepower operating capacity-installed anywhere in the world at the time. The penstock, longer than for any other plant in the Edison system-6,712 feet-connects to the outlet of the Shaver Tunnel, varying in diameter from 108 inches at the top to sixty-six near the power house. The water must be carried to each water wheel-hence the two 48-inch branches, each of these branching into two 24's. An interesting feature involving the

Water stored in the enlarged Shaver Reservoir was to be used in a new powerhouse, named No. 2A, and built adjacent to existing Powerhouse No. 2. Steel framing for the new facility was still in its early stages when this photo was taken in 1927.
Photographer unknown, from the Edison Collection

three huge "Y" pieces, reinforced by heavy steel bands, is that they were made by the once great Krupp Works in Germany. Riveted pipe, made locally, constitutes the upper portion of the penstock. The banded forge-welded central portion was made in Poland, and the bottom section, forged and seamless, was made in this country.

In a previous chapter I described the spalling of concrete on the Florence Lake Dam. As the years have passed since the Shaver Dam was completed, there has been disintegration taking place, but to a lesser degree—although the walkway along the crest has had to be refaced completely.

Disintegration was progressive on the Huntington Lake dams before and after they were increased thirty-five feet in height. We noticed, from many observations, that this condition had not occurred where the concrete was protected by a cover of earth. During the 1930s a major job of backfilling was done, covering each structure on the downstream side with a heavy layer of earth, followed with one of rock to prevent erosion. More recently, backfill has been applied to lower portions on the face of each, Dam 1, restricted by the tunnel intake, receiving the least. When the original

Powerhouse No. 2A was designed with a static head of 2,418 feet, then the highest of any hydroelectric power plant in the world. Such a great fall of water required penstock pipes of great strength to contain the high-pressure water within. Earlier chapters have told of problems encountered with American-made pipe ordered just after World War I. By the late 1920s, the American steel industry learned from the Germans how to make high-tensile steel pipe. These two views were taken in the works of the Midvale Steel Company in Pennsylvania to show how each section of penstock pipe was forged from a single large billet of steel. After forging was completed, each pipe was machined to its finished size.
Photographer unknown, from the Edison Collection

Finished sections of pipe were loaded on railroad cars at the Midvale Works in Pennsylvania, as shown in this photo. The transcontinental rail journey to Big Creek was easy until the tortuous curves of the upper division of the San Joaquin and Eastern Railroad were encountered. Each railroad car had to be unloaded at Auberry, and the pipe transferred to shorter railcars for the last portion of the journey.
Photographer unknown, from the Edison Collection

Despite the care taken in the manufacture of penstock for Powerhouse No. 2A, some sections were banded to provide a greater margin of strength. This 1927 photo shows sections of the new penstock being installed adjacent to the older, German-made penstock for Powerhouse No. 2 (foreground). Notice, too, the massive concrete anchors used to hold down the new penstock. With Powerhouse No. 2A operating on a world's record high static head, Edison's engineers were taking no chances on pipe failures, such as those that had plagued Powerhouse No. 8 in the mid-1920s.
Photographer unknown, from the Edison Collection

This rail-mounted gantry crane traveling along a temporary inclined railway was used to install each section of penstock for Powerhouse No. 2A.
Photographer unknown, from the Edison Collection

excavation was made for the Huntington Lake dams, the material was piled below each structure in several large "spoil" banks. These grew considerably in 1917 from the additional excavation preparatory to increasing the height of the dams. Years later, when Mr. Ballard was president of the company, he thought those below Dam 2 were unsightly for Huntington Lodge guests, and on several occasions made comments to me, not realizing the expense involved to remove them.

Eventually, they became part of the backfill. One day as Mr. Ward and I were walking across that dam, pointing to the "spoil" banks, I mentioned Mr. Ballard's comments. He listened most attentively, then, with a twinkle in his

200

The rotor and waterwheel shafting for each of Powerhouse No. 2A's two generating units was more intricate than any other machined components in the new plant. Here, the 44-foot-long shaft for Unit No. 1's generating rotor is about to be installed.
Photographer unknown, from the Edison Collection

This picture shows the delicate process of placing the shaft into the rotor of Unit No. 1.
Photographer unknown, from the Edison Collection

eyes, said, "If Ballard kicks any more, you tell him he doesn't know a damned thing about it." "Mr. Ward," I replied, "I am sure you can imagine me saying that to Mr. Ballard." Whereupon he added, "All right then, tell him I said it." Before the subject came up again, I was in attendance at an annual meeting of the Edison Company in Los Angeles, and Mr. Ballard, who was presiding, called on me to say something about Big Creek. Among other things, I told the above story, much to the delight of Edison Company executives, particularly Mr. Ballard. After the meeting, Mr. Ward wanted to know if I was trying to get him fired!

This May 1929 photo shows the finished product. Powerhouse No. 2A nestles on the east side of older Powerhouse No. 2. The older plant is driven by water coming down from Powerhouse No. 1, while the new addition gets its water from the recently completed Shaver Lake reservoir.
Photographer unknown, from the Edison Collection

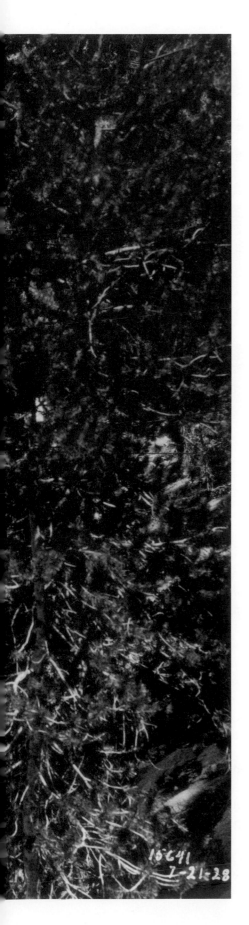

XXIII
Huntington-Pitman-Shaver Conduit

I T HAS BEEN MENTIONED previously that Shaver Lake reservoir would provide storage for excess water that could not be held in Florence Lake and Huntington Lake, the runoff from its own watershed not being sufficient to fill it. The Shaver storage is affected by use and distribution of water from the upper watersheds, as load conditions of the Big Creek plants govern such factors.

Means had to be provided to get the excess water from Florence and Huntington Lakes into Shaver reservoir. Early in 1925, we started work on the Huntington-Pitman-Shaver conduit for such diversion. Roads had to be built and camps established. The "70" series of numbers was assigned to the project, with Camp 71 at the outlet portal of the short tunnel below Dam 2; Camp 72 at the only adit; and Camp 73 located at the outlet portal of the long tunnel above Shaver. Eleven miles of road from the north end of the Shaver area were built to serve the two latter camps.

By November 1925, actual work on the tunnel got under way, efforts being concentrated on the longer section to be worked from Camp 72 to 73. We were in need of mucking equipment for the new tunnel. Messrs. Blight, Kruger and I visited Moffat Railroad Tunnel in Colorado, spending several days observing all operations in driving the huge ore and the small water tunnel paralleling it. As the result of that trip, we ordered several Conway mucking machines for our job, and they proved to be quite satisfactory.

Camp 72 was the headquarters for the work carried on at the outlet portal, and also at Camp 72, about three miles distant by road. The camp included a base hospital, in charge of Dr. W. N. Carter, but it was on a much smaller scale than any of the others we had had elsewhere.

Besides the 4.8 miles of 14-foot by 13-foot horseshoe-shaped tunnel, the conduit consists of about 3,200 feet of 8- to 10-foot steel-riveted pipe. A short section of the latter goes through Dam 2 at Huntington Lake, and connects to the short tunnel leading to the long 10-foot steel siphon, which extends across Big Creek Canyon to the tunnel, whose outlet is at Camp 73.

In all references to "siphon," such as this and the Mono-Bear, it should

A 383 3-3-26
CAMP 72
12919

The Conway mucking machine, seen in the foreground, was extensively used during the excavation of Tunnel No. 7, the Huntington-Shaver Conduit. In the background is Camp 72. Eleven months after this picture was taken, on February 15, 1927, two snow slides struck this camp in the early morning hours, killing 12 men and one woman. It was the worst disaster in the history of the Big Creek construction effort.
Photographer unknown, from the Edison Collection

be understood that an inverted one is indicated, and not the true type. Water passes through the inverted siphon by its own pressure, the intake being higher than the outlet. The 10-foot pipe through Dam 2, near its base, serves as the intake for the Huntington-Pitman-Shaver conduit. In driving the hole through the dam, the concrete was broken piece by piece by the "plug and feather" method, as the use of powder was not allowed. Two gates control the flow from Huntington Lake into the conduit-a 10-foot one on the face of the dam, supplemented at the upper end of the short flow line by an 8-foot duplex, its two leaves for opening and closing sliding horizontally.

Pitman Creek water is dropped into the main tunnel upstream from Camp 72 adit through a deep shaft. This creek, as reported by L. A. Winchell, received its name from a rancher who lived below Tollhouse and had a hunting cabin on its banks in the early days.

Considerable trouble was encountered with bad ground in the tunnel about two miles upstream from the outlet at Camp 73. A major cave-in had occurred, eventually causing a large craterlike depression on top of the mountain. It was necessary to abandon a portion of the tunnel, back up, and go around the bad area. In doing so, we did not miss it entirely, but succeeded in getting through with the use of heavy timbering, which was followed later by a lining of reinforced concrete. Repairs had to be made to this section in the winter of 1944-45, with a steel-reinforced gunite section, as cracks in the original concrete indicated fatigue from ground pressure. To reach the tunnel for these repairs, the Camp 72 adit, being the nearest approach, had to be rebuilt as it had caved in through the years. Stone & Webster did all the repair work. Another bypass while driving the main tunnel, to dodge more bad ground, had to be made where a cave-in extended to the surface upstream from Pitman Creek shaft. We had a most interesting experience in the outlet heading; quite some distance from the portal, after a round had been blasted, the flattened root of a pine or fir tree was found in a granite crevice, the shortest distance to the surface at that point being 450 feet. Undoubtedly, the root had followed the crevice to water.

Camp 72 suffered the worst disaster in the history of the Big Creek development. A snowslide struck about two a.m. February 15, 1927, followed by another about seven a.m. The slides resulted in the death of twelve men and one woman. A heavy snowstorm was raging, and all telephone lines were down. As far as can be learned, the only member of our present local personnel who experienced the slides is Leo Robinson, who was shop foreman at Camp 72 at that time. The corner of the bunkhouse in which he was sleeping was torn away, but he escaped uninjured. He and Art Kocher (the latter then connected with this office) are authority as to how the first report reached Big Creek headquarters. T. L. "Red" Coff, a lineman, made the arduous two-mile trip through the deep snow down the mountainside. Kocher had the local siren sounded about 4:30 a.m., after which hurried steps were taken to render all possible aid. It was ten days before all bodies were recovered. During the gruesome search far down the mountain, one group of men reported seeing a canary fly out after they had burrowed deeply into the snow and debris—no doubt having come down with the family residence. I was in China at the time, and did not learn of the disaster until after I arrived in Tokyo. In none of the mail from Big Creek written after February 15 was there any mention of it, the news having been omitted intentionally. On my first visit to the Tokyo Club, I was anxious to see a newspaper from my own country, and the first thing that struck me like a brick was the big headline in a weeks-old San Francisco paper.

En route back across the Pacific, I learned further details from Mr. John B. Miller, who, with Mrs. Miller, and their daughter, Carrita, was vacationing in Honolulu. After a final fling at Waikiki, we returned to San Francisco on the same ship. I enjoyed breakfasts aboard with Mr. Miller, always finding him at the early table. The second day out from Honolulu, his cabin boy looked me up on deck, as Mr. Miller was anxious to know if by chance I had any "JBM," his favorite smoking tobacco—mine too—on hand. Fortunately, I did. I had used little, as the sea, quite rough at times, did anything but create a desire for me to even smell tobacco, let alone smoke it. Needless to say, the remainder of the trip—for Mr. Miller, at least—was made much more pleasant. The "JBM" brand, from his initials, was originated by him, so he had told me years before. The clientele of the Los Angeles Spring Street tobacconist who handles it includes as devotees of that brand the names of many prominent men in this country, and up to World War 11, some in foreign countries. Any smoker could not help but be tempted after reading the

Pages 202-203: This July 1928 picture shows the just-completed intake structure to divert water from Pitman Creek into the Huntington-Shaver Tunnel. The metal grating, known as a trash rack, covers a vertical shaft that connects with the tunnel deep underground.
Photographer unknown, from the Edison Collection

To speed construction of Huntington-Shaver Tunnel, an adit was driven from Camp 72 back to the line of the tunnel. Much of this adit was driven through soft ground, requiring heavy timbering. Here, workmen are installing "spiling," overhead boards to stop the collapse of dirt from the roof of the tunnel.
Photographer unknown, from the Edison Collection

label. On each can appear two pictures—one of Big Creek Powerhouse No. 1, and one of Powerhouse No. 2. Besides these, there is the following:

HUGUNIN'S JBM MIXTURE

This mixture is prepared from old Burley leaf,

especially selected, aged for five years in wood,

stripped by hand, bound with Canadian maple sugar,

and blended with Fragrant Hollandish.

No attempt is intended here for advertising this product. It is mentioned solely because of its association with Big Creek. Although not a heavy pipe smoker, I have kept a supply on my smoke stand for years, ever since its originator introduced it to me. I never enjoy a pipeful without a recollection of the pleasant memories connected with its unusual background.

While in Japan, I was amazed at their engineers' familiarity with our Big Creek plants. Of course, many had visited not only Big Creek but other major installations throughout the United States, and they had certainly made the most of their opportunities in collecting data for use in their own country.

Work on the Huntington-Pitman-Shaver conduit was completed on April 21, 1928, when diversion into Shaver Lake from Huntington Lake began.

With completion of this conduit and Power House 2A the same year, and with the addition of a second unit in Big Creek 8 in June 1929, all major construction for that period came to an end, making Big Creek, with its 533,000-horsepower operating capacity for the turbines, and 398,000 kilowatts for the generators, the largest hydro, part of the Southern California Edison System. Although other powerhouses had been planned, the

This complex valve and venting pipe arrangement was installed just downstream from Dam No. 2 at Huntington Lake, in the steel pipeline that extends from the dam to the mouth of the Huntington-Shaver Tunnel. The 36-inch-diameter pipe that extends out of the top of the photo is a vent pipe to release trapped air from the conduit before it can cause trouble from "water hammer." The vent pipe rises to an elevation slightly higher than the crest of Dam No. 2.
Photographer unknown, from the Edison Collection

proposal to build Hoover Dam caused our picture to change, and the Edison Company joined forces in helping with that development by agreement with the United States Government to assume its share of electric power.

On the Big Creek Project, about thirty-six miles of tunnels have been driven. At various times, several of us made trips to visit such projects as Hetch-Hetchy, Don Pedro, Exchequer and Balch, to see what the other fellows were doing in the construction of their dams, power houses and tunnels. While in New York during construction of the Holland Tunnel beneath the Hudson River, I had my first experience under compressed air, when I was escorted through the air locks and down to the huge shield by the chief engineer, Cliff Holland, for whom the tunnel was named. Admittance of visitors was kept to a minimum, largely because of the conditions which they would encounter. Such underwater tunneling has to be carried on under compressed air to counteract the pressure from above and keep the water from breaking through the mud and clay into the workings. The air pressure really holds death at arm's length. A medical examination was required of every visitor, to ascertain his condition to withstand the high air pressure, which reaches as much as thirty-eight pounds, depending on the amount necessary to equalize that exerted from above. Men and material go through air locks-huge steel tanks—in which the pressure is gradually raised to equal that on the working side. Going from normal to high-pressure air takes about three to five minutes. After the lock is closed by the steel door, a valve is turned, and one can not only hear the air hissing but feel the pressure increasing. When the desired pressure is reached, the steel door in the opposite end of the chamber, or lock, is opened and one steps out into the high-pressure air. I felt a pain in my neck, literally, beneath both ears—and was most uncomfortable. Reverse passage, coming from the high pressure side out to normal, called decompression, takes much longer than going in—up to forty-five minutes.

The men who work behind the huge shield, which is forced ahead through the mud and clay by many powerful hydraulic jacks, are known as "sand hogs." Slow decompression is of vital importance to prevent the much-dreaded disability among sand hogs known as "the bends." They wear dog tags for identification, as an attack of the bends may be suffered when one is off duty and out on the street. Treatment consists of rushing the victim to the nearest compression chamber and then allowing decompression slowly. The condition comes from working under compressed air, where large amounts of nitrogen are absorbed in the bloodstream. It is supposed to be eliminated as the sand hog passes through the decompression chamber, or lock. Otherwise, the nitrogen forms bubbles in the body tissues or bloodstream, causing the various symptoms of compressed air illness, such as pains in the joints or muscles, and in the neck. Sand hogs cannot remain at work long under high air; consequently, their shifts are short, with rather long intervals in between. The plant for supplying compressed air to the section visited was in triplicate, I observed, each unit of compressors being complete in itself and having a source of power entirely independent of the others, and any one bank being capable of furnishing the required pressure. Should the pressure in the working area get too low, water and mud would rush in upon the workmen. On the other hand, should the pressure get too high, they might be blown through the mud and water to the surface. I was told that although both kinds of accidents had actually occurred, they were few and far between. In spite of such dangers, the sand hogs continue to ply their trade, putting their faith in the engineers who plan and design such undertakings. I have often wondered how many users of the tubes beneath the Hudson, regardless of the method of transportation, ever give a thought to the dangers and hardships undergone by those involved with their construction.

In the summer of 1927 we were paid a visit by a group of men from Italy, whom we referred as the Hydro Electric Commission from that country. It appeared to compare somewhat with our own Federal Power Commission. The Los Angeles office asked me to meet these gentlemen personally upon their arrival by train at Big Creek. Hurriedly I looked around, trying to find an Italian from one of our tunnel crews who could serve as an interpreter. The group was due before I met with any success, so I had to make the best of it. I sized up each man as he stepped off the train, and decided to take a chance with the one I thought to be spokesman for the group. Very much to my surprise, each individual greeted me in better English, perhaps, than most of us use ourselves. While entertaining them at Huntington Lake Lodge during their stay here, I told them of my concern, and asked how it is that practically each and every foreign visitor we have either speaks fluent English, or is capable enough to communicate without much difficulty. They told me, speaking for themselves, that they had studied English because it was their desire someday to visit the United States of America, and when that happened they wanted to be able to speak the language. Foreigners put most of us to shame when it comes to the matter of languages. Engineers, especially, have been here from all over the world. Engineers, however, are not the only ones to be credited with knowing languages other than their mother tongues. In September 1936, we had as guests a large number of delegates, mostly foreigners, to the Third World Power Conference held in Washington, D. C. Two special trainloads came west. At Fresno they split into groups for visits to various localities, including Big Creek. There was little need for interpreters. The Fresno County Chamber of Commerce gave a big dinner the evening all had returned from the day's outings. Seated on my left at the banquet was a gentleman from Uruguay, with another on my right from Chile. Both spoke English fluently and, of course, Spanish. After my complimenting them on their use of the former, they conversed briefly with each other in French for my benefit.

During the day I had asked an Italian gentleman, who had been riding with me, questions about Italy. After looking around to make sure no other member of the party was nearby, he answered in a low voice, "You should thank God you don't have a Mussolini in your country."

XXIV
Stevenson Creek Test Dam

N O DESCRIPTION OF THE Big Creek development would be complete without including something about the Stevenson Creek Test Dam, which attracted considerable attention in the engineering world during the time it was being built, tests made and reports prepared. No attempt will be made to go into the technical details of that program, but it is felt a general description is justified.

Prior to the early '20s, there had been much discussion among engineers and others concerned about the design and cost of arch dams in power development, water supply, irrigation, flood controls, etc. Involved was the question of whether such structures were being over-designed, with a consequent waste of construction materials, to say nothing of the extra cost. Up to that time many arch dams had been built in this country, some in Australia, and others were scattered over Europe. There had been no reports of failure. Engineers had no real experimental knowledge to support design theories. Some dams had been built thick and others thin. In the former, there might have been more material than necessary, and in the latter the limit of safety could have been closely approached. Throughout all discussions of the subject, uppermost in the minds of engineers especially was the permanence and safety of the structures.

In 1922, Fred A. Noetzli, a consulting engineer in Los Angeles, acting on behalf of engineers on the Pacific Coast and in the Rocky Mountain states, prevailed upon the Engineering Foundation to undertake a study of arch dams. The Engineering Foundation is an organization which functions under the direction of several of the larger national engineering societies, and is devoted specifically to research along engineering lines. As previously mentioned, many hydraulic projects involve the arch dam as a major item in development; therefore, it is extremely important to all concerned that its design be on the same scientific basis as all other parts of the entire development.

In December 1923, Mr. W. A. Brackenridge, then senior vice president of the Southern California Edison Company, suggested that an experimental

The Stevenson Creek Test Dam, an experimental thin-shell concrete-arch dam, was built during 1925 and 1926 by the Edison Company on behalf of the Engineering Foundation and the U.S. Bureau of Standards. It was intended to test the practical limits of structures of this design under field conditions. H. W. Dennis and R. C. Booth of Edison's Engineering Department supervised the construction and subsequent testing of the dam. The dam still survives today. An April 1926 progress report on the Stevenson Creek Test Dam contained this drawing showing the location of the dam and the instrument house where measuring would take place.
Drawing from the Edison Collection

arch dam be built—one comparable to some of those in existence at the time. A suitable site had to be selected, one where there would be no interference with its construction, or, as a result of the numerous tests contemplated, with anything else. Mr. Brackenridge offered on behalf of the Edison Company not only contribution of funds, but also facilities and a site in Stevenson Creek Canyon, midway between our Big Creek Plants No. 3 and No. 8. Stevenson Creek, a tributary of the San Joaquin River, is the natural outlet for Shaver Lake. The site would provide the desired small reservoir capacity, and allow tests to be made safely, even to the destruction of the dam with a full reservoir. All such tests would be made under field conditions.

The program adopted was a practical endeavor, scientifically directed to get facts from experiment and experience, all for the better guidance of engineers in the design of arch dams. There was a feeling on the part of some engineers that the data to be obtained would justify some changes in the design of arch dams, with a corresponding reduction in cost without jeopardizing the safety of such structures.

The experimental program was endorsed by the Federal Power Commission and the State Railroad Commission of California. The United States Bureau of Standards cooperated wholeheartedly, and assigned its Mr. W. A. Slater to be on hand during construction of the dam, and to remain for supervising tests, collecting data and preparing reports. Other government bureaus and agencies rendered valuable assistance in many ways. Mr. Brackenridge was appointed sole trustee for collection and distribution of funds. The Edison Company started contributions with $25,000 towards the ultimate cost, estimated at $100,000. The cooperation of others to be benefited was invited. Many companies throughout the United States responded with cash donations, or equipment, material and supplies. H. W. Dennis, of the Edison Company, supervised the construction of the dam, with R. C. Booth, of our local engineering personnel, in charge on the ground. The investigation committee, headed by Charles D. Marx of Stanford University as chairman, included, besides Mr. Dennis, several other well-known engineers in the Pacific Coast area.

By November 1, 1925, the necessary camp and facilities had been made ready and the work got under way. By April 1926, the excavation for the foundation was complete and ready for concrete, the first pour being made on the 19th. By June 4, the structure was completed to the present height of sixty feet.

During construction of the dam many instruments were imbedded in the concrete, and metal plugs and reference points carefully set for taking various measurements. According to Mr. Slater, 140 electric telemeters were scattered throughout the dam, buried in the concrete. Their purpose was to measure microscopic changes in length and temperature within the instruments themselves, by means of varying electrical resistances. Definite data were wanted on just what was going on inside the dam after the concrete had set, in the way of strains from expansion, contraction, etc. The electric telemeters used were designed by Messrs. McCullom and Peters, of the Bureau of Standards. As stated by them, the electrical telemeter "depends upon the well-known fact that if a stack of carbon plates is held under pressure, change of pressure will be accompanied by a change of electrical resistance and also a change in length of the stack." By the proper interpretation of the resistance readings registered by the telemeters, it was possible to obtain the desired data. Lead wires extending from the telemeters permitted readings to be taken at a convenient distance from the dam. The wires ended at a terminal board so that all readings could be taken at one location.

During World War II, engineers from the United States Army visited the site, having in mind the feasibility of using the structure for testing the destructive power of explosives under water and close to concrete dams. Nothing further ever came of that investigation.

Various measurements and observations were begun with the first steps of construction. For test purposes, water was first allowed to build up behind the dam to a depth of twenty feet in July. Extensive tests were made with water twenty feet deep, and at ten-foot intervals up to and including sixty feet—top of the dam. With each test a full series of measurements was made, with the small reservoir filled to the desired level, and with it empty. To take advantage of the least change in temperature, these tests were made at night. Under load tests, according to Slater's report, no crack occurred in the dam proper with a depth of water less than fifty feet, but under this head one occurred on the vertical center line, extending entirely through the dam from the downstream face to the upstream face, and down to an elevation of about forty-nine feet on the downstream face. Another crack appeared under a head of sixty feet of water on the vertical center line of the dam, extending from two inches above foundation rock to a height of about nine feet—and extending itself later to a height of thirteen feet. Each of these cracks was first discovered by means of the telemeter readings. The last load tests made started with the reservoir full—a sixty-foot depth—and continued at ten-foot intervals down to and including the thirty-foot level, the water being lowered accordingly.

The committee reported some tentative conclusions in its Volume No. 1, subject to modification in Volume No. 2, to be submitted to the Engineering Foundation at completion of the work. The committee felt that with the aid of the information being compiled from the test data, measurements and observations, arch dams of less thickness than would formerly have been considered necessary could be built on some sites. As far as I know the second volume was never finished because of Mr. Slater's death. The St. Francis Dam disaster in Southern California probably had some effect towards making any radical change in the design of all dams, even though the failure was not caused by a fault in the design of the dam itself. One thing the Stevenson Creek Test Dam did demonstrate is the great strength of a thin, reinforced, concrete-arch dam, provided it is well built on a proper foundation.

Interest in the investigation was worldwide, particularly among engineers, as previously indicated. There have been many visitors to the dam, including some engineers from foreign countries. Even today, there is seldom a visitor to the Big Creek Project, engineer or otherwise, who does not ask about the test dam, and who, if time permits, does not want to see it.

XXV
Improvements in Equipment

I T HAS BEEN INTERESTING to observe the changes and improvements that have been made, both in construction equipment and otherwise, on our job from 1912 to the present time. Along with these have come improved methods in construction.

Teams and scrapers, along with wheelbarrows, played the major role in building the San Joaquin and Eastern Railroad—in fact, they did so in the early construction of the large railroads we know today. The amount of material moved by a well-organized crew of men with wheelbarrows, "Irish Buggies," teams and scrapers, handled by real "skinners," was amazing. Today, wheelbarrows are used only where nothing else is practical, and men scoff if they are not fitted with pneumatic tires and roller bearings. Having used both the old and new types myself, I do not blame them. Even shovels, "muck sticks," have been improved in shape and material. Mule skinners who know their stuff are scarce today, and so are men who really know how to push a wheelbarrow.

In the old days, the mule skinners would feed the animals on their way to breakfast so they would be ready for the harness after the skinners had eaten. The teams would be on the job by 7:00. With the advent of the truck, instead of "twisting the mules' tails," the skinner would crank the engine, and be reminded frequently of a mule when the crank would kick back. Today, merely stepping on the starter eliminates even that hazard.

The one automobile on the Big Creek job in 1912 did not even have a truck for company. Trucks did not begin to replace horses, mules and wagons until along toward 1920, although passenger cars were becoming more numerous in the meantime. Our large stables were eventually replaced by garages, the heavy and light wagons were gradually pushed aside by various types of automotive equipment. Although there are a large number of horses and mules today, they are restricted largely to cattle ranches, riding stables, dude ranches, and packing concessions in the mountain area. It is difficult to find among members of the younger generation one who can harness a horse, let alone hitch it to a vehicle—if a horse-drawn one could be

216

Previous pages: Construction of a road down the canyon of the San Joaquin River between Powerhouse No. 8 and the site for Powerhouse No. 3 was one of the more difficult jobs on the Big Creek project. This view of the work taken in the spring of 1922 shows one of the wider points in the road, to allow opposing traffic to pass. In the distance can be seen a steam shovel at work, and a company automobile is parked in the foreground. This road is still used today, although traffic is now restricted to one-way only.
Photographer unknown, from the Edison Collection

found—but they have considerable knowledge of an automobile. What a lot they have missed!

Automotive equipment took over completely for general use during the 1920s. Tractors without dozers put in their appearance in 1925 at Florence Lake, for use in our logging operations. It was not long before they were equipped for work as bulldozers. The more maneuverable crawler steam shovel showed up during the earlier 1920s to replace the railroad type, which was restricted to use on railroad tracks. In recent years, the smaller shovels come mounted on a truck chassis, and can be moved quickly from place to place.

For moving large quantities of earth, we have used the huge carryall, towed by a tractor. As compared to the old dump wagon and even the present-day dump truck, the carryall not only gobbles up a mouthful of several cubic yards, but can carry it almost any distance before disgorging—leveling it besides. Along with such earth-moving equipment is that ingenious device, the sheep's-foot tamper, used where necessary to pack a fill instead of hand tamping. The huge roller is covered with hundreds of small steel projections resembling sheep's feet. We are told the idea was developed as the result of someone actually observing the effect from the feet of hundreds of sheep driven over a large fill—hence the name for the tamper.

The four-wheel-drive truck, "F.W.D.," without discrediting its cousin that is driven only by the rear wheels, will, as the men say, almost climb up the side of a building. Such equipment renders incalculable service, especially in snow and mud. I have had my car towed—it is more correct to say, "dragged"—over a road, while the truck's wheels were buried above the axles in mud.

In our early tunnel driving, we were plugging along with the heavy, clumsy and slow piston air drill, until the lighter, faster and more efficient

In the early 1920s, this four-wheel-drive, power-operated, rotary snowplow was tried out during winter times on the narrow road between the town of Big Creek and Huntington Lake. Although not completely successful, it was the forefather of a modern generation of snow-removal equipment.
Photographer unknown, from the Edison Collection

air hammer put in its appearance between 1914 and 1920. Tunnel drill steel was sharpened by hand before the arrival of the air-operated drill sharpener. In the old method, the helper certainly earned his money wielding the heavy sledge hammer, while at the same time developing some husky muscles. Along came the oil furnace for heating drill steel instead of using coal and coke, and as is usually the case in adopting anything new, the old-timers were somewhat skeptical, but were slowly weaned away from coal and coke and the air blower forge. Tempering drill steel requires skill; a man may be expert with a drill sharpener and fall down badly on tempering. Nothing exasperates the operator of an air hammer drill more than improperly tempered steel.

The faithful mules, too, were pushed aside when the electric locomotive came along to pull the muck cars.

To keep pace with these improvements in driving tunnels, the use of fuse for blasting gave way to the modern method of doing it electrically, with all the holes in the heading being connected to an electric circuit and the exploders detonated when the master switch, at a safe distance, was closed. The firing of the holes in proper rotation was determined by the time exploder placed in the charge of each.

We had no snow-removal equipment until the tractor came along. During the 1920s, a special piece of equipment—it could be called a "rotary,"

Original plans for the construction of Florence Lake Dam and the tunnel beneath Kaiser Ridge anticipated extension of the San Joaquin and Eastern Railroad up the South Fork of the San Joaquin River. By the time construction began, however, trucks had proven themselves, and Kaiser Pass Road was built instead. The road was the scene of intense truck traffic during the summer months. Due to heavy winter snows, the road was passable for only five or six months a year.
Photographer unknown, from the Edison Collection

mounted on a truck chassis—was given a trial on the road between Big Creek and Huntington Lake, but without success. A homemade V-shaped scraper, towed behind a truck, worked very well for the removal of light snow. With a scraper as a starter, a heavy one with hydraulic lift was later made and fitted around one of the tractors. The tractor actually sat inside the frame and pushed the plow. Another tractor was fitted with a heavy blade equipped with a hydraulic lift.

A bulldozer can move deep snow provided there is room along the roadside for the snow to be rolled over and down a bank. The present-day rotary snowplow, or "Sno-Go," as it is called, as used by the State Highway Department, has proved to be the most satisfactory type of equipment for snow removal. It moves along slowly through the deep snow and throws it aside in a heavy stream, clearing the entire roadway.

Some means had to be found for traveling over the snow other than on foot, snowshoes or skis. The first contraption tried out was motor-driven, and was supposed to be pushed ahead over the snow by a revolving worm shaft in the rear, on the order of the screw conveyor used for moving wheat in large elevators. Instead of pushing the outfit ahead, it would bury itself by digging straight down. One of our small tractors was fitted with specially made wide wooden tracks, but without success. It would go only so far, and when the snow got too soft and deep would "sit back on its haunches"—in other words, rear up with the front end up in the air and the rear burying itself by digging down to the road.

P. H. Ducker, who has headed the transportation department of the Edison Company for many years, was on the lookout for something that would travel satisfactorily over the snow. He arranged for the purchase of

The Mack "Bulldog" was the backbone of Edison's fleet of heavy trucks during the twenties.
Photographer unknown, from the Edison Collection

our present "Sno-Motor," a crawler-type piece of equipment designed by T. P. Flynn, snow equipment engineer of the U. S. Forest Service. It arrived here on February 3, 1941, and was taken on its trial trip the following day, from Big Creek to Kaiser Pass and return. Its operation was quite successful, and it has rendered excellent service for seven winters in the transportation of men and material over the snow. The main unit operates much the same as the well-known Caterpillar tractor, except that it has only one endless crawler tread which extends across the entire width of the machine, fifty-six inches, and travels completely around it. A long sled, which is towed, furnishes the fulcrum for turning. Without the sled, the machine can move only forward and backward. Steel plates four feet long, on either side of the sled, cut down into the snow, providing the means for steering—much the same as a rudder on a boat. Thirty-percent grades, and probably some steeper, have been easily made with a full load of two and one-half tons. Powder snow on grades causes some trouble, but an experienced operator will compact a trail by forward and backward movements of the machine. The Sno-Motor fulfills a long-felt need for winter transportation in our high, snowbound regions. Ours was the fifth one in use in the United States at the time of its purchase.

Hydrographic work in this area keeps expanding, and requires frequent trips in both winter and summer by hydrographers to remote stations. A lighter piece of equipment, smaller than the Sno-Motor, was needed for traveling over the snow. Mr. Ducker arranged for the purchase of a Tucker "Cat"—we call it "Sno-Cat"—made by E. M. Tucker of Grass Valley, California. It provides good transportation for two men, along with a reasonable amount of such equipment as hydrographers carry. The Sno-Cat is

Prior to the development of the "Sno-Cat," built for winter use, specially modified Caterpillar tractors were used to carry supplies over snowed-in roads. This tractor is breaking a trail for the opening of Kaiser Pass Road in the early spring of 1927.
Photographer unknown, from the Edison Collection

The first "Sno-Cat" vehicles wrought a revolution in wintertime travel at Big Creek. These rugged machines could carry snow surveyors far into the back country, where before, men could only go by walking on snowshoes. This 1940 photo shows the earliest model "Sno-Cat" on Kaiser Pass Road.
Photographer unknown, from the Edison Collection

equipped with crawler-type treads in the rear, on both sides. In front, pneumatic-tired wheels may be raised or lowered to alternate with skis, as conditions require.

Only some of the major improvements in construction equipment have been described. One can only conjecture what the saving in time and money would have been in such a huge development as this had they all been available since 1912.

Aerial photography accomplishes wonders as compared to the survey parties formerly needed on reconnaissance. In a few hours, a photography plane can cover an area that would require the arduous work of a survey party for weeks and even months. It should be said, however, that pictures taken from the air must be carefully interpreted by an expert to obtain the desired data for final field location.

Electric ranges did not come into general use by employees in this area until the early 1920s. When the free use of electricity was discontinued, all employees going on meters, there was a sudden decrease to the extent of seventy-five percent in the amount used—another example of the oft-repeated comment, "People do not appreciate anything they do not pay for." Front porch lights became conspicuous by being turned off during daylight hours.

Even though this area is in a national forest, there is pretty much of a wood famine of late, because of the difficulty in getting it—no one wants to cut it and few know how. Hence, the use of fuel oil has become the general practice.

The Engineering Construction Pay Roll #45, which had served many thousands of employees for many years, finally came to an end. The last one to be transferred from it was H. A. Barber, of the present local engineering staff, on November 1, 1931.

This chapter should end with one last story involving visitors, thousands of whom, as already mentioned, have been here during the busy construction

years and since. During the Golden Gate International Exposition, while I was having lunch in San Francisco with two chief engineers, the engineer for the Golden Gate Bridge was curious to know whether I had ever been asked a foolish question by any of our visitors. I told him of the individual who wanted to know how we got the water back into Huntington Lake after it had passed through the powerhouse! The Oakland Bay Bridge engineer thought he could go one even better. He had spent part of a day escorting a group over the two big bridges, winding up with a trip through the large Exposition buildings. While visiting the latter, he had emphasized the fact that all were to be dismantled at the close of the Fair. When saying goodbye to his party, one lady, who had displayed unusual interest in all the sights, said, "It's bad enough to think about the removal of such lovely buildings, but what really makes me sick is the thought of tearing down those two wonderful bridges."

Although gradually replaced by motor trucks, rail-mounted vehicles continued to be used on Big Creek construction projects throughout the 1920s. This 1921 view of the excavation of an area for yard tracks at Camp 42 shows the traditional Marion Model 40 rail steam shovel, accompanied by a small steam locomotive moving dump cars to be loaded by the shovel. Camp 42, also known as "Feeney," was located on the main line of the San Joaquin and Eastern Railroad, at the top of the inclined railway down to the site of Powerhouse No. 8.
Photographer unknown, from the Edison Collection

XXVI
Retrospection

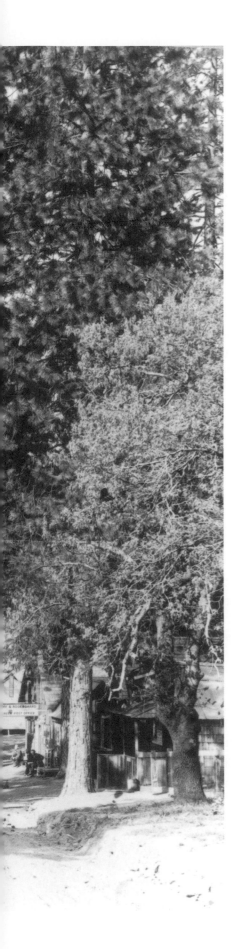

T HE GLAMOUR OF THE big construction job has disappeared, but to most of us who went through it there will always remain pleasant memories. Now and then someone asks if I have not grown tired of my long stay here. If one is really interested in his job and has good health, time does not hang heavily and he keeps reasonably contented. It matters not where one finds himself, there are always advantages and disadvantages. For a place like Big Creek it makes a difference, too, when one loves the mountains. Although the big construction job was more interesting and fascinating, much satisfaction has been derived from directing the operation of the project—the result of many years' effort by thousands of men, and one which has added so much comfort for millions of people.

There has always been enough variety to prevent monotony—visitors of note who were keenly interested, and who, in turn, added much from their own experiences. Trips in connection with the job, as well as for recreation, provided welcome changes, although for a while vacations were irregular because the job was too interesting or too important to leave.

During the 1930s I enjoyed being a member of a special consulting board of engineers with the Metropolitan Water District of Southern California, on an assignment having to do with driving the San Jacinto Tunnel, an important link in the Colorado River Aqueduct.

Looking back through the years, one of the things that stands out most clearly in the whole picture is the human element-those who made the completion of the big job possible—men like Mr. Ward, Mr. Miller and Mr. Ballard, who had the vision, the ability and the confidence to go ahead in spite of many difficulties. I mention Mr. Ward first since he had full responsibility for the huge construction program. Fortunately for all three men—each, in turn, was president—they were able to see the completion of the big job before they passed on. The Sunset Club of Los Angeles had a heavy bronze tablet placed on the east end of Powerhouse No. 1, honoring both R. H. Ballard and George C. Ward, and bearing the following inscription:

Dave Redinger stands on Kaiser Pass Road on May 11, 1940. Spring is on its way, but there is still over seven feet of snow in the pass.
Photographer unknown, from the Edison Collection

Previous pages: This circa 1915 view of the town of Big Creek shows the original Big Creek Hotel, at left.
Photographer unknown, from the Edison Collection

THE SUNSET CLUB OF LOS ANGELES
PROUD OF THE PART TAKEN IN THIS MIGHTY ENTERPRISE
BY TWO OF ITS MEMBERS
RUSSELL H. BALLARD AND GEORGE C. WARD
PLACES THIS TABLET HERE
IN GRATEFUL ADMIRATION OF THEM
AND THEIR ASSOCIATES
TO LIGHTEN THE DARKNESS OF MULTITUDES AND
TO SPEED THE WHEELS OF HUMAN PROGRESS THEY
SMOTE THE MOUNTAINOUS ROCK AND LIVING WATERS
RUSHED TO DO THEIR BIDDING
A. D. 1929

There were others, too, who, while not so outstanding perhaps, played a most important part in their respective places—men like Charlie Scott, "Doc" Dwight, T. A. Smith, Bert Wilson, "Sandy" Gilzean, "Scotty" Lawson, H. A. Noble, and last but by no means least, "Jumbo"—these gave their all and were still "in the harness" when their time came to pass beyond. They, and others like them, gave their utmost in devotion and loyalty, their one idea being to see their respective jobs done, without regard to overtime, holidays or vacations, when their services were needed. I wonder, sometimes, if they did not get something from their work and a job well done that, perhaps, the average man never experiences. I recall emergencies and how these men responded—sometimes when their own best interests, physically and otherwise, made it inadvisable. Besides being a good veterinarian, "Doc" Dwight was one of our best "cat skinners." Once while sick in bed, he learned of a vital trip to be made through deep snow, and when the large tractor left, "Doc" was in the seat, realizing he was the best qualified for that particular job. Until the day of his death, "Scotty" Lawson, who had come along the hard way, found it difficult to take overtime pay, saying that it was his duty, and if he could not do his job within eight hours it was up to him regardless of time—nights and holidays made no difference. "Jumbo" (Jevto Vasilovitch), huge of stature, had no "book larnin'," but he did have a natural know-how and the strength for doing unusual things—an excellent runner-up for Hercules himself. T. A. Smith, an excellent all-around construction man, never faltered, even during those days when he should have been in bed—men less interested in their jobs would have been. It is not possible to mention more than a few of the many men deserving credit, but nothing could be written about the major Big Creek construction without including the name of Mark Gunderson, who, as master mechanic, played a most important role. Unfortunately, he lived to enjoy only a few years of his justly earned retirement. Many were the difficult and complex problems which arose to confront him and H. A. Noble, his successor, and due credit must be given both for their unusual skill and ingenuity in handling each and every one. Both were among those unsung heroes who had no regard whatever for the clock, giving their all to help get the big job done and to keep it running afterwards. Heman Noble passed away almost on the eve of his retirement.

I am not unmindful of the wives and employees who did a wonderful job, too, through the construction years and since. Some lived in tents, some in

By the mid-1950s, helicopters were being used by the Edison Company to carry snow surveyors into the back country.
Joseph O. Fadler Photo, from the Edison Collection

cottages of more or less temporary nature, and others in more permanent quarters. All deserve much credit for standing by their husbands and providing so many of the comforts of home. It was much more trying for the wives, because the husbands had the interesting features of a huge job to hold their attention and keep them occupied, while the wives had the usual housework, along with the inconveniences and handicaps common to most camp life.

Having viewed this section of the country from a regular plane, traveled over it on snow shoes and skis, by horse and wagon, on horseback, by dog sled and automobile, and under it through many miles of tunnels, it was my pleasure to be taken on the first flight of a helicopter over Huntington Lake on July 16, 1947. The takeoff was made from "The Point." The ship rose easily, and the landing reminded me of a setting hen settling down carefully on a nest of eggs. The helicopter trip really rounded out an unusual program of diversified means of travel. Time certainly marches on!

XXVII
The Other Half

BY EDITH I. REDINGER

T HE BIG CREEK project came into being because of the imagination of civil engineer and visionary John Eastwood long before the turn of the century. He could foresee the possibility of a vast hydroelectric development using the many small streams and rivers in that part of the Sierra Nevada.

In the ensuing years it took men with imagination and money, and much hard work with very primitive tools. Remember that most of this area was an uncharted wilderness.

With the arrival of men and equipment in 1911, the project was started, and that was when the female of the species began to be a part.

I know I am just an accessory after the fact, but on the advice of counsel, I want to put down a few things on paper that might be of interest, because few people nowadays have the chance to live the kind of life I have, or get the same perspective. I have come to realize that there are very few things in this world that are really important, and that those things do not change much with the years.

I lived in an era when money was not all-important, when human relations and interest in the things you did were the only things that really counted. Born in St. Paul, Minnesota, I came from a life in the cities suddenly into an entirely new environment. With the enthusiasm of youth and, perhaps, an inherited inclination toward pioneering, I did not find it too difficult to make the adjustment.

I was then connected with a college in Fresno in the San Joaquin Valley. At the suggestion of the president, I went up into the Sierra Nevada mountains during spring vacation to look over the possibility of starting a summer school there. I returned thrilled with the idea of taking over an old, abandoned logger's camp. On my recommendation, plans were laid, and by the latter part of June, we had completed the necessary preparations for the summer session.

It was there in 1914 that I met David Redinger, the man whom I was eventually to marry. I still think the mountain air had something to do with it, because marriage at the time was furthest from my thoughts. I loved the

Edith and Dave Redinger, with their dog, Boh, at Big Creek.
Redinger Family Album, from the Edison Collection

228

work I was doing and, so far, had gotten by the diversions that had come along. We had planned to be married the following summer, but the outbreak of World War I and certain family affairs made this inadvisable, so I went back to my job. Three years later, when there was a work break and my future husband could get a few days off, we finally took the step that was to be the beginning of 60 years of a more-than-usually happy married life.

While I was still in Columbia I had a letter from Dave saying that if I expected to ride horseback, be prepared to wear a riding skirt rather than breeches. The superintendent had threatened to fire one of the boys whose mother wore breeches rather than a skirt. So I bought a beautiful brown corduroy riding habit that I never wore. All this because the mother of one of the men had appeared in riding breeches!

There were some rough spots and some funny ones, some lonesome ones and some very rewarding ones. When we arrived in Big Creek, where a big construction job was under way, we were met at the funny little mountain railway station by the townspeople. School had been let out so all the children could join in the festivities. My husband had given me some inkling of what I could expect, so I was not totally unprepared for the rousing welcome.

We had the best accommodations available—a tent with a wood stove and a corrugated iron roof to ward off the snow. Our first night in camp was not too restful. We had hardly retired when the stove began smoking because the chimney had been covered, and with the shower of rocks thrown by friends and "well-wishers," a quaint good-natured custom prevalent at the time, sleep seemed to be out of the question. Since there was no other choice, we opened the door and invited them in. They came with sandwiches, cakes and coffee, a victrola and records and spent the night with us. I have since helped a number of bewildered brides and grooms, and have enjoyed being instrumental in entertaining them.

We found our little 10 by 14-foot tent quite inadequate to house all our luggage and the boxes and barrels of wedding gifts that kept coming along, so my husband rented the tent across the way. I loved to go over to look at them.

A month later, we were moved farther up into what was to me then an uncharted wilderness where the "job" was in progress. There we had a house made of green lumber, which had been built for us in the fall before the snow came. A path had to be dug in the snow so we could get into the house and move in our belongings. We kept a big fire going to dry out the green lumber. We were occasionally startled by the cracking of the drying lumber. The house was a single-wall construction, just boards and bats, but we were lucky to have it. We had a wood stove in the kitchen and the living room, and a real bathtub that was very popular with our friends and neighbors who did not have one. A galvanized tub was all right in a tent in lieu of something better, but it was a poor substitute for a real bathtub.

There were many things to learn, and some of them I learned the hard way. Above all, the job came first. The men loved it. They did not work as men do now, with one eye on the clock. In fact, there wasn't any clock as far as I was concerned. My husband had to be on the job by 7 a.m., so we had

an early breakfast. He rarely came home for lunch, because he would be nearer some mess hall. He would come in for dinner when he got through, but by the time he had had a bath and a change of clothing, he was so tired after dinner that he usually fell asleep on the couch.

It sounds drab, but it wasn't. There was so much going on. The little railroad that brought the cars in from the electric hoist went right by our front door. I remember one day when the man who was supposed to run the hoist went to sleep on the job. One of the cars was practically wrapped around a big spindle around which the big cable was supposed to be wrapped. As the flatcar went by, I saw my husband on it, so I ran out and got aboard. He almost lost his job for that, so I learned to stay off flatcars. I had always wanted to go down on one of those cars 2,000 feet to Big Creek camp below, but after that I decided I had better not if we wanted to keep the job.

Dave had only $5 when we arrived in camp after our honeymoon, and I did not have much either. My father had tried to instill in me the necessity of saving money, but there were always so many ways to spend money that I had not profited too well by his instructions.

Life was pretty soft in those days. We got our wood and water and electricity and telephone for free. We bought our supplies from the commissary and, although our salary was only $100 a month, we began buying Liberty Bonds. We did not have a car; nobody did. In any case, my husband worked seven days a week and there wasn't any place to go anyway. We did have a canvas canoe which unfortunately was always getting holes in it because of the branches and old trees in the lake. We would go fishing when we had time. There were fish then that weren't too hard to catch.

It was at the time of World War I, and Dave was prepared to go into the service, that the Edison Company decided it would be better for him to take over the completion of the electric high line from Big Creek to Los Angeles. Dave told me that I could either go home or live in a hotel close by.

Dave and Edith on the Kern River, 1919, while working on the transmission line.
Redinger Family Album, from the Edison Collection

I said I would go with him and live in a tent. I had lived in a tent before when Father took us out to the beautiful blue lakes of Minnesota for summer vacations. It was hot in June in the San Joaquin Valley. A temperature of 112 degrees was not unusual. Still, with the flies of the tent open and a wet sheet on the floor and a good book to read, it wasn't too bad.

One day, as Dave was putting on his pants, I was startled to see him grab one side of his leg and shake out a scorpion. I killed the scorpion and did my best to suck out the poison, then gave him a belt of bootleg whiskey that had been sent surreptitiously by an eastern financier. Neither Dave nor I was used to drinking liquor of any kind.

At breakfast, we told the men about the encounter with the scorpion and the antidote that was used. The rest of the day they spent looking for a scorpion, so they, too, might have a dose of the same "medicine!"

A couple of other interesting incidents occurred while we were living in the tent. One morning early, one of the men came in to tell us that the cook had quit and that the men wanted to know where breakfast was coming from. I said that I would be there in ten minutes and that there would be "breakfast as usual." There was, and the men were all for giving me a permanent job, but Dave wasn't sold on the idea.

On another occasion, I was reading quietly with my dog Boh by my side. I saw a great big sow strolling towards the open tent fly, so I jumped upon the table and called Boh to my side. After having looked things over, the mean old pig ambled off to scavenge for food. Incidentally, Boh was a darling Australian shepherd puppy that I had picked up at a camp a little distance from where we were located. I called him Boh from one of Kipling's stories. He was my constant companion for years until he was shot, but that is another story.

One morning, the woman on whose farm our camp was located drove her span of horses and wagon into camp. During her visit, she told of her difficulty in getting help because of the war. Since I knew how to drive a team, I volunteered to help. The next day, she arrived in camp to pick me up and took me to the farm. But, instead of horses, she pointed me towards pots of steaming water and large piles of dirty clothes. Toward six in the evening when Dave arrived to pick me up, he was flabbergasted to find clothes everywhere, draped over fences and lines drying.

After the high line project was completed, we returned to Big Creek and to the house the Edison Company had ready for us. As we walked into the beautiful yard, I spotted a place behind the house that would be ideal for fruit trees—apples, cherries, pears, and maybe even grapes. However, my lord and master told me to forget it because no engineer stayed anywhere more than five years. Instead of arguing, I quietly placed an order for a dozen apple trees and some other saplings.

There were wood stoves in the kitchen and the dining room, so we were comfortable. All the boxes that had been in the extra tent were there to be unpacked. Beds had to be made on the sleeping porch. There was a small dressing room, a bathroom with a tub, etc., and a stairway leading to upstairs that had a room so we could sleep inside when it got colder. After the house had been put in order, I turned my attention to the garden and orchard. There was not much help to be had, but one man from the power house who had

The Redingers' Big Creek home in summer.
Redinger Family Album, from the Edison Collection

been there some time and had a real house and orchard lent me a kindly hand and some welcome advice.

With a little help from the available men, and wagonloads of horse manure from the Huntington Lake camp, my garden began to take shape. As soon as my plants started to germinate, I realized the necessity of putting up a fence to keep unwanted guests out.

Eventually more help was available, and a barbed-wire fence was put up around my garden. Although it was supposed to keep out intruders, a deer nevertheless found its way in every night and helped itself to the forbidden fruit. I told Dave that I would sleep out there that night to keep watch for the predator. Dave said that he would sleep out. I was sure that he would . . . sleep! So, my sleeping bag was brought out. I made myself comfortable and enjoyed the beautiful sky and the big tree that made a very nice shelter. I was on the verge of falling asleep when I was startled by a noise. I looked and found a beautiful deer ambling along in search of fresh vegetables. After a few well-chosen words, the deer took off to the spot where it could tip its head enough to get through the barbed wire, and off he went over the lawn on his last raid. The fence was mended the next day.

During our trip to China in 1927, 1 had become acquainted with Chinese peas and subsequently planted them. I made out a list of seeds that I wanted and sent to Fresno for them each spring.

A number of interesting things happened over the many years that I had my garden. I learned that root vegetables could stay in the ground under as much as four feet of snow without damage because the frost did not go very deep.

On one occasion, when the snow was deep, I asked Dave to dig down and get me some carrots. Agreeing to my request, he got out his snowshoes. Boy, the German shepherd, decided to go with him. He was used to catching a ride whenever he could on the end of the snowshoes. After Dave had dug

**Edith, apple trees and snow
behind the Big Creek house.**
*Redinger Family Album, from the
Edison Collection*

through the snow and earth to the level of the carrots, Boy was so absorbed in the goings-on that he leaned over a little too far and slid into the hole, and Dave had to dig out Boy as well as the carrots.

Our home had a wonderful basement with a concrete floor where we could store apples, squash, etc., indefinitely. The vegetables and fruit that wouldn't keep were canned and shared with friends and neighbors.

When the cherries began to ripen, I found I was not the only one interested in the fruit. Robins, too, shared my enthusiasm. If we were to get any fruit for ourselves, the trees would have to be protected. So I sent to Fresno for yards of mosquito netting to keep out the freeloaders. In this I was more or less successful, and we did have our cherries.

Beyond the orchard and across the road, we had a small building with a stall on one side for my horse, Kismet. The other side was used for chickens, with roosts and nests. They kept us supplied with fresh meat and eggs.

I recall the morning I asked Dave to get us a chicken for dinner. By the time the two had reached the house, they were fast friends and he could not bring himself to kill it. So off to the commissary it went to be cleaned and dressed.

One Sunday in the fall we went down the canyon to look at the place where the new power house was to be located. There were four of us, two engineers and their wives. While the engineers talked, we listened and tried to follow the plans they were discussing.

It was hard to visualize a big camp on the steep mountainside where we sat, with our feet propped against the boulders to keep us from sliding down the rushing stream at the bottom of the canyon hundreds of feet below us. It was such a nice, undisturbed hillside—all golden and brown and crackling in the fall sunshine—and the gorge below looked almost too narrow to hold a big powerhouse. Besides, we wondered what they would do with the all-important little creek that seemed to be so busy, and which we knew would be much busier and more important at certain times of the year.

It so happened that I went east shortly thereafter, and a short time elapsed before my next visit to the sunny hillside and the powerhouse site. In only a few weeks, the things that our engineering husbands had discussed had already come to pass or were well on the way. The hillside was no more an autumn idyll, gray-green manzanita with red stems, prickly deer brush, scrubby oaks and pines, but a tent city with the lower sides of the tents braced up on stilts, a camp of perhaps 500 men, with big mess halls, warehouses, and shops. And, instead of the little trail, a real honest-to-goodness road wound its way up the mountain to reduce the grade to enable the big trucks to negotiate the climb.

Down at the bottom of the canyon, there was no busy little creek; it had been picked up bodily and forced to flow, if at all, through a tunnel under the foot of the hill on the other side. It seemed to resent the ignominious treatment because it went growling into the tunnel and came out sputtering and fairly frothing at the mouth as it hurled itself into the river and lost its identity in the quiet deepness of the larger stream. Even the place where the little creek had been flowing for years was changed. It had been filled in and leveled and we could see where the new power house was to stand.

It seemed hardly as long as the first interval when we went down again and saw the almost-completed powerhouse, a big, white, dignified structure that, even beside the everlasting hills, seemed to have a majesty and permanence commensurate with the setting in which it was placed. The creek, released from its enforced journey through the temporary tunnel, seemed to have achieved a new sense of importance by helping to turn the big wheels that were grinding out the "juice" that was to be carried to the big city hundreds of miles away to help run the big electric trains and give comfort and convenience to millions who had never seen a powerhouse.

If my engineering husband were to see this, he would probably say that one would get no idea of the number of second-feet of water involved or the number of kilowatts turned out or the amount of money, time, and skill that had gone into the construction of this powerhouse, but this is a woman's eye view of the building of a tunnel, and "a woman is only a woman."

Having spent most of my time in three colleges studying food and nutrition, I was naturally interested in the foods used to feed 6,000 men at peak employment. The quality of the food varied, but with 30 mess halls in different locations, preparation had to be made for times when it was impossible to drive over roads, even with a dog team. It was wise to have laid in a good supply of everything. It should be borne in mind that we were working on a 17-mile tunnel from both ends at an elevation of several thousand feet, so provisions had to be brought up from the valley. They included carloads of potatoes and fresh meat on the hoof—driven up for summer grazing—to be fattened for slaughter in the fall in the slaughterhouse that had been built by the company. There was also a building where meat could be kept indefinitely. We had better meat there than was available in town. As I remember it, there were good cooks and plenty of good food. The men were voracious and hefty eaters and could put away a complete meal in eight minutes flat!

To save time, as the length of the tunnel increased, prepared food was served on covered flat railroad cars. Tables, chairs, hot food—everything the men could use was sent into the tunnel.

During the time the work was going on up there, the snow was so deep that we could see coyotes on the roof of a home belonging to the couple who spent the winters there. (They were stream gaugers.) Eventually, the crews working from both ends of the tunnel met. It was a moment of great satisfaction both for them and the company. I considered it a high privilege to be the only woman to witness this historic moment.

One day, Dave and one of the engineers went on an inspection trip after the completion of the tunnel. Dave, who was leading, stepped into a hole filled with water up to his neck. He came home soaked to the skin. Needless to say, repair followed.

One time, my niece, Marion, who was visiting us from the east, had expressed a desire for a rattlesnake skin belt. Kenneth, one of the young engineers who lived in one of the lower camps where they were more apt to have rattlesnakes, blew in and announced that he had a rattlesnake in the car. There were about a dozen of us just sitting down to the table for dinner, so I suggested his sitting down and having dinner with us and taking a look at the snake afterwards.

After dinner, Kenneth and Marion and I went out to the car and lifted the back and saw a newspaper wired closely at the top. Kenneth lifted the paper, but it was so light that we knew there was nothing in it. I suggested that we wait until morning when there was light. It seemed like a sensible idea, so the next morning we opened the car door and there the snake was, stretched out at the back under the chain . . . quite dead. We took it down and laid it on the stump of a big old tree that would make a perfect table.

While Kenneth and I were busy working on the snake, he said that he had always wanted to eat rattlesnake. There seemed to be no better time, so I called Evelyn, a young girl from the valley whom I had to help in the kitchen. I told her our idea, but she put her foot down. "Not in my kitchen," she said, so I said we would page the guests and those that did not want to eat rattlesnake could have a picnic and sandwiches outside. The plan worked, and we enjoyed the snake. I had been tempted to buy a can of rattlesnake, but it was too expensive.

Incidentally, the girl stayed with us until she married her boyfriend who had been in the service. We are still friends and she has children and grandchildren.

One time we had a visitor from Minnesota. He said that he would love to go in the lake since he was used to cold water. One day, when we were all down at the pier at Huntington Lake, this friend came running down in his bathing suit all ready for a dip in our southern waters. He dived in all right, but jumped right out and got dressed in a hurry. He had not reckoned with our icy waters. He confessed that the Minnesota streams were warm by comparison.

In 1927, Dave's supervisors insisted that he take time off and get out of the country so they could not get hold of him. Usually, when he was sent east on business, something would happen on the job and he would be summoned home.

With that order in hand, Dave came and asked where I would like to go. Without a second thought, I said, "China." It was possible then to go into any part of China we wanted to. Everything was relatively inexpensive. We were very fortunate to have picked up some Chinese treasures at bargain prices.

In the capital city of Peking, I was interested to find only one automobile belonging to an American family. When you wanted to go someplace, all you had to do was to step outside the door and summon a rickshaw by clapping your hands!

When we boarded the train going to the Great Wall, we were seated in the cab with the engineer. We were not unaccustomed to that mode of accommodation since we were quite familiar with the Big Creek railroad. We walked some distance on top of the Great Wall and, of course, we took some pictures.

The return trip was quite an experience because nobody knew when the train was coming. When it did come, we were loaded into a freight car that was very poorly lighted. A Chinese man, a total stranger, offered me his sack of beans to sit on. Now, that's what I call chivalry!

After four months in China and Japan, we decided to go home. The last

Edith and Dave in rickshaws during their China trip in 1927.
Redinger Family Album, from the Edison Collection

day in Japan, Dave went to the Men's Club in Tokyo, picked up a month-old American newspaper, and came across a story about a snow slide that had killed 14 people in a tunnel under construction between Huntington Lake and Shaver Lake. There was no way to get home in a hurry, since the only means of travel was by ship.

The memories of the trip so long ago are still vivid in my mind.

Through the years, friends and animals have occupied a special niche in our lives. It would be an oversight if I failed to mention some of the more unusual and interesting incidents.

One evening, we were having dinner with some friends whose table was in front of a plate glass window. Suddenly, we were startled to see a bear looking in hungrily.

Some friends had given us a beautiful Siamese cat with a mind of its own. It apparently preferred men to women. If I was busy at the stove or sink, it would come and nibble my ankles, demanding attention. I saw very little of it during the day, but when Dave appeared after work, he would be met at the gate by the cat. It would ride up to the house on his shoulders and wait for him to shower and change. After dinner, when Dave had settled in his big chair, it would drape itself across the back of the chair for the rest of the evening.

In front of the fireplace, we had a porch swing, seemingly put in for company to sit. After Boh, the dog in residence, had taken his evening walk, he would approach each visitor in turn "to talk all about it," placing his head on their laps.

It appeared that Boh understood the word "bath" as well as anybody, because when Dave mentioned "bath," Boh would quietly tiptoe out of the room. Dave knew that Boh was under his bed on the sleeping porch. He would talk to Boh until Boh could stand it no longer and the wagging of his tail would give him away.

I tried to bathe Boh in the bathtub. While Boh's bath was successful, I had to spend the rest of the morning cleaning up the bathroom. Later, we put his

The Redingers' house at Huntington Lake on January 25, 1952. The snow depth was 112 inches.
Redinger Family Album, from the Edison Collection

tub on the back porch. We would give his head and forequarters a thorough washing and rinsing, and then repeat the process for the hindquarters. We dried him thoroughly. After that, he would run on the front lawn with me in hot pursuit with his towel.

In the summer, we often spent quite a bit of time at our cabin at Huntington Lake, some five miles from Big Creek, taking the animals with us. The cat, which was in the habit of coming to Dave's window to get in, didn't appear one morning. When I went to the kitchen and looked out, there beside the stump was the cat, all stretched out and quite dead. Apparently it had eaten some poison put there by the forestry service for small rodents.

Most of the residents of Big Creek had pets of some sort. One family had the pleasure of entertaining and being entertained by a number of coons at dinner, on the back porch. They came every night and, as the word spread, their numbers increased until the family had to buy food by the sack!

At that time, I had a woman coming in to do housework. She always came in the back door, but one particular morning she went around the house and came up the front steps. Boh apparently resented it. He must have taken a nip on the sly. That night, Boh was shot and buried behind her house. Evidently, the boys at the construction site knew where Boh was buried. They brought him home and buried him in our lawn. A few days later, they planted a tree on his grave and brought me another puppy, this time a police dog.

One summer, we were allowed to use the cabin that was used in the winter for checking the precipitation. The cabin had the convenience of a cold shower, but if anyone wanted hot showers, he would have to walk a couple of miles to a temporary resort where hot baths were available.

The young woman who was helping us that summer had gone for an evening walk. She hurried back to camp much disturbed after seeing a rat-

The winter mail sled leaves the Big Creek post office during construction days.
Redinger Family Album, from the Edison Collection

tlesnake. We all decided to go and see if we could find it. I can still see in my mind's eye one of our young guests, high boots unlaced and flapping, leading the futile search for the elusive snake. This same young man, really a growing boy, could eat enough for two people at a regular meal. One day he went fishing with an older man and he packed their lunches. He said afterwards that that was the only time he had enough to eat!

The cabin was located at about 8,000 feet and the cold shower and sanitary provisions were adequate but primitive, consisting of several wooden structures commonly known as privies.

We did most of our cooking out-of-doors. Guests brought their tents and sleeping bags. At times we would have as many as 12 people. Dave, who was to be up only on weekends, would usually find an excuse to be there more often.

Before Dr. Herbert Stinchfield, the Chief Surgeon, passed away, he had asked to be cremated and his ashes scattered to the four winds. My nephew Ted and his wife Marion were visiting us from Kansas. Ted, a good Episcopalian, read the very moving and fitting Order for the Burial of the Dead:

> I am the resurrection and the life, saith the Lord; he that believeth in me, though he were dead, yet shall he live, and whosoever liveth and believeth in me shall never die. I know that my Redeemer liveth and that He shall stand at the latter day upon the earth: and though this body be destroyed, yet shall I see God: whom I shall see for myself, and mine eyes shall behold, and not as a stranger. We brought nothing into this world, and it is certain we can carry nothing out. The Lord giveth and the Lord hath taken away. Blessed be the name of the Lord.

It is always a question as to what to do after a busy life. After nearly 40 years with the Edison Company at Big Creek, California, Dave retired. He was asked to write *The Story of Big Creek,* which he did; it was originally published in 1949.

We then chose Laguna for our active retirement. We lived there about 15 years, traveling, making new friends and having old friends visit. Our life was very full.

We later moved to Laguna Hills, and finally to the Samarkand in Santa Barbara, California. We have lived here about six years.

In August, 1976, my beloved Dave died at the age of 92. I can only marvel at the changes that have taken place in our country. And I can truthfully say that I am thankful that I have lived my life in a less-complicated and gentler period.

XXVIII
Expansion of Big Creek
Since 1948

A N ARTICLE IN THE NOVEMBER 1947 issue of the *Edison News* reported the October 31, 1947, retirement of David Redinger:

One of the best known and best loved men in the Edison Company first entered service in August 1912 [but] his continuous service dates from March 16, 1916. His first work in 1912 was with a survey party in the driving of the tunnel from Big Creek No. I plant to West Portal [Tunnel No. 2]. From 1914 to 1916, during World War 1, when the company work on the Big Creek project was slowed down, he worked with the Bureau of Reclamation in Arizona.

From 1916 to 1920, he worked on the raising of the Huntington Lake Dams, survey work on the Big Creek transmission lines in the San Joaquin Valley, survey work in Evolution Valley, and tunnel work in connection with Kern River No. 3 construction. In 1920 he returned to Big Creek as assistant resident engineer. In 1921, he became resident engineer on the construction of the Big Creek project.

On July 1, 1929, at the completion of the construction work, he was made Division Superintendent, Northern Division Hydro, the position he held at the time of his retirement.

Even as the legendary Dave Redinger retired from active supervision of his beloved Big Creek power plants, plans were being made to add more generating capacity to the Big Creek Project. The unprecedented, and to some extent unexpected, surge in Southern California's population following World War II caused a corresponding increase in the demand for electricity. The Southern California Edison Company was faced with the need to begin a tremendous construction program to meet this demand. Not only were new generating plants needed, but new line construction as well, for much of the new growth was coming in the form of new housing tracts where only empty fields had been before.

Dave Redinger sits in front of Powerhouse No. 1, just days before his retirement in 1947. *Doug White Photo, from the Edison Collection*

BIRDSEYE VIEW
BIG CREEK-SAN JOAQUIN RIVER
Water Power Development
Of the
Southern California Edison Company

By 1924, rapidly growing energy needs in Southern and Central California caused Edison planners to expand the scope of the Big Creek development. Through 1943, the progressive construction of 18 powerhouses, along with new dams, reservoirs and conduits, was expected to raise the total output of the project to 1,957,091 horsepower (approximately 1,460,000 kilowatts). This "ultimate development" was killed by the Depression, the building of Hoover Dam, and the outbreak of World War II. Postwar construction did raise Big Creek's output to about 750,000 kilowatts by 1960.
Drawing from the Edison Collection

As recently as 1941, over 90 percent of the kilowatt hours sold by the Edison Company had been generated in hydroelectric plants, primarily those at Big Creek. Hydro power was preferred, of course, because of its lower cost compared to steam-generated electricity. So while new steam plants were a necessary part of the postwar expansion program, it was not surprising that the decision was made to develop more generating sites at Big Creek.

John Eastwood's original plans had called for four hydro plants to be built, stair-step fashion, down Big Creek and the South Fork of the San Joaquin River. Powerhouses No. 1, No. 2 and No. 3 were built in the locations Eastwood had originally stipulated. His proposed Powerhouse No. 4 had not been built, however. Eastwood had estimated the potential generating capacity of this site to be at least 67,000 horsepower (50,000 kilowatts).

Subsequently, other potential sites for generating plants had been located by Edison engineers. In a report dated 1922, four more sites were identified. Powerhouse No. 5 would be built at the outfall of a tunnel to be built between Huntington and Shaver Lakes. Powerhouse No. 6 was to be built on the banks of the South Fork of the San Joaquin River above a natural feature called Mammoth Pool. Powerhouse No. 7 was to be built further upstream from No. 6, and would receive its water from three small reservoirs at Chiquito, Jackass and Granite Meadows. Powerhouse No. 8, already in operation at the time this report was prepared, had been built at the junction of Big Creek and the San Joaquin River.

Further surveys later in the 1920s saw as many as 10 additional power plant sites identified on the upper reaches of the South Fork of the San Joaquin River and its tributaries. This so-called "West Side Development" had a total generating capacity of 309,500 horsepower (230,800 kilowatts). Federal licenses were obtained, and hydroelectric facilities would have been built at all of these sites had it not been for the onset of the Great Depression. The resulting decline in energy sales, plus financial retrenchment, caused the Edison Company to postpone the West Side Development in the early 1930s.

During the Great Depression, the federal government built Hoover Dam on the Colorado River. The Southern California Edison Company agreed to buy power from the finished dam, and to operate some of the generators for itself and other investor-owned utilities. This capacity from Hoover Dam was more than adequate for the company's needs, which provided another reason not to proceed with further construction at Big Creek in the late 1930s.

Southern California's electrical load picked up at the onset of World War II, but construction of new generation was severely curtailed by a lack of manpower and government restrictions on many vital materials. Additions to Big Creek were postponed for the duration of the war, and, in exchange, the federal government granted to Edison temporary increases in the share of energy received from Hoover Dam.

In 1948, however, construction crews reappeared at Big Creek for the first time since 1929. The first project undertaken was the addition of a fourth generator at Powerhouse No. 3. In anticipation of future needs, space for another generator had been left in the original building. All that was needed was to construct a new penstock and install the new water turbine and generator, along with related control equipment and new transformers.

This was a fairly straightforward project, but it was complicated by the fact that the old San Joaquin and Eastern Railroad had been scrapped in 1934. During the heyday of Big Creek construction, the railroad had carried with ease the huge volume of heavy materials required. With the railroad now only a memory, however, all of the new equipment for Unit No. 4 had to be carried by truck over tortuous mountain roads to Powerhouse No. 3. To accommodate these trucks, certain hairpin turns had to be widened. Several bridges had to be temporarily strengthened to support the massive weight of trucks carrying three 68-ton transformers and an 81-ton generator rotor. After months of construction work, Unit No. 4 at Powerhouse No. 3 began commercial operation on April 28, 1948.

Less than a year after the completion of this addition, the Southern California Edison Company filed applications with the (then) Federal Power Commission and the California Public Utilities Commission for the necessary licenses and permits to build a new dam and powerhouse below Powerhouse No. 3. The project proposed to build a concrete gravity dam 250 feet high that would impound water to operate a new two-unit, 84, 000-kilowatt, automatically operated generating station. Approval of this, the first major new construction at Big Creek in 20 years, was granted by the FPC on June 28, 1949.

Initial work on the project began in July 1949 under the supervision of resident construction engineer Paul B. Peecook, who reported to vice president Wallace L. Chadwick. The contractors were a consortium—of the Morrison-Knudsen and Bechtel Companies, and they were faced with a tough job, for Edison hoped to have the new units on-line by mid-1951. Such a goal was possible in part because of the major advances that had been made in heavy construction equipment in the decades since the 1920s, and in part because the lower altitude of the construction sites allowed work to go on year-round.

The first work completed was the construction of a temporary headquarters camp to house the force of 1,000 workmen hired by the contractors, as well as Edison's engineering and construction supervisory staff. The camp was erected on an oak tree-dotted hillside near the future site of the new dam, located several miles downriver from Powerhouse No. 3.

By October of 1949, a temporary cofferdam had been placed across the San Joaquin River to turn its waters through a diversion tunnel, away from the site of the foundations for new Dam No. 7. Following the clearing of the dam site, work began on the foundations, with the first concrete being placed on November 17.

At the same time, work began on the excavation of the two 24-foot-diameter tunnels that would carry water from the new reservoir to the Powerhouse. Progress on Power Tunnel No. 1 was rapid, but soft ground that required timbering slowed work on Power Tunnel No. 2. True to expecta-

The first postwar construction at Big Creek saw the installation of a long-planned fourth generator at Powerhouse No. 3. This 1948 view shows crews pouring a foundation for the new unit, which was housed inside the original powerhouse.
Doug White Photo, from the Edison Collection

By the fall of 1950, Dam No. 7 was nearing completion. This view looks upriver towards the new structure.
Photographer unknown, from the Edison Collection

tions, relatively mild winter weather enabled work on the project to continue at a rapid pace. On December 23, 1949, the 2,415-foot-long Power Tunnel No. 1 was "holed through" in the remarkable time of three months and one day! By the end of March, the reservoir site had been completely cleared of all trees and underbrush, and the dam itself was over 40 percent complete. Work had also begun on the foundations of the new powerhouse.

Through the summer and into the fall of 1950, work on the project continued at a furious pace, as all connected with the job, from supervisors to laborers, were caught up in the excitement of beating the calendar. Grizzled hard-rock miners cheered and celebrated as Power Tunnel No. 2 was holed through on September 22, after a last burst of effort that saw 239 feet of hard Sierra granite excavated in just six days. By this time, the Big Creek No. Four Project was some six months ahead of schedule.

Then, as if to scoff at these efforts, Mother Nature took charge. After a succession of dry winters, heavy rains hit the Central Sierras in November of 1950. Three days of hard rain on November 17, 18 and 19 brought flooding throughout the Central Sierras. All of Edison's hydro plants along the west side of the Sierra Nevada Range, from the Kern River to Big Creek, suffered to some degree. Big Creek Powerhouse No. 3 experienced the worst flooding in its history, as water from the San Joaquin River filled the power house from basement to turbine floor. At the new construction project downstream, floodwaters overtopped Dam No. 7 along its entire length, then rushed downriver to inundate the nearly completed Powerhouse No. 4. Superficial damage was suffered around the powerhouse, but no structural damage was done to either Dam No. 7 or Powerhouse No. 4.

Despite the fury of this, the worst flooding experienced along the San

Joaquin in decades, the construction project suffered only a temporary set-back. As soon as flood debris could be cleared away, and roads to the plant site stabilized, work began on installation of the two generating units. After months of work, the first of Big Creek No. 4's new generators was synchronized to the Edison system on June 12, 1951, and the second unit came online on July 2. To carry this new energy to Southern California, Edison construction crews had built over the previous two years a new 220,000-volt transmission line from Big Creek Powerhouse No. 4 to Magunden Substation in Kern County, and then through the Antelope Valley, over the San Gabriel Mountains and through San Gabriel Canyon to the new Mesa Substation in Monterey Park, a suburb east of Los Angeles. The cost of these major additions to the Big Creek generation and transmission system totaled $23 million, an investment of $252.75 per kilowatt of capacity gained. In fact, the construction of Big Creek No. 4 represented less than 15 percent of Edison's construction budget for the three years 1949 through 1951.

Even before the Big Creek No. 4 project was finished, Edison filed another application with the Federal Power Commission, seeking a license to build a dam and power house upstream from Big Creek No. 8 at Mammoth Pool. This was followed shortly by yet another application, this for a dam and reservoir at Vermilion Valley, a site high in the Sierra back country that had been considered for development in the twenties. The Vermilion Project's application received federal assent in 1953.

Explorations at Vermilion for a concrete dam site in 1924 revealed permeable soil lying too deep over bedrock to justify such a dam at that time, but advances in dam-building technology since that time indicated that an earthfill dam would be feasible. The unique design concept for the dam was developed by Thomas M. Leps, Edison's chief civil engineer, in consultation with Dr. Karl Terzaghi, at that time the leading international authority on earth dam design. Vermilion was the Edison Company's first earthfill dam, and it was seen to offer several advantages: it could be built cost effectively within the short construction season available at that high altitude, and it would be free of the spalling problem that plagued high-elevation concrete dams. (Spalling, the crumbling of the outer surface of a rock or a concrete structure, is induced by the alternate freezing and thawing of minute water droplets that have worked their way into tiny spaces inside the rock or concrete.) No power house was to be built in conjunction with Vermilion Dam, which was intended only to increase the storage of water available to the existing Big Creek plants, especially during dry years.

The dam site was accessible only over the old Kaiser Pass Road built by Edison in the early 1920s. The relatively short period of time available for construction, due to severe winter conditions at the 7,500-foot-high location, meant that work would have to be pressed on an accelerated schedule. Edison planned to have crews work from April to November, weather permitting, on two nine-hour shifts, six days a week. Harold Barber was Edison's resident engineer on this project, and Bechtel Corporation was selected as prime contractor.

Work in the Vermilion Valley began on April 18, 1953, with the construction of living quarters and administrative offices. Due to the isolated location of the project, some workers brought their families to live at the camp. Mrs. Margaret Barnes and Mrs. Janet Meyer, both wives of Bechtel engineers, taught the 18 school-age children living at the camp.

Small independent loggers, called "gyppos" in the lumber industry, were hired to clear the timber in the basin to be inundated by the reservoir, while work began on the foundations for Vermilion Dam. The site had everything needed to build an earthfill dam: large deposits of impervious silty soil, ideal for constructing the water-resisting core of the dam; and soil and rock to form the outer layers of the dam. The Kaiser Pass road was improved and large earth-moving equipment was brought in to the site to begin the long task of loading, hauling, spreading and compacting the fill in the dam.

A great amount of work was achieved in that first season of work. In addition to establishing the camp and clearing the site, a concrete outlet conduit through the base of the dam was built, by which the outflow from the reservoir would be controlled. Between June 16 and November 10, 1953, heavy equipment crews placed over two million cubic yards of material, bringing the growing dam to some 40 percent of its final size. By the time winter snows shut down "Project Vermilion" in November, work was ahead of schedule.

Snowplows cleared the road over 9,300-foot-high Kaiser Pass early in April of 1954 to enable construction at the site to resume. As snow melted and the ground thawed, the procession of earth-moving trucks picked up where they had stopped the previous year. In order to meet the tight schedule, it was necessary to place an average of 23,400 cubic yards of embankment and upstream impervious blanket material daily.

By September 25, 1954, 4.9 million cubic yards had been placed and compacted, with only 400,000 yards remaining to finish the dam. With an early winter threatening to shut down the project, the construction crews raced against time to wind up the work before the first big snowfall. The dam was finished early in October, and finishing touches completed by the first week in November. The total cost of Project Vermilion was $8.65 million.

In a ceremony on October 19, 1954, Southern California Edison's president and chief executive officer, Harold Quinton, dedicated the dam and unveiled a commemorative plaque. Inasmuch as the dam was completed on the 75th anniversary of the invention of the electric light bulb, the reservoir behind Vermilion Dam was named in honor of Thomas A. Edison. President Quinton reminded the audience of the great inventor's pioneering contributions to the electric utility industry, and pointed out that this same pioneering spirit marked the history of the Edison Company's development of the Big Creek hydroelectric project.

A year later, on October 24, 1955, that pioneering spirit was remembered in a more tangible way, with a special honor given to "Mr. Big Creek," David Redinger. After his retirement in 1947, Dave had written this history of the Big Creek Project, first published in 1949. To generations of Edison men and women, Dave Redinger was an integral part of this famous hydroelectric project. To symbolize this special relationship, in 1955 the company received permission from governmental authorities to name the reservoir impounded behind Dam No. 7 "David H. Redinger Lake."

Late in the summer of 1954, Vermilion Dam was nearly complete.
Photographer unknown, from the Edison Collection

The naming of facilities for company employees is a rare honor. Three company substations, Lighthipe, Barre and Hinson, carry the names of early Edison electrical engineers (James A. Lighthipe, Herbert A. Barre and Noel B. Hinson); the Poole Hydroelectric Plant is named for Charles O. Pole, chief engineer of one of Edison's predecessor companies; Ward Tunnel is named for George C. Ward; and Huntington Lake for Henry Huntington. In every case except the last, however, the honor was a posthumous one, but this precedent was broken for Dave Redinger.

In a speech at the dedication ceremony, United States Senator Thomas H. Kuchel paid tribute to Dave Redinger as a "real builder of California." The whole thing was a little overwhelming for the modest Redinger, who nonetheless entertained an after-dinner audience of Big Creek area employees and invited guests with anecdotes of Big Creek's early days, stories that appear in the early chapters of this volume.

By the mid-1950s, steam generation was by a considerable margin the major source of electricity for Edison customers. Hydro continued to be an important resource, however, still supplying around 25 percent of the company's needs, and it remained the most economical method of generation. Because of this cost-effectiveness, Edison wished to build more hydro plants, to the extent sites were available. Unfortunately, the company's application to the Federal Power Commission to build the Mammoth Pool

On October 19, 1954, Edison's president, Harold Quinton, spoke at the dedication of Vermilion Dam, naming the new reservoir for Thomas A. Edison. Dave Redinger is seated second from left.
Photographer unknown, from the Edison Collection

Dave and Edith (Dee) Redinger admire the plaque commemorating the naming of the reservoir behind Dam No. 7 "Redinger Lake."
Joseph O. Fadler Photo, from the Edison Collection

Project, first filed in June of 1951, had been repeatedly delayed. In the 1955 annual report, Edison management for the first time stated that, aside from Mammoth Pool, further large-scale hydro developments were unlikely in the future, pointing out "the company is already utilizing most of the sites which are economically feasible for hydroelectric development...."

While waiting for the Mammoth Pool project to wind its way through the halls of Washington, Edison engineers took a fresh look at a long-ignored generation site. Some of the plans for the Big Creek Project prepared back in the twenties had proposed the construction of a small generating plant at the outfall of the Florence Lake (Ward) Tunnel, but nothing had ever been done. In 1954, however, the company filed with the FPC for permission to build a facility at this location. The additional volume of water coming down the tunnel as a result of the completion of Vermilion Dam, plus the development of more efficient Francis-type reaction turbines, meant that a small

power plant at this location could be cost-effective. Construction of the Portal Powerhouse began in 1955, and was completed in December of 1956. This small, 10,000-kilowatt facility was different from any built previously at Big Creek, in that it was an outdoor design, built open to the weather. The plant was entirely automatic in operation, being controlled remotely from Big Creek Powerhouse No. 1. Portal's output feeds directly into a 33,000-volt distribution line originating at Powerhouse No. 1 that supplies customers around the Huntington Lake area.

Edison's negotiations with the Federal Power Commission to construct the long-delayed Mammoth Pool project extended into 1957. Finally, on December 30, 1957, the Commission granted Edison permission to begin work. By this time, most in the company believed that Mammoth Pool would be the "last hurrah" for major construction at Big Creek, so the project received widespread coverage in the media. Ralph W. Spencer, manager of engineering, was project engineer, and Harold Barber was Edison's resident engineer. Bechtel Corporation was awarded the prime construction contract for the dam and powerhouse, Utah Construction Company won the bid for the power tunnel work, and the diversion tunnel around the dam site was driven by a joint venture of Macco-Morrison and Knudsen-Kaiser-Shea.

Early in the spring of 1958, work began at the dam site, several miles up the South Fork of the San Joaquin River from the junction of Big Creek. Roads were cut into the area, and a construction camp set up. To provide electricity to the temporary construction camp, helicopters were used to fly in and set poles, after which ground crews borrowed from the Ontario and San Joaquin Valley Districts strung wire back to the dam site.

On May 13, hard-rock drillers completed a 2,150-foot-long, 28-foot-

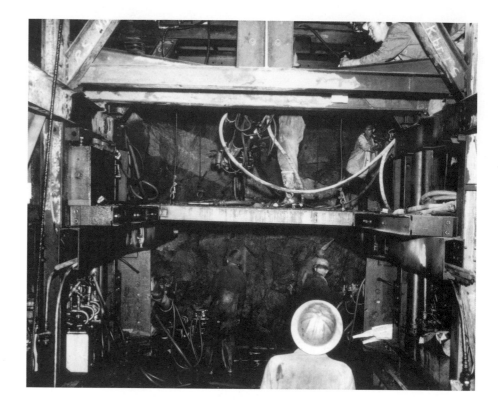

diameter diversion tunnel, dug at a pace of over 50 feet per day! The San Joaquin River was diverted through this tunnel on May 25, enabling work to begin on the foundations of the dam. Boulders, gravel and debris had to be cleared away and the riverbed excavated to a depth of over 100 feet to expose the solid granite bedrock. Just as at Vermilion, independent logging contractors were called in to clear the reservoir site of timber, after which all underbrush was removed.

While this clearing work was in progress, Utah Construction began the excavation of the eight-mile-long, 20-foot-diameter power tunnel that would carry water from the new reservoir to the new powerhouse down river. As early as June of 1958, over 700 men were employed on this phase of the project. In some ways, this tunneling effort had the appearance of the earlier tunnel jobs at Big Creek, but there were significant improvements. A giant drilling platform, nicknamed "Jumbo," had three decks from which operated a total of 11 compressed-air rock drills. After each dynamite blast, the tunnel muck was loaded onto railroad cars to be hauled out of the tunnel and deposited in dumps. Much of this excavated material was used in the construction of the dam.

Just as on the Florence Lake (Ward) Tunnel project in the early twenties, the Mammoth Pool Project's tunnel crews were very much aware of the speed at which they were excavating. Each of the three shifts competed to establish new records, as work went on around the clock, six days a week. For the week ending January 31, 1959, a crew under the supervision of Paddy O'Dowd gouged out 390 feet, which established a new world's record for a 20-foot-diameter tunnel through hard rock.

While the tunnel was being driven at this furious pace, work had begun on the new dam. Once again, Edison engineers had chosen to build an earth-fill dam, one that would be among the highest in the world at that time. Bechtel kept a force of 550 men busy on the project. Huge earth movers, bulldozers, dump trucks, shovels, graders and other types of specialized construction equipment kept loading, hauling, dumping and compacting around the clock. At times, the embankment surface at the dam resembled a freeway in rush hour, as the big trucks lumbered downhill from the borrow area by Chiquito Creek and sped out onto the fill.

Mammoth Pool Dam was designed with eight different zones of earth and gravel material, each carefully selected, placed and compacted to provide overall stability to the dam. At 11 a.m. on Saturday, October 17, 1959, a heavy-duty dump truck labored up the construction road and onto the crest of the dam, and deposited its load. A sign on the side of the truck announced that it contained the 5,154,650th, and last, load of fill material. A total of 5.5 million cubic yards had been placed to bring the dam to its finished height of 330 feet, about the height of a 30-story building.

Work had already begun on the new Mammoth Pool Powerhouse downstream. Based on the experience gained with Portal Powerhouse, Mammoth Pool was also built as an outdoor facility, to be operated remotely via a microwave link to Big Creek Powerhouse No. 8. Two Francis-type reaction turbines were installed, and the plant became operational on March 28, 1960. Exclusive of transmission lines, the Mammoth Pool Project cost $49.2 million.

After the completion of Mammoth Pool, as had been predicted by many, no more major construction projects were forecast for the Big Creek project, although minor upgrading work continued. During the fifties and sixties, the efficiency of the existing plants was improved as new transmission, metering and control equipment was installed, and improved operational techniques adopted. By 1960, Big Creek was pouring an annual average of between three and four billion kilowatt hours of energy into Edison's power grid, but the proportion of hydroelectric power to steam-generated power continued to drop, as California's economy boomed and the per-capita use of electricity increased.

During the postwar era, the general public began to seek easier access to mountain areas for recreation. As various portions of the Big Creek Project came up for license renewal, Edison was required to provide camping facilities at, and access to, several of its reservoirs. One result was the construction of Camp Edison at Shaver Lake, a campground that provided electric outlets and hot water in the showers! When licenses for Florence and Shaver lakes came up for renewal in 1971, Edison negotiated a complex agreement with the Forest Service and the California Department of Fish and Game as part of its relicensing application with the Federal Power Commission. Under this agreement, the company added nearly 1,000 new camping and day-use accommodations in areas around both lakes, and agreed to release more water to enhance fish life downstream from the two dams. In addition, boat-launching facilities, new hiking trails, and a new Visitors Information Center were provided by the company. These facilities were of benefit to all users of the national forest, and demonstrated that the Edison Company was

While the power tunnel was being driven through hard Sierra granite, a long procession of earth-moving equipment carried on the process of building the earth-fill dam across the San Joaquin River.
Joseph O. Fadler Photo, from the Edison Collection

Work on Mammoth Pool Dam went on around the clock. Photographer Joseph Fadler, renowned for his night pictures, took this dramatic view of the dam in the early stages of construction, in November of 1958.
Joseph O. Fadler Photo, from the Edison Collection

willing to strike an equitable balance between recreational and environmental needs, and the continuing need to generate low-cost hydroelectric power.

The decade of the seventies saw electric costs soar due to fuel shortages and rampant inflation, and sent Edison engineers back to the drawing boards to see if any more kilowatts could be squeezed from Big Creek's "hardest-working water in the world." On September 15, 1977, Edison announced that a fifth penstock, a new turbine and generator, and associated control equipment would be added at Big Creek Powerhouse No. 3, at a cost of $17 million. Due to improvements in generator design since the plant's earlier units had been installed, the new generator could produce 35,000 kilowatts of electric energy, as opposed to 30,000 kilowatts from each of the oldest machines. The new unit, engineered and constructed entirely by Edison forces, went on-line on February 24, 1980.

By this time, the Edison Company was deeply committed to utilizing alternative and renewable generation technologies, such as hydro, which could generate power without depleting expensive fossil fuel resources. With this in mind, the company explored several sites for new hydro plants that could make significant additions of hydroelectric power. One site was on Dinkey Creek, east of Shaver Lake, and another was on the South Fork of the San Joaquin River, above Mammoth Pool. Reflecting changes in the political and regulatory climate, both projects were to be owned by public agencies, who would sell all the electricity they generated to Edison. Despite prolonged discussions among various interested parties, to date neither of these projects has taken shape.

At the start of the decade of the 1980s, a new complexity entered the story of hydroelectric power. For years, electric utilities owned by cities, public utility districts, and other types of government agencies had been given preference in the licensing of new hydroelectric plants. Most such public entities, however, were unable, or unwilling, to raise the large sums needed to build big power projects. Traditionally, therefore, there had been little competition in the licensing of hydroelectric projects.

With the spiraling cost of fossil fuels in the seventies, however, this picture began to change, as small publicly owned power systems sought to minimize rate increases by capturing for themselves larger supplies of inexpensive hydro power. Soon this took the form of municipalities arguing for the first time that the municipal preference concept applied not only on original licensing, but also when constructed projects came up for relicensing. Two of Edison's hydroelectric projects were immediately impacted, and, because several of the Big Creek plants were due for relicensing by the end of the decade, the integrity of this entire complex, built and paid for through the free enterprise system, was jeopardized. For six tumultuous years, investor-owned utilities were forced to defend their continued ownership of hydroelectric resources against the onslaughts of public power agencies, many of which had never previously been in the electric power generation business. Finally, Congress passed the Electric Consumers Protection Act, which was signed by President Ronald Reagan on October 16, 1986. The passage of this act resolved the relicensing issue by making it clear that there is no municipal preference in the relicensing of existing hydroelectric facilities.

Edison engineers and planners recognized that hydroelectric resources were all the more desirable in an era of high fuel costs. Despite earlier predictions that no further large hydro sites remained at Big Creek, on September 14, 1978, the Southern California Edison Company filed with the Federal Energy Regulatory Commission (the former Federal Power Commission) to build a 140,000-kilowatt addition to the Big Creek Project. Named the Balsam Meadow Project, the plan called for the installation of a generating plant near the outfall of the existing Huntington-Pitman-Shaver Conduit above Shaver Lake. This was a modern, more efficient version of the old Plant No. 5 proposed back in the 1920s. Due to the increased efficiency of new hydro turbines, coupled with the high cost of electricity generated by fossil fuels, the Balsam Meadow Project seemed to be a logical addition to the existing Big Creek system.

Unfortunately, the Balsam Meadow proposal ran headlong into the midst of the relicensing controversy. The cities of Riverside and Anaheim, whose municipal power systems for decades had purchased energy from Edison, filed competing applications with the Federal Energy Regulatory

The opening of Camp Edison at Shaver Lake in the early 1960s provided improved camping facilities for the growing number of recreational visitors to the Big Creek area.
Arthur Adams Photo, from the Edison Collection

Unit No. 5 in Powerhouse No. 3 was completed in 1980. Although slightly smaller than its older companions in the background, it has a higher-rated output.
Photographer unknown, from the Edison Collection

Commission (FERC) to build the plant. Enmeshed as it was in the bitter controversy over relicensing, it took the FERC until October of 1983 to reach a decision, but the agency finally granted a license to Edison.

Edison's proposals for Balsam Meadow were impressive. To minimize the impact upon the environment, Edison planned to build the power station underground. In addition, certain alpine meadowlands that would be used during construction were to be completely restored after construction was finished. Fish habitats in Shaver Lake were to be augmented by a new artificial reef. Upon completion of construction, the new Balsam Meadow Forebay and a small surface switchyard and transmission line would be the only visible changes to the environment.

Following the traditions of the 1920s, Edison decided to manage the project through its own Engineering and Construction Department. Don Brundage was the site construction manager, reporting to Edison's project manager Bill Emrich. Dillingham-Atkinson, a joint venture of Dillingham Construction and the Guy F. Atkinson Company, was awarded the contract for the general civil construction work. In authorizing financing for the project, the California Public Utilities Commission took the unusual step of placing a strict cap of $321 million upon the work. Before final approvals were received and construction began, one major change had come about as the result of Edison's need for more peaking capacity. What had originally been planned as a 140,000-kilowatt unit was now to be built as a 200,000-kilowatt unit.

Construction work began in November of 1983, only to be briefly delayed by a last-minute court challenge from a small environmentalist group. In the spring and summer of 1984, work crews caught back up to schedule and pressed ahead with the 24,000 feet of tunnels and shafts required, including a new 5,500-foot tunnel to divert water from the existing Huntington-Shaver Tunnel No. 7 into the new Balsam Meadow Forebay; a small holding reservoir; a 3,000-foot upper power tunnel; a 1,000-foot vertical power shaft; a 1,000-foot lower power tunnel; the 15,000-square-foot Powerhouse and associated access tunnel and shafts; and a 7,500-foot tailrace tunnel. Altogether, some 650,000 cubic yards of granite were to be removed.

By March of 1985, work on the Powerhouse had progressed far enough to begin the delicate task of erecting the massive overhead crane.

This crane, running on a track laid on the long parallel walls of the chamber, would be used during construction to erect the turbine and generator, and later on for plant maintenance. A fleet of nine trucks, including three specially designed carriers, brought the crane components to the plant site, via Route 168, a tortuous mountain highway. The crane's two transverse girders, each 80 feet long, 12 feet 4 inches high and weighing 101,000 pounds, and the traverser trolley, weighing 75,000 pounds, were the first major components to be delivered to the project.

One feature of the Balsam Meadow Project that drew attention in the trade press was the drilling of the 1,000-foot vertical power shaft. This shaft was, in effect, the beginning of the "penstock" for the plant. Work began by drilling a 12-inch hole from a chamber at the end of the upper power tunnel down to a similar chamber at the end of the lower power tunnel. Then, using this hole, a special boring machine was pulled up from the lower to the upper tunnel, excavating a 13-1/2-foot-diameter shaft as it went. Three other shafts—the surge shaft, the elevator shaft and the powerhouse ventilation shaft—were also excavated using this technology.

During May of 1984, the miners working on the Balsam Meadow project smashed a long-standing record for hard-rock tunneling. Using advanced equipment and explosives, the miners excavated 1,051 feet of granite in only 22 working days, and from a tunnel larger in diameter than the old Ward Tunnel! Although weekly excavation records set during the Ward Tunnel project had been exceeded on both the Big Creek No. 4 and the Mammoth Pool Projects, the famed monthly record of 692 feet through hard granite had stood until this effort.

A major project milestone was reached just before Christmas of 1985, when hard rock miners "holed through" the 7,500-foot-long tailrace tunnel, completing the tunnel excavation work on the project. By now in their third winter of work at Balsam Meadow, the men took a brief pause for a symbolic ceremony that took place hundreds of feet below the snow-covered ground of the Sierra Nevada.

During 1985, the Edison Company decided to utilize recent advances in turbine and generator design to add as many as five new units at existing sites. Dubbed the "Big Creek Expansion Project," or "BiCEP," the $560 million project would include drilling a new 28,000-foot tunnel and enlarging the diameter of an existing 13,900-foot tunnel. "BiCEP" would raise the output of the Big Creek Project by 500,000 kilowatts, and would require a new transmission line to carry energy to Edison's major load centers.

Compare this picture of drillers working on a granite outcrop in 1985, with the photo on page 30. Although the technology is generally the same, the old "rock spiders" of 1913 have been replaced by mobile, high-capacity drills requiring only a two-man crew.
Don J. Nunes Photo, from the Edison Collection

December 1983 saw work begin on the Access Tunnel, the first tunnel for the Balsam Meadow Project. This picture by project employee Don Nunes shows placing of the first steel "sets," bracing to support the weaker, weathered rock found at the surface end of the tunnel.
Don J. Nunes Photo, from the Edison Collection

The crane lifts the 105-ton "turbine shutoff valve" off its transporter trailer inside the power station, in preparation to place it into its final location. This massive valve is used to close off the pipe carrying water from the power tunnels into the turbine, primarily whenever maintenance work must be performed on the turbine or generator.
Don J. Nunes Photo, from the Edison Collection

Also at this time, Edison decided to file an amendment to its original FERC license to enable the Balsam Meadow plant to be used as a "pumped storage" facility, whereby water flowing down from the Balsam Meadow Forebay to generate electricity during the day could be pumped back up from Shaver Lake at night, to be reused for power generation the following day. This feature had been proposed as part of the original project in 1978, and the tunneling had been designed with this capability in mind, but a decision to install the extra machinery had been delayed.

Late in 1986, Edison's chairman and chief executive officer Howard P. Allen announced that Balsam Meadow's underground powerhouse would be named in honor of the man who started it all, John Samuel Eastwood. This is a significant honor, for the original plan to harness the waters of Big Creek was Eastwood's, and his genius as an engineer has brought great benefit to generations of Californians. No more fitting tribute to John Eastwood could be made than to name for him the most modern and skillfully engineered hydroelectric plant in the system that he first envisioned nearly 90 years ago.

Were both Dave Redinger and John Eastwood alive today, they would be pleased at how "their project" has kept pace with improvements in technology to supply ever greater quantities of inexpensive hydroelectric power. For these two great engineers, for the legion of men and women who toiled to bring Big Creek into being, and for those who have kept it running smoothly over decades of change, there is no better monument than the Big Creek Powerhouses, with their spinning generators producing energy to meet the needs of' the people of' Central and Southern California.

On March 28, 1985, the first of the two massive girders for the overhead crane in Balsam Meadow's underground power-house was raised into position. The completion of this crane was a major milestone in the Balsam Meadow Project, for it would be used to install the power station's heavy components.
Don J. Nunes Photo, from the Edison Collection

In December 1985, the Balsam Meadow Project reached its halfway mark with the "holing through" of the Trailrace Tunnel. Surrounded by solid granite 400 feet below the snow-covered Sierras, Edison's Balsam Meadow project manager Don Brundage (right), congratulates Dillingham-Atkinson project manager Richard L. Kunz on completion of the project's final tunneling work.
Mark Solomon Photo, from the Edison Collection

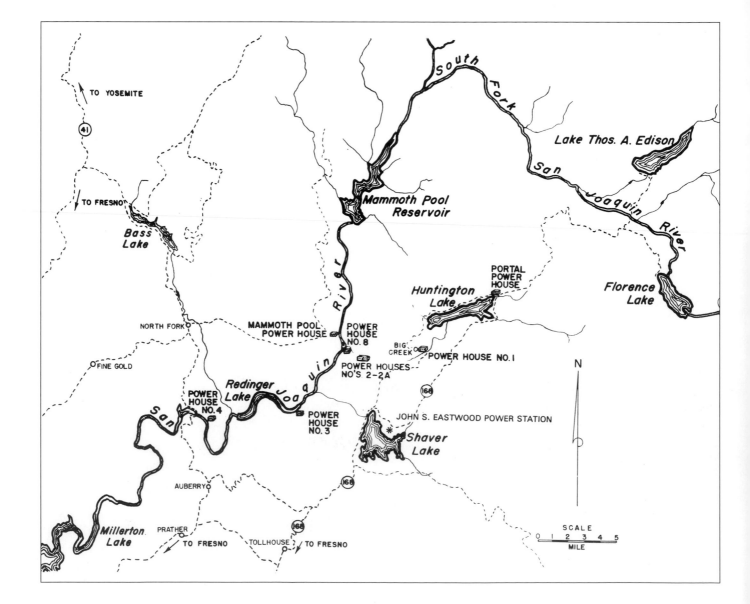

TO YOSEMITE

41

TO FRESNO

Bass
Lake

NORTH FORK

FINE GOLD

San

Redinger
Lake

POWER
HOUSE
NO. 4

POWER
HOUSE
NO. 3

AUBERRY

Millerton
Lake

PRATHER

TO FRESNO

TOLLHOUSE

TO FRESNO

166

South Fork

Lake Thos. A. Edison

San

Joaquin

River

Mammoth Pool
Reservoir

MAMMOTH POOL
POWER HOUSE

POWER
HOUSE
NO. 8

POWER HOUSES
NO'S 2-2A

BIG
CREEK

PORTAL
POWER
HOUSE

Huntington
Lake

POWER HOUSE NO. 1

166

JOHN S. EASTWOOD POWER STATION

Shaver
Lake

Florence
Lake

Joaquin

River

N

SCALE
0 1 2 3 4 5
MILE

Appendix

REFERENCE GUIDE TO
THE BIG CREEK PROJECT

T HE BIG CREEK–SAN JOAQUIN RIVER hydroelectric development
of the Southern California Edison Company is located on the western side
of California's great Sierra Nevada mountain range. The system is a com-
posite of man-made lakes, long tunnels, steel penstocks and power houses
that convert the force of falling water into electricity.

About 80 percent of a normal season's precipitation, in the form of rain
and snow, falls between December and March. The greatest part of the
"runoff" water, caused by the melting of the snow pack at the higher elevations, swells the region's streams and rivers from April to July. Because the
stream flow is so seasonal, dams and reservoirs are needed to regulate the
water supply. These reservoirs, in addition to storing water for electric generation, also provide flood control and irrigation benefits to communities in
the San Joaquin Valley below.

The total rated capacity of the Big Creek Project at time of publication
(1986), is 684,930 kilowatts, although the 22 units located in the project's
eight power houses are actually capable of producing a dependable output of
about 788,115 kilowatts. Historically, the Big Creek Project has supplied a
substantial portion of the electric energy used by customers of the Southern
California Edison Company. As recently as 1941, over 90 percent of all kilowatt hours sold were generated at hydro plants. Since then the share of hydro
power has declined, but as recently as 1985, the Big Creek plants produced
slightly more than 3.5 billion kilowatt hours of low-cost electrical power
annually for customers of Southern California Edison Company.

This remarkable amount of generation is achieved from a relatively small
amount of water. In a vertical fall of about 6,200 feet through Big Creek's
system of reservoirs, tunnels and pipelines, the water from melting snow is
used again and again to spin generators in powerhouses at successively
lower elevations. This efficient reuse of water as it cascades stair-step fashion down the system was the genius of John Eastwood's original plan, which
was expanded upon by subsequent generations of Edison engineers.

Each major component of the Big Creek–San Joaquin River hydroelectric development is described in the following. Note that the electrical output of each generator is described by its "rated capacity," usually that listed
on its nameplate. This figure is nominal and is frequently exceeded under
favorable conditions of temperature and water supply.

**This map shows the powerhouses
and main reservoirs on the Big
Creek Project as of 1986. Not
shown are the tunnels and
conduits that transfer water
between reservoirs.**
Drawing from the Edison Collection

Lake Thomas A. Edison and the upstream side of Vermilion Dam, October 1955.
Joseph 0. Fadler Photo, from the Edison Collection

The Mono Creek Dam is one of two small dams on the Mono-Bear Siphon. This picture was taken in 1985.
Greg O'Loughlin Photo, from the Edison Collection

Lake Thomas A. Edison

Lake Thomas A. Edison was completed late in 1954 by the construction of Vermilion Dam across Mono Creek, a tributary of the South Fork of the San Joaquin River. Because the project was completed on the seventy-fifth anniversary of the invention of the electric light, it was named for famed inventor Thomas Alva Edison. The dam is of the earth-fill type, 165 feet high, and 4,234 feet along its crest. The lake has a storage capacity of 125,035 acre-feet of water and is the highest in the Big Creek chain, with a spillway elevation of 7,642 feet. Water impounded in this lake travels down Mono Creek into the Mono-Bear Siphon, which diverts it into Ward Tunnel and thence into Huntington Lake.

Mono-Bear Siphon

The Mono-Bear Siphon consists of two small dams, one across Mono Creek and the other across Bear Creek; two lengths of tunnel; and a steel pipe conduit which carries the water impounded by these two dams into Ward Tunnel. This project was completed in November of 1927 after only two seasons of work. The two dams, each with a spillway elevation of 7,350 feet, divert water from tributaries of the South Fork of the San Joaquin River into tunnels which flow into steel pipelines that join together to form a single, large-diameter pipe that crosses the South Fork of the San Joaquin River as an inverted siphon. The pipe then climbs up the opposite wall of the valley and enters the Ward Tunnel at an elevation of about 7,100 feet, through an old adit remaining from construction days. By means of this ingenious siphon, water can be diverted into Huntington Lake from Lake Thomas A. Edison, Mono Creek and Bear Creek.

Florence Lake

Florence Lake Reservoir, with a drainage area of 171 square miles and a storage capacity of 64,406 acre-feet, was created by the construction of a dam across the South Fork of the San Joaquin River. The origin of the name Florence is uncertain, but is believed to have been the daughter of a local cattleman named Starr. Florence Lake Dam was built to the unique multiple-arch concrete design pioneered by John Eastwood. It rises a maximum of 154 feet above the stream bed, and is 3,156 feet along its crest. It required 56,000 cubic yards of concrete to build the structure, which was completed in August of 1926 after only two seasons of work. The spillway of Florence Lake is at an elevation of 7,327 feet, and the water stored in the reservoir is diverted into Huntington Lake by means of the Ward (Florence Lake) Tunnel.

Ward Tunnel (Florence Lake Tunnel)

The Ward Tunnel, originally known as Florence Lake Tunnel, was the major tunneling job completed at Big Creek in the 1920s. The 67,620-foot (13.5-mile) long tunnel was blasted through the hard granite of Kaiser Ridge in a record time of four and a half years. Built to a diameter of 15 feet, it diverts water from the South Fork of the San Joaquin River at Florence Lake, into Huntington Lake, and is capable of carrying 2,500 cubic feet of water per second. Its intake is at the western end of Florence Lake Dam, at an elevation of 7,220 feet. The tunnel carried its first water down into Huntington Lake on April 13, 1925. It was officially renamed in honor of Edison's late president, George C. Ward, on August 26, 1936.

Portal Forebay (Camp 61 Lake)

Portal Forebay is a small man-made lake completed in 1956, situated on the eastern slope of Kaiser Ridge astride Ward Tunnel. It lies about midway between Florence Lake and Huntington Lake, at an elevation of 7,180 feet. It has a surface area of 20 acres and a holding capacity of 330 acre-feet. It serves as a holding forebay for the Portal Powerhouse, located at the outlet of Ward Tunnel. During excavation of the tunnel, a major construction camp, No. 61, was located at this site, thus the alternate name of the lake.

Portal Powerhouse

Portal Powerhouse is the highest in the Big Creek chain, located at an elevation of 6,952 feet, at the outlet of Ward Tunnel. Its single generator, rated at 10,000 kilowatts, is powered by a vertical Francis-type reaction turbine, operating on a static head of 230 feet. The plant went into operation on December 22, 1956, and was the first on the Big Creek system to be operated unmanned, via remote "supervisory control" from Big Creek Powerhouse No. 1.

Huntington Lake

Huntington Lake Reservoir, with a drainage area of 80 square miles, was the first reservoir built as part of the "Initial Development" at Big Creek in 1911-13. It is named for Henry Edwards Huntington, the Southern California entrepreneur who financed the earliest work at Big Creek. Originally created by the construction of three dams (nos. 1, 2 and 3), Huntington Lake was enlarged in 1917-18 by the raising of those dams, and by the construction of an additional dam, No. 3A. As a result of this work, the reservoir presently has a storage capacity of 89,166 acre-feet. The four concrete gravity arch dams impounding the lake have a total length of 4,126 feet. The spillway is located at an elevation of 6,950 feet. Water from this reservoir can be sent either by Tunnel No. 1, conduit and penstock to Powerhouse No. 1 at Big Creek; or by the Huntington-Pitman-Shaver Conduit into Shaver Lake Reservoir.

Big Creek Powerhouse No. 1

This powerhouse, located at an elevation of 4,819 feet at the town of Big Creek, was the first on the Big Creek Project to be placed into commercial operation. Unit No. 2 sent energy south to Southern California on November 8, 1913. The plant's three other units were completed as follows: Unit No. 1 on November 9, 1913; Unit No. 3 on July 12, 1923; and Unit No. 4 on June 8, 1925. Each of these generators is powered by individual double overhung impulse turbines of the "Pelton" water-wheel type, all of which operate on a static head of 2,131 feet, provided by water falling from Huntington Lake Reservoir. The rated capacity of the powerhouse is 81,000 kilowatts.

Dam No. 4 and Powerhouse No. 2 Forebay

Dam No. 4 is located at an elevation of 4,810 feet, adjacent to

This view of the western end of Huntington Lake was taken in 1950, and shows the upstream side of Dam No. 2, center left, and Dam No. 1, left background. *Doug White Photo, from the Edison Collection*

Big Creek Powerhouse No. 2, right, and No. 2A, left, as they appeared in 1954. *Joseph O. Fadler Photo, from the Edison Collection*

This classic view of Big Creek Powerhouse No. 1 was taken in 1960. *Joseph O. Fadler Photo, from the Edison Collection*

Powerhouse No. 1. The dam is of concrete gravity arch construction, built in 1913 across Big Creek itself. Dam No. 4 impounds water coming from the tailrace of Powerhouse No. I and from the natural watercourses of Big Creek and Pitman Creek, to form the forebay for Big Creek Powerhouse No. 2, located several miles downstream.

Big Creek Powerhouse No. 2

Big Creek Powerhouse No. 2 was built at the same time as Powerhouse No. 1, as part of the Initial Development, and the Pelton wheel and generating equipment in the two plants is virtually identical. Located at an elevation of 2,952 feet, Plant No. 2 operates on water impounded behind Dam No. 4 that has traveled through Tunnel No. 2 and down penstocks to the four generating units. Unit No. 3 (originally No. 1) went into service on December 18, 1913; Unit No. 4 (originally No. 2) on January 11, 1914; Unit No. 5 on February 1, 1921; and Unit No. 6 on March 31, 1921. Each of these units operates on a static head of 1,858 feet, and together they have a rated capacity of 66,000 kilowatts.

Huntington-Pitman-Shaver Conduit

The Huntington-Pitman-Shaver Conduit is a tunnel 4.8 miles in length that diverts water from Huntington Lake into Shaver Lake. This conduit, also known as Tunnel No. 7, has a diameter of 13 feet and a capacity of 1,450 cubic feet per second. The conduit's intake is at an elevation of 6,885 feet, and, as completed in 1928, it discharged into the natural watercourse of the north fork of Stevenson Creek a short distance

above Shaver Lake. It is presently undergoing modification for the Balsam Meadow Project. A new 5,500-foot-long tunnel diverts the conduit's flow into the Balsam Meadow Forebay, for use in the John S. Eastwood Power Station, before the water is discharged into Shaver Lake.

Balsam Meadow Forebay

The Balsam Meadow Forebay is the regulating reservoir that controls the water flow into the John S. Eastwood underground power station. Filled by water from Huntington Lake carried down the Huntington-Pitman-Shaver Conduit (Tunnel No. 7), the forebay forms a lake with a surface area of 60 acres, containing 1,600 acre-feet of water. The forebay is impounded by a rock-fill dam 1,300 feet long along its crest and 120 feet high at its highest point. The upper side of the dam is faced with concrete. The spillway elevation of Balsam Meadow Forebay is at 6,668 feet, and the intake of the power tunnel to the Eastwood Power Station is at 6,600 feet.

John S. Eastwood (Balsam Meadow) Power Station

The Balsam Meadow Hydroelectric Project is the latest addition to the Big Creek complex. An underground facility, named the John S. Eastwood Power Station, located at an elevation of about 5,200 feet, will generate electricity from the water carried through the Huntington-Pitman-Shaver Conduit. After passing through the plant, the water will be discharged into Shaver Lake through a new tailrace tunnel. The plant,

under construction at the time of publication (1986), will have a capacity of 200,000 kilowatts, generated in one Francis-type reaction turbine that will be the largest single generating unit on the Big Creek system. This equipment will be housed in an underground cavern, 80 feet wide, 188 feet long and 153 feet high, hollowed from the native Sierra granite. The project, which includes the construction of a new forebay at Balsam Meadow, the underground powerhouse, and over 24,000 feet of new tunnels and shafts, is scheduled to begin operation in December 1987.

Shaver Lake

Shaver Lake Reservoir is the largest on the Big Creek system, having an operating capacity of 135,528 acre-feet. The reservoir is named for pioneer lumberman C. B. Shaver, who logged in this area around the turn of the century. In 1893, inside the present reservoir area, Shaver built a small rock-filled dam that impounded water to form a small millpond for lumbering operations. The present, much larger, lake was created in 1927 by the construction of a concrete gravity arch dam across Stevenson Creek. This dam has an overall length of 2,169 feet, and rises 185 feet from its foundation. Its spillway elevation is 5,370 feet, and 281,300 cubic yards of concrete were used in its construction. The drainage area for the modern Shaver Lake is small, only 30 square miles, so the majority of the water impounded in the reservoir is diverted through the Huntington-Pitman-Shaver Conduit from Huntington Lake. Water stored in Shaver Lake is sent nearly 2.5 miles through Tunnel No. 5 and penstocks to Powerhouse No. 2A.

Big Creek Powerhouse No. 2A

Big Creek Powerhouse No. 2A, located at an elevation of 2,952 feet, was constructed in 1928. Although it is adjacent to, and operated integrally with, Powerhouse No. 2, Powerhouse No. 2A utilizes water from Shaver Lake. The plant has two generators, powered by the largest double-overhung "Pelton" type impulse water wheels ever built in the United States. Unit No. 1 went into service on August 6, 1928, and Unit No. 2 on December 21, 1928. These two units operate under what was for many years the highest static head in the world, 2,418 feet, and have a rated capacity of 96,000 kilowatts.

Dam No. 5 and Powerhouse No. 8 Forebay

Dam No. 5 is a concrete gravity arch dam built across the watercourse of Big Creek just below Powerhouse No. 2 and Powerhouse 2A. It impounds the combined discharge of both plants, approximately 1,200 second-feet of water at full operation, to form a regulating reservoir and forebay for Big Creek Powerhouse No. 8 downstream.

Big Creek Powerhouse No. 8

Big Creek Powerhouse No. 8 is located at the junction of Big Creek and the South Fork of the San Joaquin River. Its out-of-sequence number results from it not having been a part of the original Big Creek Project. The plant was built in 1921 to provide additional energy quickly during a power shortage. Unit No. 1 went into operation on August 16,

1921. A second unit was added on June 8, 1929, to make use of additional water flowing from Shaver Lake through Powerhouse No. 2A upstream. Powerhouse No. 8's two Francis-type vertical reaction turbines (one built by Cramp and the other by Pelton) have a combined rated capacity of 58,000 kilowatts, operating on a static head of 713 feet.

Mammoth Pool Reservoir

The Mammoth Pool Reservoir, with an operating capacity of 119,940 acre-feet, was formed by an earth-fill dam 820 feet long and 330 feet high built across the South Fork of the San Joaquin River about eight miles upstream from its junction with Big Creek. The dam and reservoir derive their name from a natural feature in the river, first noted and named by John Eastwood during his original surveys. An interesting feature of this dam is the installation of a small 1,200-kilowatt generator in the diversion tunnel which releases water from the reservoir to sustain fish life downstream. Mammoth Pool Dam is also a key element in the chain of dams that regulate the flow of the San Joaquin River for flood control and irrigation purposes. A tunnel 20 feet in diameter and nearly eight miles long carries water from this reservoir to the Mammoth Pool Powerhouse downstream. Two small diversions carry the flow of Rock Creek and Ross Creek into the power tunnel.

Mammoth Pool Powerhouse

Mammoth Pool Powerhouse was completed and placed into service on March 28, 1960. Its two Francis-

Big Creek Powerhouse No. 8, located at the junction of Big Creek (at left) and the San Joaquin River, viewed from upstream.
Greg O'Loughlin Photo, from the Edison Collection

This interior view of Big Creek Powerhouse No. 2A shows the large Pelton wheels flanking each of the plant's two generating units. Because of the tremendous water pressure caused by the high static head on these units, two Pelton wheels, one on each side, drive each generator. This reduces stresses on the common shaft connecting the water wheels and the generator rotor.
Photographer unknown, from the Edison Collection

Dam No. 6, located just downstream from Powerhouse No. 8, impounds water to be used at powerhouse No. 3, several miles down the San Joaquin River. Occasionally, during periods of the highest spring runoff, the volume of water coming down the San Joaquin River is enough to spectacularly overtop the dam.
Joseph O. Fadler Photo, from the Edison Collection

Mammoth Pool Powerhouse in May 1960, just after going into operation.
Joseph O. Fadler Photo, from the Edison Collection

type reaction turbines operate under a static head of 1,100 feet, powering two generators having a rated capacity of 129,360 kilowatts. The plant, located at an elevation of 2,225 feet, incorporates several important design changes and operational improvements over the older Big Creek plants. It was built to an all-outdoor design, thus eliminating the expense of the powerhouse structures necessary in earlier days. The plant is also unmanned, remotely operated by "supervisory control" via a microwave link to powerhouse No. 8.

Dam No. 6 and Powerhouse No. 3 Forebay

Dam No. 6 is a concrete gravity arch dam built across the South Fork of the San Joaquin River just downstream from the junction of Big Creek. Completed in 1923, the dam has a spillway elevation of 2,230 feet and forms a small reservoir with a surface area of 23 acres, containing 993 acre-feet of water. This reservoir is the forebay for powerhouse No. 3 several miles downstream.

Tunnel No. 3

Tunnel No. 3 was completed in 1923 after several years of work, to carry water from Dam No. 6 down to powerhouse No. 3. The tunnel, built almost entirely through hard Sierra granite, was driven through the cliffs along the eastern side of the precipitous canyon of the San Joaquin River. Those who travel through this canyon over the famous "Million Dollar Mile" road, can see three places where "adits" were driven into the canyon wall to provide additional work faces to speed construc-

tion of the tunnel. The largest of these adits, which today serves to provide access to the tunnel for inspection purposes, is located at Stevenson Creek Falls, at the former site of Construction Camp 35. Tunnel No. 3 has a diameter of 21 feet and can carry 2,600 cubic feet of water per second.

Big Creek Powerhouse No. 3

When Big Creek powerhouse No. 3 first went into operation in 1923, the trade press hailed it as "the Electrical Giant of the West," for its (then) 99,000 kilowatts of rated capacity made it the largest hydroelectric plant in the West. Since that time, two additional units have been added to the plant, giving it a rated capacity of 171,000 kilowatts. Unit No. 1 went into service on October 3, 1923; Unit No. 2 on September 30, 1923; Unit No. 3 on October 5, 1923; Unit No. 4 on April 28, 1948; and Unit No. 5 on February 24, 1980. Each of these units is powered by a Francis-type vertical reaction turbine operating on a static head of 827 feet. Located at an elevation of 1,412 feet, powerhouse No. 3 is the operating headquarters for the Big Creek system, housing the control center for the entire project. From a switchyard located near the powerhouse, 220,000-volt transmission lines carry the electrical energy produced at Big Creek to customers in Southern and Central California.

Dam No. 7 and Redinger Lake

Dam No. 7 was completed in 1951 across the South Fork of the San Joaquin River to impound water to form David H. Redinger Lake, the water from which is used to operate powerhouse No. 4 downstream. The reservoir holds 26,119 acre-feet of water. The massive concrete gravity dam is 891 feet long and stands 250 feet high. Its spillway is at an elevation of 1,403 feet. Dam No. 7 also contains a small 350-kilowatt generator to generate electricity from the water that is continuously released from the dam to maintain fish life downstream.

Big Creek Powerhouse No. 4

Powerhouse No. 4 is the lowest in the chain of plants on Edison's Big Creek system, located at an elevation of 988 feet above sea level. Two sections of tunnel, and a section of steel pipe forming an inverted siphon across Willow Creek, carry water from Redinger Lake to the powerhouse. The tunnel is 24 feet in diameter, and the conduit totals 10,520 feet in length. powerhouse No. 4 has two Francis-type reaction turbines that operate on a static head of 416 feet. Unit No. 1 went into operation on June 12, 1951, and Unit No. 2 on July 2, 1951, and together have a rated capacity of 91,000 kilowatts.

The Transmission System

With the exception of Portal powerhouse and the "small fish" water generators at several dams, all of Big Creek's power plants deliver their electricity into the 220,000-volt transmission network of the Southern California Edison Company. When the Initial Development at Big Creek was completed in 1913, the energy was delivered to Eagle Rock Substation in Los Angeles over a 243-mile-long, 150,000-volt power line, then the longest and highest-voltage power line in the world. With the development of additional capacity on the Big Creek system in 1923, the transmission voltage was raised to its present 220,000 volts, another world's record that won widespread acclaim for Edison Company engineers. From the switchyard near powerhouse No. 3, three transmission lines carry the energy southward to the San Joaquin Valley and Southern California. Two of these lines are the original 1913-era lines, rebuilt in 1922-23 to carry 220,000 volts. The third line is the so-called "Vincent" line, completed in 1927 via a separate right-of-way. Major substations at Springville and Vestal (Richgrove) in Tulare County, and at Vincent, Gould, Eagle Rock and Laguna Bell in Los Angeles County feed Big Creek energy to Edison customers.

Powerhouse No. 4 is the final point at which waters of the San Joaquin River and its many tributaries are used to generate electricity for the customers of the Southern California Edison Company. From the tailrace of the plant, the water is discharged back into the river, and flows downstream into the Pacific Gas & Electric Company's Kerckhoff Reservoir. The water generates electricity at PG&E's Kerckhoff Powerhouse before flowing into Millerton Lake, impounded by Friant Dam. This last reservoir, owned by the Federal Government's Central Valley Project, is the last major flood control dam on the San Joaquin River, as well as an important source of irrigation water for the central San Joaquin Valley through the Friant-Kern and Madera Canals.

Big Creek Powerhouse No. 3 as it appeared in 1985.
Greg O'Loughlin Photo, from the Edison Collection

Big Creek Powerhouse No. 4 presents a stark appearance compared to the older facilities on the project.
Doug White Photo, from the Edison Collection

Glossary
OF
HYDRO AND ELECTRICAL TERMS

This glossary has been prepared for the benefit of readers who are not familiar with the technical terminology used in the electric power industry, or with the specialized terms used around hydro plants, and terms included in this book .

ACRE-FOOT: The volume of water that will cover one acre one foot deep—about 326,000 gallons of water.

ADIT: A tunnel cut into the side of a hill or mountain to provide access to the main axis of a tunnel under construction; such an access tunnel can speed up the excavation of the main tunnel by providing additional working faces.

BUS: Short for "bus-bar," the main conductor, often a bar of copper or aluminum, that interconnects different input and output points of the same voltage in a generating plant or a substation.

CIRCUIT BREAKER: A device for interrupting the flow of electric current.

CONDUCTOR: Any material through which electricity can flow easily; in electric utility jargon, the copper or aluminum wire on a power line.

CYCLE (HERTZ): The complete alternation of current, i.e., forward or backward, in the conductor. Edison operates at 60 cycles per second, or 60 Hertz, which is the standard frequency of all electric utilities in North America.

DISTRIBUTION LINES: Overhead or underground lines originating at power plants or substations that operate at a voltage of 33,000 volts or lower, which feed electricity to customers.

FOREBAY: A pond or lake which is that part of the water supply system for a hydroelectric power plant from which water is fed into the penstocks for delivery to the water wheel or water turbine; a forebay may be the same as, in addition to, or in lieu of, a reservoir, depending upon the geography and water supply of the area in which the hydro plant is located.

FRANCIS TURBINE: A reaction-type turbine, often looking like a snail's shell, where the force of water under great pressure moving around the circular "scroll case" imparts a spinning motion to an impeller, thus creating the rotary motion needed to spin a generator; prime movers of this type are generally used in low- or medium-head hydro plants having a greater volume of water.

GENERATOR: A device for the conversion of mechanical energy into electrical energy; in a hydroelectric plant, the generator is spun by a water wheel or water turbine prime mover turned by the force of falling water.

HEAD: Sometimes called static head; the distance from the surface of the water at the intake of the conduit in a reservoir or forebay to the point of release at the water wheel or turbine; the higher the head, the greater the amount of electricity that can be generated by a given amount of water.

HIGH VOLTAGE: On the Edison system, voltages ranging from 33,000 volts to 500,000 volts that are used to transmit electricity long distances; as a rule of thumb, the higher the voltage, the longer the distance it can be sent over wires.

HORSEPOWER: A unit of mechanical power equivalent to the work done to lift

The large size of the Pelton wheels used at Big Creek can be seen from this picture taken during a repair project in 1948.
Photographer unknown, from the Edison Collection

a 150-pound weight 220 feet in one minute; in the early days of the electric utility industry, this term was used in place of "kilowatt" to refer to the capacity of a generating plant. To get kilowatts from horsepower, multiply the number of horsepower by 0.746.

HYDRO PLANT: A power plant whose generators are turned by the force of falling water; also known as a hydroelectric plant.

KILOVOLT: A kilovolt is 1,000 volts, and is abbreviated as KV; this term is used in referring to power lines. For example, a 220 KV power line is a 220,000-volt line (see HIGH VOLTAGE).

KILOWATT: A kilowatt is a unit of electrical energy equal to 1,000 watts, and is one-third greater than one horsepower. This term is replacing the older "horsepower" in referring to the capacity of a power plant; to get horsepower from kilowatts, multiply the number of kilowatts by 1.341.

KILOWATT-HOUR: Kilowatts multiplied by hours; this is the unit that measures the electrical energy created by one kilowatt acting for one hour; for example, if a 100-watt light bulb burns for 10 hours, it has produced one kilowatt-hour's worth of work, in this case, light.

MEGAWATT: A megawatt is one million watts, or 1,000 kilowatts. This term is often used to describe the capacity of large generators. For example, the generator at the John Eastwood underground powerhouse is rated at 200,000 kilowatts, or 200 megawatts.

MINER'S INCH: A measurement of the volume of water passing a given point, defined as 1.5 cubic feet per minute.

PEAK POWER: Power supplied by a plant for only a few hours during the day to assist other plants in carrying the load during times of maximum demand for electricity; when a plant produces such short-term power, it is said to be "peaking."

PELTON WHEEL: A Pelton Wheel is a type of impulse water wheel, originally perfected by Lester A. Pelton, that is often used as the prime mover in older hydroelectric plants. It is ideal for use where small amounts of water are used under a high static head, these wheels have specially designed buckets fixed around a wheel, and a stream of water under great pressure spins the wheel by hitting each bucket in turn.

PENSTOCK: A closed conduit or pipe, usually built of high-tensile-strength steel to withstand great pressures, which conveys water down a steep drop to the turbine or water wheel of a hydro plant.

RATED CAPACITY: The capacity of a generator to produce electrical output, generally given in kilowatts; this rating, often called the nameplate rating, is a conservative estimate that can often be exceeded under favorable conditions.

REGULATOR: In electricity, a type of transformer which varies the voltage

according to customer demands at any given moment.

RESERVOIR: A body of water, of varying size, that is used to store water for future use.

ROTOR: The rotating part of a generator.

SECOND-FOOT: A measurement of the flow of water past a given point, defined as one cubic foot per second, or approximately two acre-feet per day.

An Edison snow surveyor prepares to force a hollow tube into the snow. Measurements made from the resulting core sample will reveal the water content of the snow. When coupled with the depth of the snow pack, hydrographers can estimate the amount of runoff water that will be available in the upcoming spring and summer. From this data, Edison planners can estimate how much hydroelectric generation will be available for the system in coming months.
Photographer unknown, from the Edison Collection

SNOW SURVEY: A method of determining the water content in the snow pack. These surveys are done to predict the amount of water runoff when the snow melts.

STATOR: The stationary part of a generator.

STREAM FLOW: The quantity of water flowing past a given point in a

stream, generally expressed in cubic feet per second.

STREAM FLOW PLANT: A hydroelectric plant where there is no reservoir to store water against periods of low runoff; as a result, the amount of water available for electric generation is limited to the amount of water flowing in the stream at any given time. A few of Edison's oldest small hydro plants are stream flow plants.

SUBSTATION: An electrical facility, located at key points throughout an electric transmission and distribution system, capable of raising or lowering voltages, as necessary. In addition, a substation usually also has switches, circuit breakers and other equipment needed to switch electric power between various circuits.

SWITCH(ING) YARD: At a power plant, that portion of the facility containing transformers, circuit breakers and switching equipment needed to feed the output of the plant's generators into the utility's transmission system.

TAILRACE: The passage by which the water leaves the water wheel or water turbine after performing the work of turning that prime mover.

TRANSFORMER: An electrical device that changes electric energy from one voltage to another in an alternating current system (see also HIGH VOLTAGE, above).

TRANSMISSION LINE: Electric power lines operated at high voltages that carry large quantities of power over long distances (see also HIGH VOLTAGE, above).

TURBINE: A prime mover, driven by water, steam or gas in a rotary motion to turn a generator to produce electric energy.

Index